Undergraduate Topics in Computer Science

'Undergraduate Topics in Computer Science' (UTiCS) delivers high-quality instructional content for undergraduates studying in all areas of computing and information science. From core foundational and theoretical material to final-year topics and applications, UTiCS books take a fresh, concise, and modern approach and are ideal for self-study or for a one- or two-semester course. The texts are all authored by established experts in their fields, reviewed by an international advisory board, and contain numerous examples and problems, many of which include fully worked solutions.

The UTiCS concept relies on high-quality, concise books in softback format, and generally a maximum of 275–300 pages. For undergraduate textbooks that are likely to be longer, more expository, Springer continues to offer the highly regarded Texts in Computer Science series, to which we refer potential authors.

More information about this series at http://www.springer.com/series/7592

Noel Kalicharan

Julia - Bit by Bit

Programming for Beginners

Noel Kalicharan
Department of Computing and IT
University of the West Indies
St. Augustine, Trinidad and Tobago

ISSN 1863-7310   ISSN 2197-1781   (electronic)
Undergraduate Topics in Computer Science
ISBN 978-3-030-73935-5   ISBN 978-3-030-73936-2   (eBook)
https://doi.org/10.1007/978-3-030-73936-2

This Springer imprint is published by the registered company Springer Nature Switzerland AG
The registered company address is: Gewerbestrasse 11, 6330 Cham, Switzerland

Dedication

James & Clara

Claudette & Samuel

Jeff & Jenny

Margaret & Stephen

Kenrick & Debbie

Jennifer & Andrew

Anushka & Michael

Saskia & Vaishnavi

Special Thanks

Hubert Dupont

Shellyann Sooklal

For their meticulous, insightful and helpful comments on the manuscript. Their eye for detail was truly impressive. Each brought their special, but different, strengths to bear, making this a better book than it would have been without their input.

Preface

Julia—Bit by Bit attempts to teach computer programming to the complete beginner using *Julia*—a relatively new programming language. Created in 2009 by Jeff Bezanson, Stefan Karpinski, Viral B. Shah and Alan Edelman, *Julia* was launched in 2012. Their goal? "To create a free language that was both high-level and fast." Since its launch, *Julia* has undergone several version changes. As of November 9, 2020, it had matured to Version 1.5.3.

The book assumes you have no knowledge whatsoever about programming. And if you are worried that you are not good at high-school mathematics, don't be. It is a myth that you must be good at mathematics to learn programming. In this book, a knowledge of primary school mathematics is all that is required—basic addition, subtraction, multiplication, division, finding the percentage of some quantity, finding an average or the larger of two quantities.

Some of our most outstanding students over the last forty years have been people with little mathematics background from all walks of life—politicians, civil servants, sports people, housewives, secretaries, clerical assistants, artists, musicians and teachers. On the other hand, we've had professionals like engineers and scientists who didn't do as well as might be expected. So it's not about how "qualified" you are.

What *will* be an asset is the ability to think logically or to follow a logical argument. If you are good at presenting convincing arguments, you will probably be a good programmer. Even if you aren't, programming is the perfect vehicle for learning logical thinking skills. You should learn it for these skills even if you never intend to become a serious programmer.

The main goal of this book is to teach fundamental programming principles using *Julia*, one of the fastest growing programming languages in the world today. *Julia* can be classified as a "modern" language, possessing many features not available in more popular languages like C and Java.

Best of all, *Julia* is easy to learn. In fact, I would go so far as to say that, of all the many languages I have learnt and taught over the last forty years, *Julia* is the easiest to learn. This is particularly important for someone learning programming for the first time. You can concentrate on acquiring problem-solving skills without being overwhelmed by the language. I've known many students who got turned off learning programming because they found the basics of the language too difficult to grasp.

Julia strips away the "fluff" of most languages, the "overhead" you need to write even the simplest programs. It's not fussy about things like semi-colons or having to "declare" the type of every variable you need to use. You just use it the way you want—*Julia* will figure out the type for you. But if you really *want Julia* to enforce "typing", it can do that as well.

Nevertheless, this book is as much about teaching basic problem-solving principles as it is about teaching *Julia*. Remember, a language is useless if you can't use it to solve a problem. But once you learn the *principles* well, they can be applied to any language.

Chapter 1 gives an overview of the programming process. It shows you how to write your first *Julia* program and introduces some of the basic building blocks needed to write programs.

Chapter 2 is all about *numbers*—integers, floating-point, operators, expressions—how to work with them and how to print them. It also explains how to write programs that use *sequence logic*—statements are executed one after the other, from first to last.

Chapter 3 shows how to write programs which can make decisions. It explains how to use `if` and `if...else` statements.

Chapter 4 explains the notion of 'looping' and how to use this powerful programming idea to solve more interesting problems. Looping is implemented using `for` and `while` statements. We also explain how to read data from a file and write results to a file.

Chapter 5 formally treats with functions. These enable a (large) program to be broken up into smaller manageable units but which work together to solve a given problem.

Chapter 6 is devoted to Characters and Strings. These present some difficulty in other languages but, in *Julia*, we can work with them as seamlessly as we do numbers.

Chapter 7 tackles the nemesis of many would-be programmers—array processing. However, this is significantly easier in Julia than other languages. Master array processing and you would add to your repertoire a tool that will significantly increase the range of problems you can solve.

Chapter 8 is mainly about sorting and searching techniques. Sorting puts data in an order that can be searched more quickly/easily, and makes it more palatable for human consumption.

Chapter 9 introduces *structures*. These enable us to group data in a form that can be manipulated more easily an a unit.

Chapter 10 deals with two useful data structures—dictionaries and sets. These enable us to solve certain kinds of problems more easily and conveniently than we can without them.

The first step in becoming a good programmer is learning the syntax rules of the programming language. This is the easy part and many people mistakenly believe that this makes them a programmer. They get carried away by the cosmetics— they learn the *features* of a language without learning how to use them to solve problems. Of course, you must learn *some* features. But it is far better to learn a few features and be able to use them to solve many problems rather than learn many features but can't use them to solve anything. For this reason, this book emphasizes solving many problems from just a few features.

This book is intended for anyone who is learning programming for the first time, regardless of age or institution. The presentation is based on our experience that many people (though not all) have difficulty learning programming. To try and overcome this, we use an approach which provides clear examples, detailed explanations of very basic concepts and numerous interesting problems (not just artificial exercises whose only purpose is to illustrate some language feature).

While computer programming is essentially a mental activity and you *can* learn a fair amount of programming from just *reading* the book, it is important that you "get your hands dirty" by writing and running programs. One of life's thrills is to write your first program and get it to run successfully on a computer. Don't miss out on it.

But do not stop there. The only way to learn programming well is to write programs to solve new problems. The end-of-chapter exercises are a very rich source of problems, a result of the author's more than 40 years in the teaching of programming.

Thank you for taking the time to read this book. I hope your venture into programming is a successful and enjoyable one.

Noel Kalicharan

Contents

Chapter 1   **Elementary Concepts**   1
         1.1   Programs, Languages and Compilers   1
         1.2   How a Computer Solves a Problem   3
                1.2.1 Define the Problem   3
                1.2.2 Analyze the Problem   3
                1.2.3 Develop an Algorithm to Solve the Problem   4
                       1.2.3.1 Data and Variables   4
                       1.2.3.2 Example – Develop the Algorithm   5
                1.2.4 Write the Program for the Algorithm   5
                1.2.5 Test and Debug the Program   7
                1.2.6 Document the Program   8
                1.2.7 Maintain the Program   8
         1.3   How a Computer Executes a Program   8
         1.4   Data Types   9
         1.5   Characters   10
         1.6   Welcome to Julia Programming   11
         1.7   A Program With Input   12
         1.8   Writing Output with `print`/`println`   13
                1.81 The Newline Character, \n (backslash n)   14
                1.8.2 `println()`   15
                1.8.3 Escape Sequences   15
         1.9   Print the Value of a Variable   16
         1.10   Comments   17
         1.11   Julia Basics   18
                1.11.1 The Julia Alphabet   18
                1.11.2 Julia Tokens   18
                1.11.3 Reserved Words   20
                1.11.4 Identifiers   20
                1.11.5 Some Naming Conventions   21
         Exercises 1   22

Chapter 2   **Numbers**   23
         2.1   Introduction   23
         2.2   How to Read Integers   23
         2.3   How to Read Floating-Point Numbers   25
         2.4   Example - Average   26
         2.5   Example - Square a Number   27
         2.6   Example - Banking   28
         2.7   Example - Football Tickets   31
         2.8   Integers - Int   34
                2.8.1 Integer Expressions   36
                2.8.2 Precedence of Operators   37
                2.8.3 Print an Integer Using a *Field Width*   38
         2.9   Floating-point Numbers   40
                2.9.1 Print Float64 and Float32 Variables   41
                2.9.2 Assignment Between `Float64` and `Float32`   42
                2 9 3 Floating-point Expressions   43

		2.9.4 Mixed Expressions	44
2.10	Assignment Operator		45
2.11	Updating Operators		45
2.12	trunc, ceil, floor, round		46
	Exercises 2		51

Chapter 3	**Selection Logic**		**53**
3.1	Introduction		53
3.2	Boolean Expressions		53
		3.2.1 AND, &&	54
		3.2.2 OR, ||	55
		3.2.3 NOT, !	55
3.3	The type Bool		56
3.4	The if Statement		56
		3.4.1 Find the Sum of Two Lengths	59
3.5	The if…else Statement		61
		3.5.1 Calculate Pay	63
3.6	On Program Testing		64
3.7	Symbolic Constants		65
3.8	The if…elseif…else Statement		66
		3.8.1 Print a Letter Grade	67
		3.8.2 Classify a Triangle	68
	Exercises 3		69

Chapter 4	**The for and while Statements**		**72**
4.1	Introduction		72
4.2	The for Statement		72
		4.2.1 Multiplication Tables	75
		4.2.2 Temperature Conversion	78
4.3	The Expressive Power of for		80
4.4	break/continue in for		82
4.5	Read Data From File		83
		4.5.1 Keep a Count	85
		4.5.2 Find Average	85
4.6	Find Largest Number		86
		4.6.1 Find 'Largest' Word	88
		4.6.2 Find Longest Word	89
		4.6.3 Find Smallest Number	89
4.7	Nested for Statement		90
4.8	Read Data From File, Cont'd		92
4.9	The while Statement		95
		4.9.1 Sum of Numbers (Prompt)	97
		4.9.2 Sum, Count, Average (Prompt)	98
		4.9.3 Greatest Common Divisor	99
4.10	Send Output to a File		100
4.11	Payroll		101
4.12	break/continue in while		104
	Exercises 4		106

Chapter 5	**Functions**		**109**
5.1	Introduction		109
5.2	Function Basics		110

           5.2.1 How an Argument Is Passed to a Function   113
  5.3   Function - Examples   114
           5.3.1 How to Swap Two Variables   114
           5.3.2 Yesterday, Today and Tomorrow   115
           5.3.3 GCD, Greatest Common Divisor   116
           5.3.4 Using GCD to Find LCM   118
           5.3.5 Factorial and Big Integers   118
           5.3.6 Combinations   121
           5.3.7 Calculate Pay   123
           5.3.8 Sum of Exact Divisors   123
           5.3.9 Perfect, Abundant or Deficient   124
           5.3.10 Letter Position in Alphabet   125
  5.4   Introduction to Recursion   126
           5.4.1 GCD, Greatest Common Divisor   128
           5.4.2 Fibonacci Numbers   128
           5.4.3 Decimal to Binary   129
           5.4.4 Towers of Hanoi   130
           5.4.5 The Power Function   132
           5.4.6 Find Path Through Maze   133
  Exercises 5   137

Chapter 6   **Characters & Strings**   **140**
  6.1   Character Sets   140
  6.2   Character Constants and Values   141
  6.3   The Type char   142
  6.4   Some char Functions   143
           6.4.1 Uppercase To/From Lowercase   144
  6.5   Read and Print Characters   146
  6.6   Count Space Characters   148
  6.7   Compare Characters   149
  6.8   Echo Input, Number Lines   150
  6.9   Convert Digit Characters to Integer   151
  6.10 String Basics   154
  6.11 Compare Strings   156
  6.12 Index Into a String   157
  6.13 Example - Sum of Distances   159
  6.14 Concatenation   161
  6.15 Example - Get Words From Random Data   162
  6.16 Example - Palindrome   164
  6.17 A Flexible getString Function   166
  6.18 Example - Geography Quiz Program   167
  6.19 Other String Functions   169
           6.19.1 findfirst   170
           6.19.2 findlast   171
           6.19.3 findnext   171
           6.19.4 findprev   173
           6.19.5 occursin   174
  6.20 Array of Characters   174
  6.21 For the Curious Reader   176
  Exercises 6   180

Chapter 7	**Arrays**	**181**
	7.1 Introduction	181
	7.2 Simple vs Array Variable	182
	7.3 Array Declaration	182
	7.4 Store Values in an Array	186
	7.5 Average and Differences from Average	190
	7.6 Letter Frequency	191
	7.7 Array as Argument to a Function	194
	7.8 Name of Day Revisited	194
	7.9 Find Largest, Smallest in Array	195
	7.9.1 `min`, `max`, `minimum`, `maximum`	197
	7.10 A Voting Problem	198
	7.10.1 How to Handle Any Number of Candidates	202
	7.10.2 How to Sort the Results	202
	Exercises 7	205
Chapter 8	**Searching, Sorting and Merging**	**207**
	8.1 Sequential Search	207
	8.2 Selection Sort	209
	8.2.1 Analysis of Selection Sort	211
	8.3 Insertion Sort	212
	8.3.1 Analysis of Insertion Sort	216
	8.3.2 Sort Unlimited Data	216
	8.4 Sort Parallel Arrays	217
	8.5 Binary Search	219
	8.6 Word Frequency Count	221
	8.7 Merge Sorted Lists	224
	Exercises 8	228
Chapter 9	**Structures**	**230**
	9.1 The Need for Structures	230
	9.2 How to Write a `struct` Declaration	231
	9.2.1 Pass `struct` as Argument to a Function	232
	9.3 Array of Structures	234
	9.3.1 Sort `struct` Array	236
	9.4 Nested Structures	238
	9.5 Fractions	239
	9.5.1 Manipulate Fractions	240
	9.5.2 Rational Numbers	241
	9.6 Voting Problem Revisited	243
	9.6.1 On using `isless` in `sort`	247
	Exercises 9	250

Chapter 10   **Dictionaries & Sets**   **252**
                        10.1 Dictionaries   252
                               10.1.1 Letter-Frequency   254
                               10.1.2 Dict Functions - haskey, in, delete!   256
                        10.2 Sets   257
                               10.2.1 Set Operations   258
                               10.2.2 Find All Unique Words   263
                        10.3 Thesaurus   264
                        10.4 Scrabble   267
                        Exercises 10   277

Appendix A   **Install Julia/Atom/Juno**   **279**

Index   **286**

CHAPTER 1

Elementary Concepts

In this chapter, we will explain the following:

- How a computer solves a problem
- The various stages in the development of a computer program: from problem definition to finished program
- How a computer executes a program
- What is a *data type* and its fundamental role in writing a program
- The role of *characters*—the basic building blocks of all programs
- The concepts of *constants* and *variables*
- The distinction between *syntax* and *logic* errors
- How to produce output in Julia using `print/println` statements
- What is an escape sequence
- How descriptive or explanatory comments can be included in your program
- What is an *assignment statement* and how to write one in Julia

1.1 Programs, Languages and Compilers

We are all familiar with the computer's ability to perform a wide variety of tasks. For instance, we can use it to play games, write a letter or a book, perform accounting functions for a company, learn a foreign language, listen to music on a CD, send a fax or search for information on the Internet. How is this possible, all on the same machine? The answer lies with programming—the creation of a sequence of instructions which the computer can perform (we say "execute") to accomplish each task. This sequence of instructions is called a *program*. Each task requires a different program:

- To play a game, we need a game-playing program.
- To write a letter or a book, we need a word processing program.
- To do accounts, we need an accounting program.
- To learn Spanish, we need a program that teaches Spanish.
- To communicate with others around the world, we need a program like WhatsApp.
- To create/play karaoke music, we need an appropriate karaoke program.
- To use the Internet, we need a program called a *Web browser*.

For every task we want to perform, we need an appropriate program. And in order for the computer to run a program, the program must be stored (we sometimes say loaded) in the computer's memory.

© The Author(s), under exclusive license to Springer Nature Switzerland AG 2021
N. Kalicharan, *Julia - Bit by Bit*, Undergraduate Topics in Computer Science,
https://doi.org/10.1007/978-3-030-73936-2_1

But what is the nature of a program? First, we need to know that computers are built to execute instructions written in what is called *machine language*. In machine language, everything is expressed in terms of the binary number system—1s and 0s. Each computer has its own machine language and the computer can execute instructions written *in that language only*.

The instructions themselves are very simple, for example, add or subtract two numbers, compare one number with another or copy a number from one place to another. How, then, can the computer perform such a wide variety of tasks, solving such a wide variety of problems, with such simple instructions?

The answer is that no matter how complex an activity may seem, it can usually be broken down into a series of simple steps. It is the ability to analyze a complex problem and express its solution in terms of simple computer instructions that is one of the hallmarks of a good programmer.

Machine language is considered a *low-level* programming language. In the early days of computing (1940s and 50s) programmers had to write programs in machine language, that is, express all their instructions using 1s and 0s.

To make life a little easier for them, *assembly language* was developed. This was closely related to machine language but it allowed the programmer to use mnemonic instruction codes (such as ADD and names for storage locations (such as sum) rather than strings of binary digits (bits). For instance, a programmer could refer to a number by sum rather than have to remember that the number was stored in memory location 1000011101101011.

A program called an *assembler* is used to convert an assembly language program into machine language. Still, programming this way had several drawbacks:

- It was very tedious and error prone.
- It forced the programmer to think in terms of the machine rather than in terms of his problem.
- A program written in the machine language of one computer could not be run on a computer with a different machine language. Changing your computer could mean having to rewrite all your programs.

To overcome these problems, *high-level* or *problem-oriented* languages were developed in the late 1950s and 60s. The most popular of these were FORTRAN (FORmula TRANslation) and COBOL (COmmon Business-Oriented Language). FORTRAN was designed for solving scientific and engineering problems which involved a great deal of numerical computation. COBOL was designed to solve the data-processing problems of the business community.

The idea was to allow the programmer to think about a problem in terms familiar to him and relevant to the problem rather than have to worry about the machine. So, for instance, if he wanted to know the larger of two quantities, A and B, he could write

```
IF A IS GREATER THAN B THEN BIGGER = A ELSE BIGGER = B
```

rather than have to fiddle with several machine or assembly language instructions to get the same result. Thus high-level languages enabled the programmer to concentrate on solving the problem at hand, without the added burden of worrying about the idiosyncrasies of a particular machine.

However, the computer *still* could *execute* instructions written in machine language only . A program called a *compiler* is used to translate a program written in a high-level language to machine language. (And, just so you know, there are different *kinds* of compilers.)

We speak of a FORTRAN compiler or a C compiler for translating FORTRAN and C programs, respectively. But that's not the whole story. Since each computer has its own machine language, we must have, say, a FORTRAN compiler for a Lenovo ThinkPad computer and a FORTRAN compiler for a MacBook computer. Ultimately, though, a compiler translates code written in a high-level language to code which can be executed by the *processor* of a particular machine.

1.2 How a Computer Solves a Problem

Solving a problem on a computer involves the following activities:

1. Define the problem.
2. Analyze the problem.
3. Develop an algorithm (a method) for solving the problem.
4. Write the computer program which implements the algorithm.
5. Test and debug (find the errors in) the program.
6. Document the program. (Explain how the program works and how to use it.)
7. Maintain the program.

There is normally some overlap of these activities. For example, with a large program, a portion may be written and tested before another portion is written. Also, documentation should be done at the same time as all the other activities; each activity produces its own items of documentation which will be part of the final program documentation.

1.2.1 Define the Problem

Suppose we want to help a child work out the areas of squares. This defines a problem to be solved. However, a brief analysis reveals that the definition is not complete or specific enough to proceed with developing a program. Talking with the child might reveal that she needs a program which requests her to enter the length of a side of the square; the program then prints the area of the square.

1.2.2 Analyze the Problem

We further analyze the problem to

- Ensure that we have the clearest possible understanding of it.
- Determine general requirements such as the main inputs to the program and the main outputs from the program. For more complex programs, we would, for instance, also need to decide on the kinds of files which may be needed.

If there are several ways of solving the problem, we should consider the alternatives and choose the best or most appropriate one.

In this example, the input to the program is the length of one side of the square and the output is the area of the square. We only need to know how to calculate the area. If the side is s, then the area, a, is calculated by this:

```
a = s × s
```

1.2.3 Develop an Algorithm to Solve the Problem

An *algorithm* is a set of instructions which, if faithfully followed, will produce a solution to a given problem or perform some specified task. When an instruction is followed, we say it is *executed*. We can speak of an algorithm for finding a word in a dictionary, for changing a punctured tyre or for playing a video game.

For any problem, there will normally be more than one algorithm to solve it. Each algorithm will have its own advantages and disadvantages. When we are searching for a word in the dictionary, one method would be to start at the beginning and look at each word in turn. A second method would be to start at the end and search backwards. Here, an advantage of the first method is that it would find a word faster if it were at the beginning, while the second method would be faster if the word were towards the end.

Another method for searching for the word would be one which used the fact that the words in a dictionary are in alphabetical order—this is the method we all use when looking up a word. In any situation, a programmer would usually have a choice of algorithms, and it is one of her more important jobs to decide which algorithm is the best, and why this is so.

In our example, we must write the instructions in our algorithm in such a way that they can be easily converted into a form which the computer can follow. Computer instructions fall into three main categories:

1. *Input* instructions, used for supplying data from the *outside world* to a program; this is usually done via the keyboard or a file.
2. *Processing* instructions, used for manipulating data inside the computer. These instructions allow us to add, subtract, multiply and divide; they also allow us to compare two values, and act according to the result of the comparison. Also, we can move data from one location in the computer's memory to another location.
3. *Output* instructions, used for getting information out of the computer to the outside world.

1.2.3.1 Data and Variables

All computer programs, except the most trivial, are written to operate on *data*. For example:

- The data for an action game might be keys pressed or the position of the cursor when the mouse is clicked.
- The data for a word processing program are the keys pressed while you are typing a document.
- The data for an accounting program would include, among other things, expenses and income.
- The data for a program that teaches Spanish could be an English word that you type in response to a question.

Recall that a program must be stored in the computer's memory for it to be run. When data is supplied to a program, that data is also stored in memory. Thus we think of memory as a place for holding programs and data. One of the nice things about programming in a high-level language (as opposed to machine language) is that you don't have to worry about which memory locations are used to store your data. But how do we refer to an item of data, given that there may be many data items in memory?

Think of memory as a set of boxes (or storage locations). Each box can hold one item of data, for example, one number. We can give a name to a box, and we will be able to refer to that box by the given name. In our example, we will need two boxes, one to hold the side of the square and one to hold the area. We will call these boxes s and a, respectively.

s   a

If we wish, we can change the value in a box at any time; since the values can vary, s and a are called variable names, or simply *variables*. Thus a variable is a name associated with a particular memory location or, if you wish, it is a *label* for the memory location. We can speak of giving a variable a value, or setting a variable to a specific value, 1, say. Important points to remember are:

- A box can hold only one value at a time; if we put in a new value, the old one is lost.
- We must not assume that a box contains any value unless we specifically store a value in the box. In particular, we must not assume that the box contains zero.

Variables are a common feature of computer programs. It is very difficult to imagine what programming would be like without them. In everyday life, we often use variables. For example, we speak of an *address*. Here, *address* is a variable whose value depends on the person under consideration. Other common variables are telephone number, name of school, subject, size of population, type of car, television model, etc. (What are some possible values of these variables?)

1.2.3.2 Example – Develop the Algorithm

Using the notion of an algorithm and the concept of a variable, we develop the following algorithm for calculating the area of a square, given one side:

Algorithm for calculating area of square, given one side

1. Ask the user for the length of a side
2. Store the value in the box s
3. Calculate the area of the square (s × s)
4. Store the area in the box a
5. Print the value in box a, appropriately labelled
6. Stop

When an algorithm is developed, it must be checked to make sure that it is doing its intended job correctly. We can test an algorithm by 'playing computer', that is, we execute the instructions by hand, using appropriate data values. This process is called *dry running* or *desk checking* the algorithm. It is used to pinpoint any errors in logic before the computer program is actually written. We should *never* start to write programming code unless we are confident that the algorithm is correct.

1.2.4 Write the Program for the Algorithm

We have specified the algorithm using English statements. However, these statements are sufficiently 'computer-oriented' for a computer program to be written directly from them. Before we do this, let us see how we expect the program to work from the user's point of view.

First, the program will type the request for the length of a side; we say the program *prompts* the user to supply data. The screen display might look like this:

```
Enter length of side:
```

The computer will then wait for the user to type the length. Suppose the user types 12. The display will look like this:

```
Enter length of side: 12
```

The program will then accept (we say *read*) the number typed, calculate the area and print the result. The display may look like this:

```
Enter length of side: 12
Area of square is 144
```

Here we have specified what the *output* of the program should look like. For instance, there is a blank line between the prompt line and the line that gives the answer; we have also specified the exact form of the answer. This is a simple example of *output design*. This is necessary since the programmer cannot complete the program unless he knows the precise output required.

In order to write the computer program from the algorithm, a suitable *programming language* must be chosen. We can think of a *program* as a set of instructions, *written in a programming language*, which, when executed, will produce a solution to a given problem or perform some specified task.

The major difference between an algorithm and a program is that an algorithm can be written using informal language without having to follow any special rules (though some *conventions* are usually followed) whereas a program is written in a programming language and *must* follow all the rules (the *syntax* rules) of the language. (Similarly, if we wish to write correct English, we must follow the syntax rules of the English language.)

In this book, we will be showing you how to write programs in Julia, the programming language developed by Jeff Bezanson, Stefan Karpinski, Viral B. Shah, and Alan Edelman. They set out to create a free language that was both high-level and fast. It was officially launched in 2012, and has rapidly grown in popularity.

Program P1.1 is a Julia program which requests the user to enter the length of a side and prints the area of the square:

```
# Program P1.1 - Area of Square
# Given length of side, calculate area of square
function areaOfSquare()
    print("Enter length of side: ")
    s = parse(Int, readline()) # fetch the length typed by the user
    a = s * s                  # calculate area; store in a
    println("\nArea of square is $a")
end

areaOfSquare()  # call the function to get the action started
```

It is not too important that you understand anything about this program at this time. The first two lines are *comments*. (In Julia, they begin with #.) Comments help to explain things about a program but have no effect when the program is run.

Next, observe that this program has a *function* called `areaOfSquare` followed by opening and closing brackets. Then there are four statements called the *body* of the function. The first two prompt and fetch a number typed by the user (*read*). The third does a calculation (*evaluate*) and the fourth outputs the answer (*print*). * denotes multiplication. The *reserved word* end indicates the end of the function. And the last statement `areaOfSquare()` *calls/invokes* the function `areaOfSquare` to do its job. All of this will be explained in detail in due course.

Terminology: A program written in a high-level language is a *source program* or *source code*.

1.2.5 Test and Debug the Program

Having written the program, the next job is to *test* it to find out whether it is doing its intended job. Testing a program involves the following steps:

1. *Compile the program*: recall that a computer can execute a program written in *machine language only*. Before the computer can run our Julia program, the latter must be converted to machine language. We say that the *source code* must be converted to *object code* or *machine code*. The program which does this job is called a *compiler* or *interpreter*. Appendix A tells you how you can acquire a Julia compiler for writing and running your programs.

   Among other things, a compiler/interpreter will check the source code for *syntax errors*—errors which arise from breaking the rules for writing statements in the language. For example, suppose we wrote this:

   ```
   print("Enter length of side: )
   ```

   We would get an error about a missing double quote.

   If the program contains syntax errors, these must be corrected before compiling it again. When the program is free from syntax errors, the compiler will convert it to machine language and we can go on to the next step.

2. *Run the program*: here we request the computer to execute the program and we supply data to the program *for which we know the answer*. Such data is called *test data*. Some values we can use for the length of a side are 3, 12 and 20.

   If the program does not give us the answers 9, 144 and 400, respectively, then we know the program contains at least one *logic* error. A logic error is one which causes a program to give incorrect results for valid data. A logic error may also cause a program to *crash* (come to an abrupt halt).

   If a program contains logic errors, we must *debug* the program; we must find and correct any errors that are causing the program to produce wrong answers.

To illustrate, suppose the statement which calculates the area was written (incorrectly) as this:

```
a = s + s;
```

When the program is run, the user enters 10. (Below, 10 is underlined to indicate it is typed by the user.) Now we *know* the area should be 100. But when the program is run, it prints this:

```
Enter length of side: 10
Area of square is 20
```

Since this is *not* the answer we expect, we know that there is an error (perhaps more than one) in the program. Since the area is wrong, the logical place to start looking for the error is in the statement which calculates the area. If we look closely, we should discover that + was typed instead of *. When this correction is made, the program works fine.

1.2.6 Document the Program

The final job is to complete the documentation of the program. So far, our documentation includes the following:

- The statement of the problem.
- The algorithm for solving the problem.
- The program listing.
- Test data and the results produced by the program.

These are some of the items that make up the *technical documentation* of the program. This is documentation that is useful to a programmer, perhaps for modifying the program at a later date.

The other kind of documentation which must be written is *user documentation*. This enables a non-technical person to use the program without needing to know about the internal workings of the program. Among other things, the user needs to know how to load the program in the computer and how to use the various features of the program. If appropriate, the user will also need to know how to handle unusual situations which may arise while the program is being used.

1.2.7 Maintain the Program

Except for things like class assignments, programs are normally meant to be used over a long period of time. During this time, errors may be discovered which previously went unnoticed. Errors may also surface because of conditions or data that never arose before. Whatever the reason, such errors must be corrected.

But a program may need to be modified for other reasons. Perhaps the assumptions made when the program was written have now changed due to changed company policy or even due to a change in government regulations (e.g. changes in income tax rates). Perhaps the company is changing its computer system and the program needs to be *migrated* to the new system. We say the program must be *maintained*.

Whether or not this is easy to do depends a lot on how the original program was written. If it was well-designed and properly documented, then the job of the *maintenance programmer* would be made so much easier.

1.3 How a Computer Executes a Program

First, recall that a computer can execute a program written in machine language only. For the computer to execute the instructions of such a program, those instructions must be *loaded* into the computer's *memory* (also called *primary storage*), like this:

| instruction 1 |
| instruction 2 |
| instruction 3 |
| etc. |

You can think of memory as a series of storage locations, numbered consecutively starting at `0`. Thus you can speak of memory location `27` or memory location `31548`. The number associated with a memory location is called its *address*.

A computer *runs* a program by executing its first instruction, then the second, then the third, and so on. It is possible that one instruction might say to jump over several instructions to a particular one and continue executing from there. Another might say to go back to a previous instruction and execute it again.

No matter what the instructions are, the computer faithfully executes them exactly as specified. That is why it is so important that programs specify precisely and exactly what must be done. The computer cannot know what you *intend*, it can only execute what you *actually write*. If you give the computer the wrong instruction, it will blindly execute it just as you specify.

1.4 Data Types

Every day we meet names and numbers—at home, at work, at school or at play. A person's name is a type of data; so is a number. We can thus speak of the two *data types* called *name* and *number*. Look at this statement:

```
Caroline bought 3 dresses for $199.95
```

In it, we can find:

- An example of a name: `Caroline`.
- Two examples of numbers: `3` and `199.95`.

Usually, we find it convenient to divide numbers into two kinds:

1. Whole numbers, or *integers*.
2. Numbers with a decimal point, so-called *real* or *floating-point* numbers. (Since `real` has a special place in Julia for working with *complex* numbers, we will use *floating-point number* or *float*.)

In the example, `3` is an *integer* and `199.95` is a *float*.

Exercise: Identify the data types—names, integers and floats—in the following:

1. Bill's batting average was `35.25` with a highest score of `99`.
2. Abigail, who lives at `41` Third Avenue, worked `36` hours at `$11.50` per hour.
3. In his `8` subjects, Richard's average mark was `68.5`.

Generally speaking, programs are written to manipulate data of various types. We use the term *numeric* to refer to numbers (integer or floating-point). We use the term *string* to refer to non-numeric data such as a name, address, job description, title of a song or vehicle number (which is not really a number as far as the computer is concerned—it usually contains letters, e.g. `PTW6052`). (Note, however, that hexadecimal numbers *can* contain the letters `A-F`, e.g. `3D`, written in Julia as `0x3D`, which has the decimal value `61`.)

Programming languages precisely define the various types of data which can be manipulated by programs written in those languages. Integer, floating-point, character (a single character such as `'K'` or `'+'`) and string data types are the most common.

Each data type defines *constants* of that type. For example,

- Some integer constants are 3, -52, 0 and 9813.
- Some float constants are 3.142, -5.0, 345.21 and 1.16.
- Some character constants are 't', '?', '8' and 'R'. (Character constants are enclosed in *single* quotes.)
- Some string constants are "Hi there", "Wherefore art thou, Romeo?" and "Julia World". (String constants are enclosed in *double* quotes.)

In many languages, before we use a variable, we have to say what type of data we intend to store in that variable—we say we must *declare* the variable. One major difference between Julia and other major languages is that you don't *have to* declare variables explicitly in Julia. If you don't declare the type of a variable, Julia will determine its type from the way you use it.

For example, if you write b=7, Julia will set the type of b to Int64 (integer); if you write b=17.75, b will have type Float64; and if you use b="Hi", b will have type String.

Julia data types will be discussed in detail starting from the next chapter.

1.5 Characters

In computer terminology, we use the term *character* to refer to any one of the following:

- A digit from 0 to 9.
- An uppercase letter from A to Z.
- A lowercase letter from a to z.
- A special symbol like (,), $, =, <, >, +, -, /, *, etc.

The following are commonly used terms:

letter – one of a to z or A to Z

lowercase letter – one of a to z

uppercase letter – one of A to Z

digit – one of 0, 1, 2, 3, 4, 5, 6, 7, 8, 9

special character – any symbol except a letter or a digit e.g. +, <, $, &, *, /, =

control character – this is a character which, when pressed, does not type anything but creates an *effect.* Examples are tab, new line, new page and backspace.

alphabetic – used to refer to a letter

numeric – used to refer to a digit

alphanumeric – used to refer to a letter or a digit

Characters are the basic building blocks used in writing programs.

Point to note: In this book, we will deal mainly with characters from the ASCII character set. But note, in general, Julia can handle any Unicode characters; these include, among others, accented characters, and those found in languages such as Hindi, Greek, Chinese, Arabic and Korean.

We put characters together to form *variables* and *constants*.

We put variables, constants and special characters to form *expressions* such as

```
(a + 2.5) * (b - c)
```

We add special words such as `if`, `else`, `while` and `end` to form *statements* such as this:

```
if a > 0
    b = a + 2
else
    b = a - 2
end
```

And we put statements together to form *programs*.

1.6 Welcome to Julia Programming

We take a quick peek at the Julia programming language by writing a program to print the message

```
Welcome to Trinidad & Tobago
```

One solution is Program P1.2.

Program P1.2 - Welcome

```
println("Welcome to Trinidad & Tobago")
```

That's it! Just a single `println()` statement. Here, the thing to be printed (called the *argument* to `println`) is a string (a set of characters enclosed in double quotes). When the program is run, the *value* of the string (the characters not including the quotes) is printed.

This, of course, is the simplest program we will ever write—a one-line program.

We now rewrite the program to do the same thing but with a bit more structure. We do this to set the stage early for what is to come. We show it as Program P1.2a.

Program P1.2a - Welcome

```
function welcome()
    println("Welcome to Trinidad & Tobago")
end

welcome()
```

Here, we have a *function* called `welcome`. A Julia program normally consists of one or more units called functions. A function consists of

- a *header*—`function welcome()`—the word `function` followed by a name of your choosing followed by parentheses
- a *body*; here it consists of the single `println()` statement (but could have as many statements as we wish)
- the *keyword* `end`

The statement `welcome()` *calls* (invokes) the function `welcome` to do its job, which is to execute the *body*—the `println()` statement. When it does, the following is displayed (printed) on the screen:

```
Welcome to Trinidad & Tobago
```

Here, the `println()` statement consists of one *argument* written inside the brackets—the string `"Welcome to Trinidad & Tobago"`. When executed, the *value* of the string (the characters without the quotes) is printed.

Caution: In `println(...)` there must be no space between n and (.

Tip: The statement `println()`, with nothing inside the brackets, prints a blank line.

1.7 A Program With Input

Many programs require the user to type some input at the keyboard. The next program illustrates this. When run, we would like the program to work as follows (normally, we will underline items typed by the user; everything else is typed by the computer):

```
Hi, what's your name? Vaishnavi
Delighted to meet you, Vaishnavi
```

Here is the program:

```
# Program P1.3 - Greeting

function greet()
    print("Hi, what's your name?")
    name = readline()
    println("Delighted to meet you, $name")
end

greet()
```

Observe the use of `print` (rather than `println`) to ask for the name. When we use `print`, the computer waits on the same line as the prompt for the name. Had we used `println`, it would wait on the next line, like this:

```
Hi, what's your name?
Vaishnavi
```

Note, again, the function *header*, the *body* which now has three statements, and the word `end`. The statement `greet()` calls the function `greet` to do its job.

By now, we have an idea what `println` does. But look at this statement:

```
name = readline()
```

`readline()` waits for the user to type something and press `Return/Enter` on the keyboard. Whatever is typed is stored in (we say *assigned to*) the *variable* `name` on the left hand side. (Recall, a variable is a label for a place where we can store data to be retrieved later.) The program then continues with the next statement. This is

```
println("Delighted to meet you, $name")
```

Here, again, the argument consists of a string (enclosed in double quotes) but with a difference—`$name`. This tells Julia to print the *value* of the *variable* `name` (whatever is stored there). In the example, the *value* of `name` is `Vaishnavi`. In general, when the string is printed, *$variable* is replaced by the value of *variable*.

We sometimes refer to $name as a *placeholder*. One definition of *placeholder* is "a symbol used in a logical or mathematical expression to represent a quantity that is not yet specified but may occupy that place later".

When we are writing the program, we do not know what value a user may enter as their name, so we do not know what name to print when we write the program. We use $name as a placeholder which will be replaced by the *value* of name when println() is executed.

We note, in passing, that we could get the same effect of program P1.3 with the following only (no need to write a function):

```
print("Hi, what's your name? ")
name = readline()
println("Delighted to meet you, $name")
```

However, the structure we've used will help us to cope better with the demands of writing more complex programs.

Let's expand the example a little. We want to write a program which 'talks' a bit more. When run, it should work as follows:

```
Hi, what's your name? Vaishnavi
Delighted to meet you, Vaishnavi

Where are you from? Princes Town
Oh, I hear Princes Town is lovely
```

The *structure* of the new part is the same as what we had before. The program asks a question, the user responds and the program prints something. The details are shown in program P1.4.

```
# Program P1.4 - Name and Place
function namePlace()
    print("Hi, what's your name? ")
    name = readline()
    println("Delighted to meet you, $name")
    println()
    print("Where are you from? ")
    place = readline()
    println("Oh, I hear $place is lovely")
end

namePlace()
```

Note the use of println(), with nothing inside the brackets, to print a blank line. We could have achieved the same thing by omitting println() and adding \n to the next line, like this:

```
print("\nWhere are you from?")
```

\n (see Section 1.8.1) says *go to the beginning of the next line*, effectively skipping a line. What do you think would happen if you put \n\n? Try it and see.

1.8 Writing Output with print/println

In the previous section, we used println to print a line of output. Now we take a closer look at print/println—the two most common statements for printing output.

We want to write a program to print the following lines from *The Gitanjali* by Rabindranath Tagore:

```
Where the mind is without fear
And the head is held high
```

A first attempt might be this:

```
function Gitanjali()
    print("Where the mind is without fear")
    print("And the head is held high")
end

Gitanjali()
```

However, when run, the program will print this:

```
Where the mind is without fearAnd the head is held high
```

The two strings are joined together (we say they are *concatenated*). This happens because print does not automatically supply a *newline* character after printing its argument(s). Put another way, print does not terminate a line it is printing, unless this is specified explicitly. A newline character would cause subsequent output to begin at the left margin of the next line.

In the example, a newline character is *not* supplied after fear is printed; And the head... is printed on the same line as fear and immediately after it.

1.8.1 The Newline Character, \n (backslash n)

To get the desired effect, we must tell print to supply a newline character after printing ...without fear. We do this using the character sequence \n (backslash n) as in Program P1.5.

```
# Program P1.5 - Gitanjali
function Gitanjali()
    print("Where the mind is without fear\n")
    print("And the head is held high\n")
end

Gitanjali()
```

The first \n says terminate the current output line; subsequent output will start at the left margin of the next line. Thus, And the... will be printed on a new line. The second \n terminates the second line. If it were not present, the output will still come out right, but only because this is the last line of output. When a program is about to terminate, pending output is *flushed*.

As an embellishment, suppose we want to put a blank line between our two lines of output:

```
Where the mind is without fear

And the head is held high
```

Each of the following sets of statements will accomplish this:

```
1. print("Where the mind is without fear\n\n")
   print("And the head is held high\n")

2. print("Where the mind is without fear\n")
   print("\nAnd the head is held high\n")

3. print("Where the mind is without fear\n")
   print("\n")
   print("And the head is held high\n")
```

We just have to make sure and put \n twice between fear and And. The first \n ends the first line; the second ends the second line, in effect, printing a blank line. Julia gives us a lot of flexibility in how we write statements to produce a desired effect.

1.8.2 println()

println() is provided for convenience; it doesn't do anything we couldn't do with print. It has the effect of printing a newline character after printing its argument(s). In other words, subsequent output will always begin at the leftmost position of the next line. The function Gitanjali could have been written like this:

```
function Gitanjali()
    println("Where the mind is without fear")
    println("And the head is held high")
end
```

With println, there is no need to put \n for the output to come out right.

Exercise: What would be printed if we put \n after fear or before And or both?

1.8.3 Escape Sequences

Within the string argument of print (and println), the backslash (\) signals that a special effect is needed. The character following the backslash specifies what to do. This combination (\ followed by another character) is referred to as an *escape sequence*. We have met \n which has the effect of going to the next line.

The following are some of the more common escape sequences:

\n	newline (line feed)
\$	dollar sign
\\	backslash
\"	double quote
\'	single quote
\r	carriage return
\b	backspace
\t	horizontal tab
\f	form feed (new page)

For example, using an escape sequence is probably the easiest way to print a double quote as part of our output. Suppose we want to print the line

```
Use " to begin and end a string
```

We might try this:

```
println("Use " to begin and end a string\n")
```

Julia would assume that the double quote *after* Use ends the string (causing a subsequent error when it can't figure out what to do with to). Using the escape sequence \", we can correctly print the line with this:

```
println("Use \" to begin and end a string")
```

Julia provides another option: enclose the string using three double quotes, like this:

```
println("""Use " to begin and end a string""")
```

This also will print

```
Use " to begin and end a string
```

With a triple-quoted string, we can put " within the string without an escape sequence.

Consider how we might print the following:

```
"Hands in the air!" he commanded
```

Each of the following will do the job:

```
println("""Hands in the air!" he commanded""")
println("\"Hands in the air!\" he commanded")
```

You can decide which you prefer to use.

1.9 Print the Value of a Variable

So far, we have used `print` (and `println`) to print the *value* of a string (enclosed in double quotes) which *may* include a reference to a *string* variable (such as `$name`). However, we can also include references to other kinds of variables.

We do this in pretty much the same manner since, in Julia, we are not required to explicitly declare the type of a variable if we choose not to. One variable looks the same as any other with *usage* determining their type. For instance, in the following, when we assign `52` to `classSize`, since `52` is an integer, Julia figures out that `classSize` should be an integer variable. We'll discuss this in more detail in Chapter 2.

Consider this:

```
classSize = 52
println("The number of students = $classSize")
```

It will print:

```
The number of students = 52
```

In `println`, `$classSize` is replaced by the value of `classSize`; this is `52`. Another example:

```
b = 14
c = 25
println("The sum of $b and $c is $(b + c)")
```

This will print the following:

```
The sum of 14 and 25 is 39
```

In `println`, `$b` is replaced by `14` (value of b), `$c` is replaced by `25` (value of c) and `$(b + c)` is replaced by the value of (14+25), that is, `39`.

Caution: There must be no space between $ and the variable, or $ and (.

In `$(b + c)`, there can be an arbitrary expression (provided it could be evaluated when the statement is executed) between the brackets. The spaces around + are not required; we could have written `$(b+c)`. However, we would get an error if we wrote `$(b+c+d)` but d was undefined or had an incompatible value like "hi" (a string). Even if d had the value "7" (a string containing a number), we would get an error because it's still considered a string.

What do you think will be printed by the following?

```
println("$b + $c = $(b+c)")
```

You'd be right if you said this:

```
14 + 25 = 39
```

Whatever the values of b and c, println will give the correct answer.

Tip: Since we did not declare a type for b (and c), Julia deduces the type based on what we assign to it. Since we assigned the integer 14 to b, Julia will set its type to Int64. On another computer, it might be Int32. To find out what it is on yours, type this:

```
julia> typeof(b)
Int64
```

This means that, on the computer I'm using, an integer is represented using 64 bits unless I declare a different size. We will discuss this in more detail in the next chapter.

1.10 Comments

All programming languages let you include *comments* in your programs. Comments can be used to remind yourself (and others) of what processing is taking place or what a particular variable is being used for. They can be used to explain or clarify any aspect of a program which may be difficult to understand by just reading the programming statements.

This is very important since the easier it is to understand a program, the more confidence you will have that it is correct. It is worth adding anything which makes it easier to understand a program.

Remember that a comment (or lack of one) has absolutely no effect on how the program runs. If you remove all the comments from a program, it will run exactly the same way as with the comments.

Each language has its own way of specifying how a comment must be written. In Julia, we introduce a comment using the special character #. We can have a comment on a line by itself, like this:

```
# This program prints a greeting
```

We can have a comment as part of a line, like this:

```
c = pi * r * r    # calculate area of circle
```

The comment extends from # to the end of the line.

Julia also lets us put multi-line comments in a program. Such a comment starts with #= and can extend over one or more lines until terminated by =#. Here's an example:

```
#= This program reads characters one at a time and
   counts the number of letters found. It also counts
   the number of vowels found. It then calculates
   the percentage of letters that were vowels.
=#
```

If you wish, =# could be placed as above or at the end of the last line (...vowels. =#).

1.11 Julia Basics

We now discuss some basic concepts you need to know in order to write programs in Julia.

A programming language is similar to speaking languages in many respects. It has an *alphabet* (more commonly referred to as a *character set*) from which everything in the language is constructed. It has rules for forming *words* (also called *tokens*), rules for forming statements and rules for forming programs. These are called the *syntax rules* of the language and *must* be obeyed when writing programs. If you violate a rule, your program will contain a *syntax error*. When you attempt to compile/run the program, the compiler/interpreter will inform you of the error. You must correct it and try again.

The first step to becoming a good programmer is learning the syntax rules of the programming language. This is the easy part and many people mistakenly believe that this makes them a programmer. It is like saying learning some rules of English grammar and being able to write some correctly formed sentences makes one a novelist. Novel-writing skills require much more than learning some rules of grammar. Among other things, it requires insight, creativity and a knack for using the right words in a given situation.

In the same vein, a good programmer must be able to creatively use the features of the language to solve a wide variety of problems in an elegant and efficient manner. This is the difficult part and can be achieved only by long, hard study of problem-solving algorithms and writing programs to solve a wide range of problems. But we must start with baby steps.

1.11.1 The Julia Alphabet

In Section 1.5 we introduced the idea of a character. As we indicated then, the Julia alphabet consists of *any* character you can type in *any* language; but for our purposes, we will work mainly with the ASCII (American Standard Code for Information Interchange, pronounced ass-key) character set.

This is a character standard which includes the letters, digits and special characters found on a standard English keyboard. It also includes *control* characters such as backspace, tab, line feed, form feed and carriage return. Each character is assigned a numeric code. The ASCII codes run from 0 to 127.

The programs in this book will be written using the ASCII character set.

Character handling will be discussed in detail in Chapter 6.

1.11.2 Julia Tokens

The *tokens* of a language are the basic building blocks which can be put together to construct programs. A token can be a reserved word (such as `function` or `end`), an identifier (such as `b` or `sum`), a constant (such as `25` or `"Alice in Wonderland"`), a delimiter such as `(` or `#`, or an operator (such as `+` or `=`).

For example, consider the following portion of Program P1.1:

```julia
function areaOfSquare()
    print("Enter length of side: ")
    s = parse(Int, readline()) # fetch the length typed by the user
    a = s * s                  # calculate area; store in a
    println("\nArea of square is $a")
end
```

Starting from the beginning, we can list the tokens in order:

token	type
function	reserved word
areaOfSquare	identifier
(	left bracket, delimiter
)	right bracket, delimiter
print	function name
(	left bracket, delimiter
"..."	string constant
)	right bracket, delimiter
s	variable
=	assignment operator
parse	function name
(	left bracket, delimiter
Int	type name
,	comma, delimiter
readline	function name
(	left bracket, delimiter
)	right bracket, delimiter
)	right bracket, delimiter
#	start of comment

and so on. Therefore, we can think of a program as a *stream of tokens*, which is precisely how the compiler views it. So that, as far as the compiler is concerned, the above could have been written like this:

```
function
    areaOfSquare(
    )
    print(
    "Enter length of side: "
    )
    s = parse(Int,
    readline()) # fetch the length typed by the user
    a =
    s * s                      # calculate area; store in a
    println(
    "\nArea of square is $a")
end
```

The order of the tokens is exactly the same; to the compiler, it *is* the same program (but not as readable, *to us*, as the first). Generally, only the order of the tokens is important. However, Julia imposes some restrictions such as no space between a function name and the left bracket that follows e.g. `areaOfSquare(` or `print(`. But even though Julia gives us that flexibility, we will use a line layout and appropriate spacing to make our programs more readable to human beings.

1.11.3 Reserved Words

Julia uses a number of *keywords* such as `if`, `for` and `while`. A keyword has a special meaning in the context of a Julia program and can be used for that purpose only. For example, `while` can be used only in those places where we need to specify that we want to execute a piece of code repeatedly.

All keywords must be written exactly as specified. For instance, `while` is a keyword but `While` and `whIle` are not. Keywords are reserved, that is, you cannot use them as *your* identifiers. As such, they are usually called *reserved words*. At the time of writing, this is the list of Julia reserved words:

```
baremodule begin      break      catch      const      continue do        else
elseif     end        export     false      finally    for      function  global
if         import     let        local      macro      module   quote     return
struct     true       try        using      while
```

1.11.4 Identifiers

The Julia programmer needs to make up names for things such as variables, function names and symbolic constants (see next section). A name that he makes up is called a *user identifier*.

Julia is extremely flexible in the naming of identifiers but, for our purposes, we will use the following rules:

- It must start with a letter (`a-z` or `A-Z`) or underscore, `_`.
- If other characters are required, they can be any combination of letters, digits or underscore.

(Just so you know, the following are all valid identifiers in Julia: αβθ, ☎, π.)

Examples of valid identifiers:

```
r
R
sumOfRoots1and2
_XYZ
maxThrowsPerTurn
TURNS_PER_GAME
R2D2
root1
```

Examples of invalid identifiers:

```
2hotToHandle    # does not start with a letter or underscore
Net Pay         # contains a space
ALPHA:BETA      # contains an invalid character  :
```

Important points to note:

- Spaces are not allowed in an identifier. If you need one which consists of two or more words, use a combination of uppercase and lowercase letters (as in `numThrowsThisTurn`) or use the underscore to separate the words (as in `num_throws_this_turn`). We prefer the uppercase/lowercase combination.

- In general, Julia is *case-sensitive* (an uppercase letter is considered different from the corresponding lowercase letter). Thus `r` is a different identifier from `R`. And `sum` is different from `Sum`, which is different from `SUM`, which is different from `SuM`.
- You cannot use a Julia reserved word as one of your identifiers.

1.11.5 Some Naming Conventions

Other than the rules for creating identifiers, Julia imposes no restriction on what names to use, or what format (uppercase or lowercase, for instance) to use. However, good programming practice dictates that some common-sense rules should be followed.

An identifier should be meaningful. For example, if it's a variable, it should reflect the value being stored in the variable; `netPay` is a much better variable than `x` for storing someone's net pay, even though both are valid. If it's a function, it should give some indication of what the function is supposed to do; `playGame` is a better identifier than `plg`.

It is a good idea to use upper and lower case combinations to indicate the kind of item named by the identifier. In this book, we use the following conventions:

- A *variable* is normally written in lowercase, for example, `sum`. If we need a variable consisting of two or more words, we start the second and subsequent words with an uppercase letter, for example, `voteCount` or `sumOfSeries`.
- A *symbolic* (or *named*) *constant* is an identifier which can be used in place of a constant such as `100`. Suppose `100` represents the maximum number of items we wish to process in some program. We would probably need to use the number `100` in various places in the program.

  But suppose conditions change and we need to cater for 500 items. We would have to change all occurrences of `100` to `500`. However, we would have to ensure we do *not* change an occurrence of `100` used for some purpose other than the maximum number of items (in a calculation like `principal*rate/100`, say).

  To make it easy to adapt, we can set the identifier `MaxItems` to `100` and use `MaxItems` whenever we need to refer to the maximum number of items. If conditions change, we would just need to set `MaxItems` to the new value *in one place*.

  In our programs, we begin a symbolic constant with an uppercase letter. (Some languages use all uppercase.) If it consists of more than one word, we will start each word with uppercase, as in `MaxThrowsPerTurn`.
- In Julia, we can use the keyword `const` to declare a symbolic *const*ant:

  ```
  const MaxItems = 100
  ```

Now that we have a general idea of some programming basics, we are ready to get down to the nuts and bolts of Julia programming.

EXERCISES 1

1. What makes it possible to do such a variety of things on a computer?
2. Computers can execute instructions written in what language?
3. Give two advantages of assembly language over machine language.
4. Give two advantages of a high-level language over assembly language.
5. Describe two main tasks performed by a compiler.
6. Describe the steps required to solve a problem on a computer.
7. Distinguish between an algorithm and a program.
8. Programming instructions fall into 3 main categories; what are they?
9. Distinguish between a syntax error and a logic error.
10. What is meant by "debugging a program"?
11. Name 3 data types commonly used in programming and give examples of constants of each type.
12. What are the different classes into which characters can be divided? Give examples in each class.
13. What is the purpose of comments in a program?
14. Write a program to print `Welcome to Julia` on the screen.
15. Write a program to print the following:

    ```
    There is a tide in the affairs of men
    Which, taken at the flood, leads on to fortune
    ```

16. Write a program to print any 4 lines of your favourite song or poem.
17. Same as exercise 16, but print a blank line after each line.
18. In the ASCII character set, what is the range of codes for (a) the digits (b) the uppercase letters and (c) the lowercase letters?
19. What is a token? Give examples.
20. Spaces are normally not significant in a Julia program. Give examples where spaces are significant.
21. What is a reserved word? Give examples.
22. Give the rules for making up an identifier.
23. What is a symbolic constant and why is it useful?
24. Give examples of integer constants, floating-point constants and string constants.

CHAPTER 2

Numbers

In this chapter, we will explain the following:

- Integer data types - `Int`, `Int32`, `Int64`
- Floating-point data types - `Float32`, `Float64`
- How to read `Int` and `Float` values
- What happens when `Int` and `Float` values are mixed in the same expression
- What happens when we assign `Int` to `Float` and vice versa
- How to print an integer using a field width
- How to print a floating-point number to a required number of decimal places
- What happens when you use expressions with different types
- Assignment operators
- Updating operators
- The functions `trunc`, `ceil`, `floor`, `round`

2.1 Introduction

Numbers play a big role in the lives of many of us. It is no wonder, then, that they are fundamental to almost all programming languages, and Julia gives them the respect they deserve. Regardless of what you want to do with numbers, regardless of their size, regardless of their type, Julia's got you covered. The language provides all the types (even complex numbers) and all the operations the most demanding of us may require. In this introductory text, we will cover the ones most commonly used.

We will discuss the integer types—`Int`, `Int32`, `Int64` and the floating-point types—`Float32` and `Float64`. We discuss operations within each type and what happens when you mix them in expressions. We'll meet some special-purpose functions and we'll solve several problems that illustrate the concepts that we discuss.

2.2 How to Read Integers

We have seen how to *assign* a value to a variable with statements like these:

```
b = 13
c = 29
```

© The Author(s), under exclusive license to Springer Nature Switzerland AG 2021
N. Kalicharan, *Julia - Bit by Bit*, Undergraduate Topics in Computer Science,
https://doi.org/10.1007/978-3-030-73936-2_2

But how do we get the user to *enter* values for b and c? We might try this:

```
print("Enter a whole number: ")
b = readline()
print("Enter a whole number: ")
c = readline()
sum = b + c
```

Let's run it and see what happens:

```
Enter a whole number: 13
Enter a whole number: 29
ERROR: LoadError: MethodError: no method matching +(::String, ::String)
```

It doesn't work! The error message tells us that we are trying to add two strings. Strings? But I entered two numbers! Yes, but…

Any data fetched by readline() is treated as a string. So, as far as Julia is concerned, b and c contain strings and we cannot add two strings, even if the strings contain numbers only.

(A more technical explanation hinges on the fact that the *integer* 13 is represented by 00000000 00001101—its binary equivalent using 16 bits—but the *string* representation is 00110001 00110011—completely different.)

We have to get Julia to convert the string read ("13", say,) to the number (*integer*) 13. This can be done with the standard Julia function, parse, as follows:

```
b = parse(Int, readline())
```

As before, readline() will fetch whatever is typed; parse will then *try* to convert the input to a whole number; that's the purpose of Int.

Tip: Depending on your computer, Int could be either 32-bit or 64-bit. To find out which it is, type Int at the julia> prompt. On my computer, I got this:

```
julia> Int
Int64
```

When prompted for input here, if you type anything other than an integer, you will get an error. For instance, typing hi or 2.5 will give an error since neither is an integer.

But if you type a valid integer (positive, negative or zero), parse will convert it correctly. The converted value (now an integer) is stored in the variable on the left hand side. The *type* of this variable becomes Int. We now rewrite the code as shown in Program P2.1.

```
# Program P2.1 - Read Integer
function readInt()
    print("Enter a whole number: ")
    b = parse(Int, readline())
    print("Enter a whole number: ")
    c = parse(Int, readline())
    sum = b + c
    println("The sum of $b and $c is $sum")
end # readInt

readInt()
```

This will run correctly without error provided we enter valid integers when prompted.

```
Enter a whole number: 13
Enter a whole number: 29
The sum of 13 and 29 is 42
```

As you may know by now, the `sum` and `println` statements could be replaced by this:

```
println("The sum of $b and $c is $(b+c)")
```

2.3 How to Read Floating-Point Numbers

We just saw how our program can read an integer typed by the user. How can we get it to read a *floating-point* number, one with a decimal point? It's easy once you know the names of the two most common floating-point number types—`Float32` and `Float64`.

Use `Float32` for single-precision numbers (6 or 7 significant digits) and `Float64` for double-precision (13 or 14 significant digits). When in doubt, use `Float64`. We'll use `Float64` in our examples.

We rewrite program P2.1 as program P2.2 to work with floating-point numbers. We replace `Int` by `Float64` in two places, and remove the word 'whole' from the prompts.

```
# Program P2.2 - Read Floating-point Number
function readFloat()
    print("Enter a number: ")
    b = parse(Float64, readline())
    print("Enter a number: ")
    c = parse(Float64, readline())
    sum = b + c
    println("The sum of $b and $c is $sum")
end # readFloat

readFloat()
```

Look at this statement from the program:

```
b = parse(Float64, readline())
```

As before, `readline()` fetches whatever the user types. But this time `parse` converts it to a `Float64` number; this number is stored in `b`.

Since a `Float64` number is stored in `b`, its type becomes `Float64`, regardless of what it was before.

We can see this by typing the following at the `julia>` prompt:

```
julia> b = 13;
julia> typeof(b)
Int64
julia> b = parse(Float64, readline()); # waits for the user to type a number
8.3
julia> typeof(b)
Float64
```

Similar remarks apply to `c`.

The following shows a sample run of Program P2.2:

```
Enter a number: 1.3
Enter a number: 2.9
The sum of 1.3 and 2.9 is 4.2
```

Now we can enter any valid numbers—positive or negative, with or without a point—and the program will run correctly. However, as before, if we enter data that isn't a valid number (like a word), an error will result.

If we enter a number without a point (an integer), Julia will convert it to a floating-point number (e.g. 13 to 13.0) before doing the calculation. Here's an example:

```
Enter a number: 13
Enter a number: 2.9
The sum of 13.0 and 2.5 is 15.9
```

2.4 Example - Average

Now that we've seen how to read numbers, let's look at an example which requires us to read three numbers and find their average. Here's what a sample run of the program could look like:

```
Enter a whole number: 29
Enter a whole number: 10
Enter a whole number: 17

Their average is 18.67
```

A solution is shown as Program P2.3. We print the average to 2 decimal places.

```
# Program P2.3 - Find average of 3 numbers
function average3()
# prompt for 3 numbers and find their average
    print("Enter a whole number: ")
    a = parse(Int, readline())
    print("Enter a whole number: ")
    b = parse(Int, readline())
    print("Enter a whole number: ")
    c = parse(Int, readline())
    average = round((a+b+c)/3,digits=2)
    println("\nTheir average is $average")
end

average3()
```

Points to note about Program P2.3:

- If whole numbers are not entered, the program will crash. This would happen because parse expects an Int. If we want the program to work for numbers that may have a decimal point, change Int to Float64 in the parse statements (and drop 'whole' from the prompts).
- In the println statement, \n produces the blank line in the output.
- Note the statement that calculates average:
  ```
  average = round((a+b+c)/3,digits=2)
  ```
  After the average is calculated, it is rounded to 2 decimal places, using the option digits=2. To round to a whole number, use digits=0.
  round() is an example of a built-in (standard) function. Julia provides many functions which enable us to be more productive. We will see several examples as we progress.

2.5 Example - Square a Number

In Section 1.2.4 we wrote Program P1.1 which, given the length of a side of a square, prints its area. We are now in a position to fully understand how it works. Here is a slightly modified version which finds the square of a number:

```
# Program P2.4 - Square a Number
function square()
# Request a number; print its square

    print("Enter a whole number: ")
    num = parse(Int, readline())
    numSq = num*num
    println("\nSquare of $num is $numSq")
end # square

square()
```

And here's a sample run:

```
Enter a whole number: 6

Square of 6 is 36
```

For this problem, numSq isn't necessary. We could print the same output with this println statement:

```
println("\nSquare of $num is $(num*num)")
```

The program assumes an integer will be entered; if anything other than an integer is entered, the program will crash. Entering 6.0 will also crash the program since, as far as Julia is concerned, 6.0 is not an Int.

To cater for numbers with a point, we just need to change Int to Float64 in the assignment statement so it becomes this:

```
num = parse(Float64, readline())
```

Now we can enter *any* valid number—positive or negative, with or without a point—and the program will run correctly. Here are some sample runs (we also drop 'whole' from the prompt):

```
Enter a number: 7.5

Square of 7.5 is 56.25
```

```
Enter a number: -7.5

Square of -7.5 is 56.25
```

```
Enter a number: 6

Square of 6.0 is 36.0
```

All correct, except the last is not aesthetically pleasing. If we enter a number without a point, can we give the output without a point?

We can, but it requires a little more work. How to do it is shown in Program P2.5. This assumes we know the `if..else` statement. If you do not understand all of it, wait until we cover the `if..else` statement or peek ahead to Section 3.5.

```
# Program P2.5 - Improved Area of Square
function square1()
# Request a number; print its square

    print("Enter a number: ")
    num = parse(Float64, readline())
    if isinteger(num)      # isinteger is a standard Julia function
        println("\nSquare of $(Int(num)) is $(Int(num*num))")
    else
        println("\nSquare of $num is $(num*num)")
    end
end

square1()
```

When a number is entered, the program uses `isinteger(num)` to check if `num` is an integer. If it is, it executes the first `println`; if not, it executes the second `println`.

Study this statement:

```
println("\nSquare of $(Int(num)) is $(Int(num*num))")
```

Here, what follows `$` is not a variable but an *expression*, which must be enclosed in brackets, with no space between `$` and `(`. The expression is evaluated, and the answer converted to `Int`. This `Int` value is then printed. The following is a sample run:

```
Enter a number: 6

Square of 6 is 36
```

As we wanted. Suppose we insert this statement just before the end of the function:

```
println("Type of num: $(typeof(num))")
```

When we run the program, it prints this:

```
Type of num: Float64
```

The *type* of `num` is still `Float64`. `Int(num)` converts the *value* of `num` to `Int` (provided it is convertible: `6.0` is convertible, `6.5` is not) but doesn't change the type of `num`.

2.6 Example - Banking

The following data are given for a customer in a bank: name, account number, average balance and number of transactions made during the month. It is required to calculate the interest earned and service charge.

The interest is calculated as follows:

interest = 3% of average balance

and the service charge is calculated by this:

service charge = 75 cents per transaction

Write a program to read the data for the customer, calculate the interest and service charge, and print the customer's name, average balance, interest and service charge.

When the program is run, we want the output to look like this:

```
Name? Alice Wonder
Account number? RBL4901119250056048
Average balance? 2500
Number of transactions? 13

Name: Alice Wonder
Average balance: $2500.00
Interest: $75.00
Service charge: $9.75
```

A solution is shown as Program P2.6.

```
# Program P2.6 - Bank Calculations
function banking()
    print("Name? ")
    customer = readline()
    print("Account number? ")
    acctNum = readline()
    print("Average balance? ")
    avgBal = parse(Float64, readline())
    print("Number of transactions? ")
    numTrans = parse(Int, readline())

    interest = avgBalance * 0.03
    service = numTrans * 0.75

    println("\nName: $customer")
    println("Average balance: \$$(round(avgBal, digits=2))")
    println("Interest: \$$(round(interest, digits=2))")
    println("Service charge: \$$(round(service, digits=2))")
                        # prints 2 or 1 decimal places
end

banking()
```

This problem is a little more complicated than those we have seen so far. It involves more data and more processing. But we can simplify its solution if we tackle it in small steps.

Firstly, let us outline an algorithm for solving the problem:

```
prompt for and read each item of data
calculate interest earned
calculate service charge
print required output
```

The logic here is fairly straightforward and a little thought should convince us that these are the steps required to solve the problem.

Next, we must choose variables for the data items we need to store. We choose the following:

```
customer - name of customer
acctNum - account number
avgBal - average balance
numTrans - number of transactions
interest - interest earned
service - service charge
```

Prompting for and reading the data are similar to what we've done before. We need only emphasize that when numeric data is being entered, it must be a numeric constant. We cannot, for instance, enter the average balance as $2500 or as 2,500. We must enter it as a pure number— 2500 or 2500.0 or 2500.00.

The calculation of the interest and service charge presents the biggest challenge. We must specify the calculation in a form which the computer can understand and execute.

We cannot, for instance, write this:

```
interest = 3% of avgBal
```

or this:

```
interest = 3% * avgBal
```

or this:

```
service = 75 cents per transaction
```

We must express each right-hand side as a proper arithmetic expression, using appropriate constants, variables and operators. Therefore,

"3% of average balance" must be expressed as `avgBal*0.03` or `0.03*avgBal` or `avgBal*3/100` and "75 cents per transaction" must be expressed as `0.75*numTrans` or `numTrans*0.75` or something equivalent.

Printing the output requires some explanation. Even though, for example, we cannot use $ when entering data for average balance, we can print a dollar sign in front of it when we print its value. All we need to do is print $ as part of a string.

But how do we print $ given that it serves a special purpose within a `println` string? We must use \$.

Since `avgBal`, `interest` and `service` represent dollar amounts, we want to print them to two decimal places. We illustrate using `avgBal`:

```
println("Average balance: \$$(round(avgBal,digits=2))")
```

We use the `digits=2` option within `round` to round `avgBal` to two decimal places before we print it. Note, again, the expression which follows $ must be enclosed within brackets with no space between $ and (.

Similarly, we print `interest` and `service` to two decimal places, labelled with a dollar sign.

This should have been the end of the discussion but an irksome matter arises. When we print `avgBal`, `service` and `interest` for the sample data, this is what we actually get:

```
Average balance: $2500.0
Interest: $75.0
Service charge: $9.75
```

Correct, as numbers, but the first two show only one decimal place, even though we asked for two with `digits=2`. This is due to a quirk of `round`. If, after rounding, the second digit after the point is 0, it is omitted. We see this with the following example:

```
julia> x = 6.5038
6.5038
julia> round(x, digits=2)
6.5
julia> round(x, digits=3)
6.504
```

Is there a way to fix this so we get exactly what we ask for (2 decimal places)? Yes, but not with `print/println`; we must use `@printf`. (If you are familiar with the C language, it's essentially Julia's version of C's `printf` function.)

We will explain `@printf` in more detail in Section 2.8.3 but, for now, take it on faith that we can get what we want with this:

```
@printf("Average balance: \$%0.2f\n", avgBal)
# always prints exactly 2 places
```

As above, we use \$ to print the dollar sign.

We use the specification %0.2f for printing avgBal. Here, ".2" means two decimal places; "0" says to print the value using the exact number of columns needed. This ensures the value of avgBal is printed right next to the dollar sign.

Similarly, we can print interest and service to exactly two decimal places.

Need to know: In order to use @printf you must type using Printf at the julia> prompt before you run the program. Alternatively, you can put using Printf as the first statement in the file containing the program or, at least, before all functions and executable statements. We will show how in the next program.

2.7 Example – Football Tickets

At a football match, tickets are sold in 3 categories: reserved, stands and grounds. For each of these categories, you are given the ticket price and the number of tickets sold. Write a program to prompt for these values and print the amount of money collected from each category of tickets. Also print the total number of tickets sold and the total amount of money collected.

We will write a program which, when run, operates as follows:

```
Price of reserved ticket? 100
Number sold? 500
Price of stands ticket? 75
Number sold? 4000
Price of grounds ticket? 40
Number sold? 8000

Reserved sales: $50000.00
Stands sales: $300000.00
Grounds sales: $320000.00

Total tickets sold: 12500
Total money collected: $670000.00
```

As shown, we prompt for and read the price and the number of tickets sold for each category.

We calculate the sales by multiplying the ticket price by the number of tickets sold.

The total number of tickets sold is calculated by summing the number of tickets sold for each category.

The total money collected is calculated by summing the sales for each category.

An outline of the algorithm for solving the problem is as follows:

```
prompt for and read reserved price and tickets sold
calculate reserved sales

prompt for and read stands price and tickets sold
calculate stands sales

prompt for and read grounds price and tickets sold
calculate grounds sales

calculate total tickets
calculate total sales
print required output
```

A solution is shown as Program P2.7. The prices can be entered with or without a decimal point. The number of tickets sold *must* be entered as a whole number; if not, the program will crash.

As explained earlier, we use @printf (rather than print) to ensure the dollar amounts are always printed to two decimal places.

```
# Program P2.7 - Football Tickets
using Printf
# needed in order to use @printf

function tickets()
    print("Price of reserved ticket? ")
    rPrice = parse(Float64, readline())
    print("Number sold? ")
    rTickets = parse(Int, readline())
    rSales = rPrice * rTickets

    print("Price of stands ticket? ")
    sPrice = parse(Float64, readline())
    print("Number sold? ")
    sTickets = parse(Int, readline())
    sSales = sPrice * sTickets

    print("Price of grounds ticket? ")
    gPrice = parse(Float64, readline())
    print("Number sold? ")
    gTickets = parse(Int, readline())
    gSales = gPrice * gTickets

    tTickets = rTickets + sTickets + gTickets
    tSales = rSales + sSales + gSales

    @printf("\nReserved sales: \$%0.2f\n", rSales)
    @printf("Stands sales: \$%0.2f\n", sSales)
    @printf("Grounds sales: \$%0.2f\n", gSales)
    @printf("\nTotal tickets sold: %d\n", tTickets)
    @printf("Total money collected: \$%0.2f\n", tSales)
end

tickets()
```

For advanced users (may be omitted at a first reading)

Caution: This rest of this section requires knowledge of *array* terminology.

Let us pose the following question: what if the price of a ticket and the number sold were on the same line? The prompt might look like this:

```
Reserved price and tickets sold? 100 500
```

or, even this (noting that the price could have a decimal point):

```
Reserved price and tickets sold? 99.95 500
```

How can we read more than one value from the same line?

Consider this:

```
rPrice, rTickets = [parse(Float64, x) for x in split(readline())]
```

Suppose two numbers are typed in response to readline():

```
3.84 25
```

`split` will convert this into a 2-element `String` array with elements "3.84" and "25". Then, for each of these two elements, `parse` will convert it to a `Float64` number. It assigns the first (3.84) to `rPrice` and the second (25.0) to `rTickets`.

The *array brackets* [and] indicate that the values are to be treated as an array. Because we specified two variables on the left hand side, the first value (3.84) is assigned to the first variable (`rPrice`) and the second value (25) is assigned to the second variable (`rTickets`). Since we used `Float64` in `parse`, the values are floating-point so the value of `rTickets` is 25.0. In essence, this statement declares `rPrice` and `rTickets` to be of type `Float64`.

Let us explore this statement some more:

```
rPrice, rTickets = [parse(Float64, x) for x in split(readline())]
```

The square brackets on the right hand side ([and]) indicate an array is created. But suppose we wrote this (one variable on the left hand side (LHS)):

```
reserved = [parse(Float64, x) for x in split(readline())]
```

and, again, typed this as input in response to `readline()`:

```
3.84 25
```

Now `reserved` is a *2-element Float64 array* with `reserved[1]` = 3.84 and `reserved[2]` = 25.0.

Strictly speaking, when we write this:

```
rPrice, rTickets = [parse(Float64, x) for x in split(readline())]
```

and supply two values, two 1-element *arrays*, `rPrice` and `rTickets`, are created. It is valid to talk about `rPrice[1]` (and `rTickets[1]`) but not `rPrice[2]` (or `rTickets[2]`). When we use `rPrice`, say, in a calculation, it's the same as using `rPrice[1]`.

To elaborate further, consider this statement:

```
arr = [parse(Int, x) for x in split(readline())]
```

When this statement is executed, `arr` becomes an *n*-element integer array if *n* values are supplied in response to `readline()`. Suppose we enter the following:

```
7 3 9 6
```

This creates a 4-element array with `arr[1]=7`, `arr[2]=3`, `arr[3]=9` and `arr[4]=6`. The following shows a sample interaction with Julia:

```
julia> arr = [parse(Int, x) for x in split(readline())]
7 3 9 6
4-element Array{Int64,1}:
 7
 3
 9
 6

julia> arr[1]*4
28

julia> print(arr*4)
[28, 12, 36, 24]

julia> print(arr)
[7, 3, 9, 6]

julia> brr = arr*4
4-element Array{Int64,1}:
 28
```

```
12
36
24
julia> print(brr)
[28, 12, 36, 24]
```

In the next few sections, we delve a little deeper into the basic number types.

2.8 Integers - `Int`

An `Int` variable is used to store an *integer* (whole number) value. An integer value is one of 0, ±1, ±2, ±3, ±4, etc. However, on a computer, the largest and smallest integers which can be stored are determined by the *number of bits* used to store an integer.

Typically, an `Int` variable occupies 32 bits on a 32-bit computer and 64 bits on a 64-bit computer. To find out what it is on *your* computer, just type `Int` at the Julia prompt. I got this:

```
julia> Int
Int64
```

Another person might get a response of `Int32`. Note that this is just the default type for `Int` on the computer you happen to be using. If your default is `Int32` but you need `Int64`, just declare your variables to be `Int64`.

Julia does not require us to declare variables explicitly. Depending on how we use a variable, Julia will try to determine its type. Suppose we write this:

```
n = 99
```

Since 99 is an integer, the type of `n` will be the default size for `Int` (`Int64` on most computers; `Int32` on others). We can find out with `typeof(n)`.

If we wish, we can declare our integers to be exactly the size we want. If we wanted to work with 16-bit integers, we could write a statement like this within our function:

```
num::Int16 = 0
```

If you wish, you can have spaces on either side (or both sides) of `::`. This is valid:

```
num :: Int16 = 0
```

Caution: Julia will complain if you try to declare a variable without assigning a value. Suppose you wrote the following in a function or at the `Julia>` prompt:

```
num::Int16
```

You will get an error message:

```
ERROR: UndefVarError: num not defined
```

However, as of this writing, you can use the word `local` to declare a variable without assigning a value, like this:

```
local num::Int16
```

We can declare several in one statement, like this:

```
local aa::Int16, bb::Int8, cc::Int64
```

We can assign a value in the declaration but *only if we are declaring one item*. We can do this:

```
local num::Int16 = 27
```

but not this:

```
local aa::Int16=99, bb::Int8=79
```

Even if we attempt to assign one value, we'll get an error, like here:

```
local aa::Int16=99, bb::Int8
```

Julia lets us work with *unsigned integers*. To illustrate, with 8 bits we can store bit patterns from 00000000 to 11111111. To represent positive and negative numbers, Julia uses 00000000 to 01111111 for integers from 0 to 127; and 10000000 to 11111111 for negative integers from -128 to -1. The *range* of numbers which can be stored in 8 bits is -128 to 127, or -2^7 to $+2^7-1$.

However, if we are not interested in working with negative integers, we could use the whole range from 00000000 to 11111111 to represent non-negative integers only, from 0 to 255.

With *n* bits, we can store *unsigned* integers from 0 to 2^n-1 and *signed* integers from -2^{n-1} to $+2^{n-1}-1$.

To declare unsigned integers, we put U in front of the integer types Int8, Int16, Int32, Int64 and Int128 to get UInt8, UInt16, UInt32, UInt64 and UInt128. The range of numbers that can be stored for each of these types is shown here:

Type	Range
Int8	-128 to 127
UInt8	0 to 255
Int16	-32,768 to 32,767
UInt16	0 to 65,355
Int32	-2,147,483,648 to +2,147,483,647
UInt32	0 to 4,294,967,295
Int64	-9,223,372,036,854,775,808 to 9,223,372,036,854,775,807
UInt64	0 to 18,446,744,073,709,551,615
Int128	-2^{127} to $2^{127}-1$
UInt128	0 to $2^{128}-1$

Note the following:

```
n::Int8 = 200   # invalid, 200 is outside the range -128 to 127
n::UInt8 = 200  # valid since 200 is within the range 0 to 255
```

If you are testing this at the Julia prompt, make sure and type local, like this:

```
local n::UInt8 = 200
```

If not, you will get the following error:

```
julia> n::UInt8 = 200
ERROR: syntax: type declarations on global variables are not yet supported
```

Variables used at the julia> prompt are considered *global*.

2.8.1 Integer Expressions

An integer constant is written in the manner we are all accustomed to, for example, `354`, `-1`, `639`, `30705` and `-4812`. Note that you can use only a possible sign followed by digits from `0` to `9`. In particular, you *cannot* use commas as you might do to separate thousands; `32,732` is *not* a *valid* integer constant—you must write it as `32732`.

Tip: Julia lets you use the underscore (`_`) in writing numbers. You can use it anywhere you choose. The following are valid: `32_767`, `12_34`, `43_6.31_592` (`436.31592`). The value of a number is the same with or without `_`.

An integer expression can be written using the following *arithmetic operators* (among others):

+	add
−	subtract
*	multiply
/	divide
÷	integer divide
%	remainder
^	power/exponentiation

For example, suppose `a`, `b` and `c` are integers. The following are all valid expressions:

```
a + 39
a + b - c * 2
b % 10          # the remainder when b is divided by 10
c+(a*2+b*2)/2
28 ÷ 8          # discard remainder; ans: 3
3^4             # 3 to the power 4; ans: 81
```

The operators `+`, `-` and `*` all give the expected results. However, `/` performs *normal division*: `25/4` gives `6.25`. Use `÷` for *integer division*; if there is any remainder, it is thrown away. So `25÷4` gives `6` and `19÷5` gives `3`. We say integer division *truncates*.

Tip: To type `÷` on MacOS, type Option-`/`. On a Windows keyboard with a numeric keypad, make sure `Num Lock` is on, and type `Alt-246` or `Alt-0247` (press and hold `Alt`, type `246` or `0247`) Note that you *must* use the keypad, not the number keys above the letters. At the `julia>` prompt, type `\div` and press the `Tab` key.

The value of `-19/5` is `-3.8`. But what about `-19÷5` or `19÷(-5)`? The answer in both cases is `-3`. After division, the fractional part is discarded. Since the exact value of both divisions is `-3.8`, discarding the fraction gives `-3`.

The `%` operator gives the *remainder* when one integer is divided by another. For example,

```
19 % 5 gives 4
h % 7 gives the remainder when h is divided by 7
```

You can use it to test, for instance, if a number `h` is even or odd. If `h % 2` is `0` then `h` is even; if `h % 2` is `1`, `h` is odd.

The % operator is fairly easy to understand with positive numbers. But it can be quite tricky when negative numbers are involved. For instance, what's the value of `-19 % 5` or `19 % (-5)` or `-19 %(-5)`. The answers might surprise you.

To gain some insight, consider `19 % 5`. The quotient (`3.8`), truncated, is `3`; `3×5 = 15`. How much to get to `19`? `4`. So `19 % 5` is `4`.

Let's apply the same process to `-19 % 5`. The quotient (`-3.8`), truncated, is `-3`; `-3×5 = -15`. How much to get to `-19`? `-4`. So `-19 % 5` is `-4`.

What about `19 % (-5)`? The quotient (`-3.8`), truncated, is `-3`; `-3×(-5) = 15`. How much to get to `19`? `4`. So `19 % (-5)` is `4`.

Apply similar reasoning to deduce that `-19%(-5)` is `-4`.

Tip: It is helpful to remember that the value of `x % y` is of the same sign as `x`, and smaller in magnitude than `y`.

2.8.2 Precedence of Operators

Julia evaluates an expression based on the *precedence* of operators that appear in the expression. In the most common case, multiplication and division are done *before* addition and subtraction. We say multiplication and division have (the same) *higher precedence* than addition and subtraction (which have the same precedence). For example, look at this expression:

```
5 + 3 * 4
```

It is evaluated by *first* multiplying `3` by `4` (giving `12`) and *then* adding `5` to `12`, giving `17` as the value of the expression.

As usual, we can use brackets to force evaluation in the order we want. Consider this:

```
(5 + 3) * 4
```

We add `5` and `3` (giving `8`), then multiply `8` by `4`, giving `32`.

When two operators which have the *same* precedence appear in an expression, they are evaluated *from left to right* (we say they *associate* from left to right), unless specified otherwise by brackets. For example,

```
24 / 4 * 2
```

is evaluated as

```
(24 / 4) * 2
```

(giving `12`) and

```
12 - 7 + 3
```

is evaluated as

```
(12 - 7) + 3
```

giving `8`. However,

```
24 / (4 * 2)
```

is evaluated as expected, giving `3`, and

```
12 - (7 + 3)
```

is evaluated as expected, giving `2`.

The remainder operator % and the integer divide operator ÷ have the same precedence as multiplication (*) and division (/).

Of particular interest is the exponentiation operator ^ which raises a number to a given power. It's interesting because it's one of the few operators which associates *from right to left*. Consider this:

```
3^2^3
```

This is evaluated as $3\verb|^|(2\verb|^|3) = 3\verb|^|8$, giving 6561. But $(3\verb|^|2)\verb|^|3 = 9\verb|^|3 = 729$.

Even if *you* know the order of evaluation, the person reading your code may not, so it's a good idea to use brackets to remove any possible doubt.

Exercise: What is printed by the following? Verify your answer by typing and running the program.

```
function exercise()
    a = 15
    b = 24
    println("$(b - a + 7), $(b - (a + 7))")
    println("$(b - a - 4), $(b - (a - 4))")
    println("$(b % a ÷ 2), $(b % (a ÷ 2))")
    println("$(b * a ÷ 2), $(b * (a ÷ 2))")
    println("$(b ÷ 2 * a), $(b ÷ (2 * a))")
    println("$((b ÷ 12) ^ (a ÷ 5) ^ 2)")
end

exercise()
```

2.8.3 Print an Integer Using a *Field Width*

Earlier, we introduced the @printf statement which allowed us to print money values to two decimal places. But it can do much more than that. In general, it allows us to have more control over our output format than we have with print/println. We now explore @printf in a bit more detail.

Suppose n is an integer with value 782 representing a number of marbles. We can print n with the following:

```
@printf("Number of marbles = %d\n", n)
```

This will print

```
Number of marbles = 782
```

%d is called a *format specification*. When the string is printed, %d will be replaced by the value of n, the variable after the comma. Since the value of n has 3 digits, it will be printed using 3 print columns. If its value was 65535, it would be printed using 5 print columns.

While this is usually sufficient for most purposes, there are times when it is useful to be able to tell Julia how many print columns to use. For example, if we want to print the value of n in 5 print columns, we can do so by specifying a *field width* of 5, as in:

```
@printf("%5d", n)
```

Instead of %d, we now use %5d. The field width is placed between % and d. The value of n is printed *in a field width of* 5.

Suppose n is 279; there are 3 digits to print so 3 print columns are needed. Since the field width is 5, the number 279 is printed with 2 spaces before it, like this: ◊◊279 (◊ denotes a space). We also say *printed with 2 leading blanks/spaces* and *printed padded on the left with 2 blanks/spaces.*

A technical way of saying this is "n is printed *right-justified* in a field width of 5". *Right-justify* means that the number is placed as far right as possible in the field and spaces added in *front* of it to make up the field width.

 If the number is placed as far *left* as possible and spaces are added *after* it to make up the field width, the number is *left-justified*. For example, 2790◊ is left-justified in a field width of 5.

The minus sign can be used to specify *left-justification*; %-wd (w is a positive integer) will print a value left-justified in a field width of w. For example, to print an integer left-justified in field width of 5, we use %-5d.

For another example, suppose n is -7 and the field width is 5. Printing n requires two print columns (one for - and one for 7); since the field width is 5, it is printed with 3 leading spaces: ◊◊◊-7.

You may ask, what will happen if the field width is too small? Suppose the value to be printed is 23456 and the field width is 3. Printing this value requires 5 columns which is greater than the field width 3. In this case, Julia ignores the field width and simply prints the value using as many columns as needed (5, in this example).

In general, suppose the integer value v is printed with the specification %wd where w is a positive integer, and suppose n columns are needed to print v. There are 3 cases to consider:

1. If n is less than w (the field width is bigger), the value is padded on the left with (w-n) spaces. If w is 7 and v is -345 so n is 4, the number is padded on the left with (7-4) = 3 spaces and printed as ◊◊◊-345.

2. If n is equal to w (field width is the same), the value is printed using n print columns.

3. If n is greater than w (field width is smaller), w is ignored and the value printed using n print columns.

A field width is useful when we want to line up numbers one below the other. Suppose we have three Int variables a, b and c with values 9876, -3 and 501, respectively. The statements

```
@printf("%d\n", a)
@printf("%d\n", b)
@printf("%d\n", c)
```

will print this:

```
9876
-3
501
```

Each number is printed using just the number of columns required. Since this varies from one number to the next, they do not line up. If we want to, we could get the numbers lined up using a field width of 5, say. The statements

```
@printf("%5d\n", a)
@printf("%5d\n", b)
@printf("%5d\n", c)
```

will print this (◊ denotes a space):

```
◊9876
◊◊◊-3
◊◊501
```

which will look like this (without ◊), all nicely lined up:

```
9876
  -3
 501
```

Just so you know, we don't really need three @printf statements. We can replace them with this:

```
@printf("%5d\n%5d\n%5d\n", a, b, c)
```

Each \n forces the following output onto a new line.

2.9 Floating-point Numbers

We introduced *floating-point* numbers in Section 2.3. We now discuss the topic in more detail.

A floating-point number is one which may have a fractional part. A *floating-point constant* can be written in one of two ways:

- The normal way, with an optional sign, and including a decimal point; for example, -3.75, 0.537, 47.0.

- Using *scientific* notation, with an optional sign, including a decimal point and including an *exponent* part. For example, we can write 42.715 as 0.42715E2 which means "0.42715 multiplied by 10 to the power 2".

  Similarly, 0.537 can be written as 5.37e-1, that is, 5.37×10^{-1}. The exponent can be specified using either e or E.

- There are several ways to write the same number. For example, the following all represent the same number 27.96:

  27.96E00 2.796e1 2.796E+1 2.796E+01 0.2796e+02 279.6E-1

  Caution: There must be no space anywhere between the first digit of the number and the last digit of the exponent.

We declare a floating-point variable using either Float32 or Float64. A Float32 value is stored as a 32-bit floating-point number, giving 6-7 significant digits. This is usually referred to as *single-precision*.

A Float64 value is stored as a 64-bit floating-point number, giving 13-14 significant digits. We call this *double-precision*.

A floating-point *constant*, written in the usual way, is of type Float64 unless specified otherwise. So 3.75 and -47.2 are of type Float64. If a number is written in scientific notation using e or E, it's also Float64.

On the other hand, if a number is written in scientific notation using f (but not F), it is considered Float32. So, for instance, 3.45f1 is the Float32 equivalent of 34.5. Suppose we write this:

```
num = 3.45f1
```

num becomes a Float32 variable with value 34.5. We could achieve the same result with this:

```
num = Float32(34.5)
```

Most calculations are done using Float64 precision. Float32 is useful if you need to store lots of floating-point numbers and wish to use as little storage as possible (and do not mind just 6-7 digits of precision).

Almost always, we will use Float64 for working with floating-point numbers.

2.9.1 Print Float64 and Float32 Variables

We have been using the *format specification* %d in @printf statements to print the value of an integer variable. If we wish to print the value of a floating-point variable, we use %f. For example, consider the following:

```
d::Float64 = 987.458321
@printf("%f \n", d)
```

This will print the value 987.458321.

However, if d were assigned 987.4583216, the value printed would be 987.458322 (rounded to 6 decimal places).

But if d were 9.87, the value printed would be 9.870000.

Similarly, if x is of type Float32, its value could be printed using this:

```
@printf("%f \n", x)
```

The specification %f prints the number to a pre-defined number of decimal places. Most times, though, we want to say how many decimal places to print and, sometimes, how many columns to use. For example, if we want to print d, above, to 2 decimal places in a field width of 6, we could use this:

```
@printf("%6.2f \n", d)
```

Between % and f, we write 6.2, that is, the field width, followed by a . (point), followed by the number of decimal places. The value is *rounded* to the stated number of decimal places and then printed. Here, the value printed will be 987.46, which occupies exactly 6 print columns.

If the field width were bigger, the number will be padded on the left with spaces. If the field width were smaller, it is ignored, and the number is printed using as many columns as necessary.

As another example, consider this:

```
b = 245.77
@printf("%6.1f \n", b)
```

In the specification %6.1f, 1 says to *round* the number to 1 decimal place; this gives 245.8, which requires 5 columns for printing.

6 says to print 245.8 in six columns; since only five columns are needed for printing the number, one space is added at the beginning to make up 6 columns, so the number is printed as ◊245.8 (◊ denotes a space).

Similarly,

```
@printf("%6.0f \n", b)
```

will print b as ◊◊◊246 (rounded to 0 decimal places and printed in a field width of 6).

If the specification were %3.1f and the value to be printed is 245.8, it would be printed using 5 print columns, even though the field width is 3. Again, when the field width specified is *smaller* than the number of print columns required, Julia ignores the field width and prints the value using as many columns as needed.

We can sometimes use this to our advantage. If we do not know how big a value might be, we can deliberately use a small field width to ensure it is printed using the exact number of print columns required for printing the value.

Tip: When the size of the number to print can vary or is unpredictable, but you know how many decimal places you need, it's good practice to use a field width of 0, as in %f0.3 (assuming you need 3 decimal places).

In general, suppose the `Float` value v is to be printed with the specification %w.df where w and d are integers. First, the value v is *rounded* to d decimal places. Suppose the number of print columns required to print v, including a possible point (there will be no point if d = 0; the value is to be rounded to a whole number) and a possible sign, is n. There are 2 cases to consider:

1. If n is less than w (the field width is bigger), the value is padded on the left with (w-n) spaces. For example, suppose w is 7 and the value to be printed is -3.45 so that n is 5. The number is padded on the left with (7-5) = 2 spaces and printed like this: ◊◊-3.45.

2. If n is greater than or equal to w (field width is the same or smaller), the value is printed using n print columns.

As with integers, a field width is useful when we want to line up numbers one below the other. Assume we have three `Float64` variables a, b and c with values 419.563, -8.7 and 3.25, respectively. Suppose we want to print the values to 2 decimal places, lined up on the decimal point, like this:

```
419.56
 -8.70
  3.25
```

Since the biggest number requires 6 print columns, we can line them up using a field width of at least 6. The following statements will line them up as above:

```
@printf("%6.2f \n", a)
@printf("%6.2f \n", b)
@printf("%6.2f \n", c)
```

If we use a field width bigger than 6, the numbers will still line up but with leading spaces.

For example, if we use a field width of 8, we will get this (◊ denotes a space):

```
◊◊419.56
◊◊◊-8.70
◊◊◊◊3.25
```

Again, we can use one @printf instead of three to achieve the same effect:

```
@printf("%6.2f \n%6.2f \n%6.2f \n", a, b, c)
```

Each \n forces the following output onto a new line.

2.9.2 Assignment Between Float64 and Float32

As expected, you can store a `Float32` value in a `Float32` variable and a `Float64` value in a `Float64` variable.

Since `Float32` is smaller than `Float64`, you can store a `Float32` value in a `Float64` variable without any problems.

However, if you assign a `Float64` to a `Float32`, some precision may be lost. Consider the following:

```
d6 = Float64(987654321.12345)
d3 = Float32(d6)
@printf("Float64: %f, Float32: %f \n", d6, d3)
```

When executed, these statements print this:

```
Float64: 987654321.123450, Float32: 987654336.000000
```

The `Float64` variable is printed correctly but the `Float32` variable has retained only seven digits of precision.

As an exercise, see what values are printed on your computer.

2.9.3 Floating-point Expressions

Floating-point expressions can be written using the same operators we used for integers. There are others but these are the ones most commonly used:

+	add
-	subtract
*	multiply
/	divide
÷	divide; discard remainder
%	remainder
^	power/exponentiation

The operators +, -, * and / all give the expected results. In the case of ÷, it performs the division and discards the remainder, as we see in this example:

```
julia> 25.0/6.5
3.8461538461538463
julia> 25.0 ÷ 6.5
3.0
```

In the following, observe that the type of b changes according to the type of the operands. If both operands are `Int`, the result is `Int`; if at least one is `Float`, the result is `Float`.

```
julia> b = 19 ÷ 5
3
julia> typeof(b)
Int64
julia> b = 19 ÷ 5.0
3.0
julia> typeof(b)
Float64
```

When we discussed integers, we saw that the % operator gives the remainder when one integer is divided by another. For example, 19 % 5 = 4.

The *process* to arrive at the answer starts with asking, which (integer) multiple of 5 is closest to 19 but less than or equal to 19? The answer is 3. Then, by how much is 3×5 less than 19? We get our answer 4.

But what does *remainder* mean with floating-point numbers? Consider this:

```
b = 24.8 % 6.4
```

What value is assigned to b? We can use the process just described to get the answer.

We ask, which integer multiple of 6.4 is closest to 24.8 but less than or equal to 24.8? The answer is 3. And 3×6.4=19.2. Then, by how much is 19.2 less than 24.8? We get our answer 5.6.

Let's try this: 24.8 % 6.8. We have 3×6.8=20.4. How much is 20.4 less than 24.8?

Answer: `24.8` - `20.4` = `4.4`. In Julia, we get this:

```julia
julia> b = 24.8 % 6.8
4.400000000000001
```

Not quite what we were expecting! Because most floating-point numbers cannot be represented exactly in a `Float64` (or any other) type, answers are almost always an approximation to the mathematical answer.

The expression `19.0 % 5.1` gives this: `3.700000000000001` instead of `3.7` (`19.0` - `3×5.1`).

As with integers, the `%` operator can be quite tricky when negative floats are involved. But the process of figuring out the answer is the same as for integers. The following shows how:

```julia
# The general principle is to determine which integer multiple of the divisor is
# closest to the dividend; the distance from the dividend is the "remainder".

julia> 19.7 % 5.1
4.4                      # the amount to get to 19.7 from 3×5.1=15.3

julia> -19.7 % 5.1
-4.4                     # the amount to get to -19.7 from (-3)×5.1=-15.3

julia> 19.7 % (-5.1)
4.4                      # the amount to get to 19.7 from (-3)×(-5.1)=15.3

julia> -19.7 % (-5.1)
-4.4                     # the amount to get to -19.7 from 3×(-5.1)=-15.3

julia> -19.6 % 5.1
-4.3000000000000025      # the mathematical answer is -4.3

julia> 19.6 % (-5.1)
4.3000000000000025       # the mathematical answer is 4.3

julia> -19.6 % (-5.1)
-4.3000000000000025      # the mathematical answer is -4.3
```

What happens if we have an expression with `Float32` and/or `Float64` values? If `op1` and `op2` are the two operands of an operator, the following shows the *type* of calculation performed and, hence, the type of the answer:

op1	op2	type of calculation
Float32	Float32	Float32
Float32	Float64	Float64
Float64	Float32	Float64
Float64	Float64	Float64

`Float32` is performed only if both operands are `Float32`; otherwise, `Float64` is performed.

2.9.4 Mixed Expressions

It is quite common to use expressions involving both integer and floating-point values, for example,

```
a/3 where a is Float64
n*0.25 where n is Int32
```

In Julia, the rule for such expressions is this:

If either operand of an arithmetic operator is floating-point, the calculation is done in floating-point arithmetic. The calculation is done in Float64 *unless both operands are* Float32, *in which case the calculation is done in* Float32.

In the first example above, the integer 3 is converted to Float64 and the calculation is done in Float64. In the second example, n is converted to Float64 (since 0.25 is Float64) and the calculation is done in Float64.

The following should shed a bit more light on how the *type* of a calculation is determined.

```
julia> b = 24f0
24.0f0
julia> typeof(b)
Float32

julia> c = b/3
8.0f0
julia> typeof(c)
Float32
# The Int 3 is promoted to Float32, the type of b; result is Float32
# Note: the result 8.0f0 should also tell you the type of c is Float32

julia> c = b/3.0
8.0
julia> typeof(c)
Float64
# The value of b is promoted to Float64, the type of 3.0; the result is Float64
# The result 8.0 (Float64 constant) should also tell you the type of c is Float64

julia> typeof(b)
Float32
# The type of b has not changed
```

2.10 Assignment Operator

So far, we have used the assignment operator, =, to assign the value of an expression to a variable, as in the following:

```
c = a + b
```

The entire construct consisting of the variable, = and the expression is referred to as an *assignment statement*. The *value* of an assignment statement is simply the value assigned to the variable; if a is 15 and b is 20, then the following statement assigns the value 35 to c:

```
c = a + b
```

The value of the (entire) assignment statement is 35.

Multiple assignments are possible, as in

```
a = b = c = 13
```

The operator = evaluates from *right to left*, so the above is equivalent to this:

```
a = (b = (c = 13))
```

The rightmost assignment is done first, then the one to the left, and so on.

2.11 Updating Operators

Julia provides a number of special operators, more for convenience than necessity. The most common of these are the *updating operators*. For example, to add 5 to n, we can write this:

```
n = n + 5
```

However, we can achieve the same thing with this:

```
n += 5
```

Here, += is an updating operator which *adds* the value of the right-hand-side to the variable on the left.

We can use the following to add the value of num to sum:

```
sum += num
```

Other updating operators include -=, *=, /=, ÷=, %= and ^=.

If op represents any of +, -, *, /, ÷, % or ^, then

```
variable op= expression
```

is equivalent to

```
variable = variable op expression
```

For example, if c = 27,

```
c ÷= 4      # same as c = c ÷ 4
```

will assign 6 to c.

It may be useful to remember that an updating operator *could* change the *type* of the variable on the left-hand side. We illustrate with the following:

```
julia> n = 7;
julia> typeof(n)
Int64
julia> n += 1
8
julia> typeof(n)       # n is still Int64
Int64
julia> n += 1.0        # this will change the type of n
9.0
julia> typeof(n)
Float64
```

We point out that we could write all our programs without using any of these special operators. However, sometimes, they permit us to express certain operations more concisely, more conveniently and, possibly, more clearly.

2.12 trunc, ceil, floor, round

Suppose b is Float64 and n is Int64. Consider this:

```
n = b # attempt to assign Float64 to Int64
```

The assignment is valid only if the value of b is an integer (like 7 or even 7.0). Any other value of b (e.g. 7.4) would give an *InexactError*. In this case, the error would be

```
InexactError: Int64(7.4)
```

This means we want to convert 7.4 to Int64, which is not a valid operation. So, in general, we cannot assign a float value to an Int variable.

In Julia, we can use functions like trunc, ceil, floor and round to convert a floating-point value to integer.

trunc

Consider the following:

```
julia> b = 7.3;
julia> n = trunc(b)
7.0
julia> typeof(n)
Float64
```

As we see, trunc *discards the fractional part* of b and assigns 7.0 to n, making it a Float64 variable. We continue:

```
julia> n = trunc(Int32, b)
7
julia> typeof(n)
Int32
```

Here we see a modified form of trunc in which the first argument is an integer type and the second is the value to truncate. The fractional part of b is discarded and the value converted to Int32.

The same thing happens if b is negative; if b is -7.3, trunc(Int32, b) returns -7 and trunc(b) returns -7.0.

If we use the option trunc(T, x) but x is not representable as type T, an error will result. For example, trunc(Int8, 200.8) will give an InexactError since Int8 is too small to hold the value 200. (The largest value we can store in Int8 is 127.)

ceil

ceil(x) returns the nearest integral value *of the same type* as x that is greater than or equal to x.

```
julia> ceil(7.0)
7.0
julia> b = ceil(7.4)
8.0
```

The type of 7.4 is Float64. The next integer *greater than* 7.4 (and of type Float64) is 8.0.

Compare the following:

```
julia> b = ceil(Int64, 7.4)
8
```

ceil takes an optional first argument, the type to be returned. Here it returns 8, of type Int64.

Be careful with negative arguments. The next integer *bigger than* -7.4 is -7, so ceil(Int64, -7.4) returns -7.

If we use the option ceil(T, x) but x is not representable as type T, an error will result. For example, ceil(Int8, 200.8) will give an InexactError since Int8 is too small to hold the value 201. (The largest value we can store in Int8 is 127.)

floor

floor(x) returns the nearest integral value *of the same type* as x that is less than or equal to x.

```
julia> floor(7.0)
7.0
julia> b = floor(7.4)
7.0
```

The type of 7.4 is Float64. The next integer *smaller than* 7.4 (and of type Float64) is 7.0.

Compare the following:

```
julia> b = floor(Int64, 7.4)
7
```

`floor` takes an optional first argument, the type to be returned. Here it returns 7, of type `Int64`.

Be careful with negative arguments. The next integer *smaller than* -7.4 is -8; `floor(Int64, -7.4)` returns -8.

If we use the option `floor(T, x)` but x is not representable as type T, an error will result. For example, `floor(Int8, 200.8)` will give an `InexactError` since `Int8` is too small to hold the value `200`. (The largest value we can store in `Int8` is `127`.)

round

The function `round` is very versatile with a dizzying array of options available. We will explain some of the more common ones. The first few examples are self-explanatory.

```
julia> round(7.4)
7.0

julia> round(Int64, 7.4)
7

julia> round(Int64, 7.8)
8

julia> round(Int64, -7.8)
-8

julia> round(Int64, -7.4)
-7
```

All fairly straightforward, but...

```
julia> round(Int64, 3.5)
4
```

As expected. However,

```
julia> round(Int64, 4.5)
4
```

Huh? Not what we learnt in school! The technical reason is this: Julia uses the IEEE754 standard for rounding. This rounds to the nearest integer, with fractional values of 0.5 being rounded to the *nearest even* integer. We get the answer 4 because 4 is the nearest even integer to 4.5. Round(3.5) works as expected because 4 is the nearest even integer to 3.5.

In any case, this seeming anomaly is merely the default behaviour of `round`. Julia provides many options for rounding.

One such option is `RoundNearestTiesAway`. It is used as follows:

```
julia> round(Int64, 4.5, RoundNearestTiesAway)
5
```

The option `RoundNearestTiesAway` rounds to the nearest integer, with fractional values of 0.5 rounded away from zero. Using this rule, we would get -5 as the answer to this:

```
julia> round(Int64, -4.5, RoundNearestTiesAway)
-5
```

The following are some other options you can use with `round`.

`RoundNearestTiesUp` - rounds to nearest integer, with fractional values of 0.5 rounded towards positive infinity. For example:

```
julia> round(Int64, 4.5, RoundNearestTiesUp)
5

julia> round(Int64, -4.5, RoundNearestTiesUp)
-4
```

```
julia> round(Int64, -4.8, RoundNearestTiesUp)
-5
```

RoundToZero - this is an alias for `trunc`

RoundUp - alias for `ceil`

RoundDown - alias for `floor`

In the examples above, we rounded to a whole number. But `round` can round to any number of decimal places we desire. Suppose we want to round to two decimal places. The following illustrates how:

```
# digits=2 specifies rounding to two decimal places
julia> round(7.3486,digits=2)
7.35

julia> round(7.3566,digits=2)
7.36

julia> round(7.3693,digits=2)
7.37
```

But note this: if the third decimal place is 5, and is followed by 0s or nothing, the second decimal place determines the answer; if it is even, it remains the same and if it is odd, 1 is added to it. In other words, the digit in the second decimal place is rounded to *the nearest even* digit.

```
julia> round(7.365,digits=2)
7.36
# second decimal place, 6, is even so it's unchanged

julia> round(7.3650,digits=2)
7.36
# trailing zeroes don't affect the rule or result

julia> round(7.375,digits=2)
7.38
# second decimal place, 7, is odd so it's rounded up

julia> round(7.36501,digits=2)
7.37
# second decimal place, 6, is even but since there is something non-zero after the 5,
# the 6 is rounded up to 7.
```

In general, if we want to round to d decimal places, we look at the digit in the $(d+1)$st position. If it is less than or greater than 5, the usual rules of rounding apply.

If it *is* 5, and is followed by 0s or nothing, the digit in the dth position is rounded to the nearest *even* digit. If the 5 is followed by *any* non-zero value, the digit to the left is incremented.

Here's an example with $d=4$. What is `round(4.3216500,digits=4)`?

The 5th digit, 5, is followed by zeroes. The 4th digit is 6; this is even so it remains unchanged and we get the answer 4.3216. But if the number was 4.32175, we would get the answer 4.3218. (7 is odd so it is incremented to 8.)

Here are some other examples:

```
julia> round(4.32165001, digits=4)
4.3217
# 5 is followed by a non-zero value so 6 is incremented to 7

julia> round(4.3216499, digits=4)
4.3216
# 5th digit is 4 (less than 5) so 6 is unchanged
```

```
julia> round(4.3216499, digits=3)
4.322
```

As a matter of interest, what follows `digits=` doesn't have to be an integer *constant*; it can be an integer *variable* or an integer *expression*.

```
julia> d=2;

julia> round(8.345679, digits=d-1)
8.3        # to 1 decimal place

julia> round(8.346789, digits=d)
8.35       # to 2 decimal places

julia> round(8.345679, digits=d+1)
8.346      # to 3 decimal places

julia> round(8.345679, digits=2d)
8.3457     # to 4 decimal places

julia> round(8.345679, digits=2d+1)
8.34568    # to 5 decimal places
```

For completeness, we point out that what follows `digits=` can be a negative integer. But, for instance, what does `round(456.78, digits=-1)` mean?

When we write `digits=d`, it has the following meaning:

```
d=0 means round to the nearest whole number
d=1 means round to the nearest tenth
d=2 means round to the nearest hundredth, and so on
```

With negative `d`, we go left from the decimal point. So

```
d=-1 means round to the nearest ten
d=-2 means round to the nearest hundred
d=-3 means round to the nearest thousand, and so on
```

Our example `round(456.78, digits=-1)` says to round `456.78` to the nearest `10`, which is `460`.

Here are some other examples:

```
julia> round(8754.345, digits=-1)
8750.0       # to the nearest 10

julia> round(8754.345, digits=-2)
8800.0       # to the nearest 100

julia> round(8754.345, digits=-3)
9000.0       # to the nearest 1000

julia> round(875.0000, digits=-1)
880.0        # 0s follow 5, 7 is odd so it is incremented to 8

julia> round(865.0000, digits=-1)
860.0        # 0s follow 5, 6 is even so it does not change

julia> round(865.0001, digits=-1)
870.0        # non-zero follows 5, so 6 is incremented to 7
```

One last observation: the values returned are `Float64`. You might think that since we're rounding to the nearest `10`, `100`, and so on, `round` would return an integer or, at least, allow an *option* like this:

```
round(Int32, 8736.745, digits=-1)  # wrong - can't do this
```

(Recall, you *can* use `round(Int32, 8736.745)` to get `8737`.)

But it doesn't. However, we can easily get around this by using `Int` (or `Int32`, `Int64`, etc.):

```
julia> b = Int(round(8736.745, digits=-1))
8740

julia> b = Int32(round(8736.745, digits=-2))
8700

julia> b = Int64(round(8736.745, digits=-3))
9000
```

EXERCISES 2

1. Name 5 operators which can be used for writing integer expressions and give their precedence in relation to each other.

2. Give the value of (a) 39 % 7 (b) 88 % 4 (c) 100 % 11 (d) -25 % 9

3. Give the value of (a) 39 / 7 (b) 88 / 4 (c) 100 / 11 (d) -25 / 9

4. Write a statement to print the value of the integer variable sum, right justified in a field width of 6.

5. You are required to print the values of the integer variables b, h and n. Write a statement which prints b with its rightmost digit in column 10, h with its rightmost digit in column 20 and n with its rightmost digit in column 30.

6. Write statements which print the values of b, h and n lined up one below the other with their rightmost digits in column 8.

7. Using scientific notation, write the number 345.72 in 4 different ways.

8. Write a statement which prints the value of the Float64 variable total to 3 decimal places, right justified in a field width of 9.

9. You need to print the values of the Float32 variables a, b and c to 1 decimal place. Write a statement which prints a with its rightmost digit in column 12, b with its rightmost digit in column 20 and c with its rightmost digit in column 32.

10. Write statements to print the values of 3 Float64 variables a, b and c, to 2 decimal places, The values must be printed one below the other, with their rightmost digits in column 12.

11. How can you print the value of a Float64 variable, rounded to the nearest whole number?

12. What happens if you try to print a number (any type) with a field width and the field width is too small? What if the field width is too big?

13. Name the common operators which can be used for writing floating-point expressions.

14. Describe what happens when we try to assign an Int value to a Float variable.

15. Describe what happens when we try to assign a Float value to an Int variable.

16. Write a statement to increase the value of the Int variable quantity by 10.

17. Write a statement to decrease the value of the Int variable quantity by 5.

18. Write a statement to double the value of the Int variable quantity.

19. Write a statement to set a to 2 times b plus 3 times c.

20. The Float64 variable price holds the price of an item. Write a statement to increase the price by (a) $12.50 (b) 25%.

21. If a is 29 and b is 14, what is printed by the following statements?

```
@printf("%d + \n", a)
@printf("%d\n", b)
@printf("--\n")
@printf("%d\n", a + b)
```

22. If a is 29 and b is 5, what is printed by each of the following statements?

```
@printf("The product of %d and %d is %d\n", a, b, a * b)
@printf("%d + %d = %d\n", a, b, a + b)
@printf("%d - %d = %d\n", a, b, a - b)
@printf("%d x %d = %d\n", a, b, a * b)
```

23. If rate = 15, what is printed by the following:

```
(a) @printf("rate\n")?
(b) @printf("%d\n", rate)?
```

24. Suppose rate = 15. What is printed by each of the following?

```
@printf("Maria earns rate dollars an hour\n")
@printf("Maria earns %d dollars an hour\n", rate)
```

25. What will happen when the computer attempts to execute the following:

```
p = 7
q = 3 + p
p = p + r
@printf("%d\n", p)
```

26. If m is 3770 and n is 123, what is printed by each of the following?

```
(a) @printf("%d%d\n", n, m)
(b) @printf("%d\n%d\n", n, m)
```

CHAPTER 3

Selection Logic

In this chapter, we will explain the following:

- What are Boolean expressions
- How Julia represents Boolean values
- How to write programs using `if`
- How to write programs using `if…else`
- How to write programs using `if…elseif…else`
- How a program should be tested
- Symbolic constants, why they are useful and how to use them

3.1 Introduction

In the Chapter 2, we showed how to write programs using *sequence* logic—programs whose statements are executed "in sequence" from the first to the last.

In this chapter, the programs will use *selection* logic—they will *test* some *condition* and take different courses of action based on whether the condition is true or false. In Julia, selection logic is implemented using the `if`, `if…else` and `if…elseif…else` statements.

3.2 Boolean Expressions

A *Boolean expression* (named after the famous English mathematician George Boole) is one that is either `true` or `false`. The simplest kinds of Boolean expressions are those that compare one value with another. Some examples are:

```
k is equal to 999
a is greater than 100
a² + b² is equal to c²
b² is greater than or equal to 4ac
name is not equal to "Mary"
```

Each of these can be either true or false. These are examples of a special kind of Boolean expression called *relational expressions*. Such expressions simply check if one value is equal to, not equal to, greater than, greater than or equal to, less than and less than or equal to another value. We write them using *relational operators*.

In Julia, the relational operators (with examples) are:

N. Kalicharan, *Julia - Bit by Bit*, Undergraduate Topics in Computer Science,
https://doi.org/10.1007/978-3-030-73936-2_3

==	equal to	k == 999, name == "Mary"
!=	not equal to	s != 0, name != "John"
>	greater than	a > 100, ch > '0'
>=	greater than or equal to	b*b >= 4.0*a*c
<	less than	n < 0, ch < 'A'
<=	less than or equal to	score <= 65

Boolean expressions are normally used to control the flow of program execution. For example, we may have a variable (h, say) which starts off with a value of 0. We keep increasing it by 1 and want to know when its value reaches 100. We wish to know when the *condition* h == 100 is true. A condition is the common name for a Boolean expression.

The real power of programming lies in the ability of a program to *test* a *condition* and determine whether it is true or false. If it is true, the program can perform one set of actions and if it is false, it can perform another set, or simply do nothing at all.

For example, suppose the variable score holds the score obtained by a student in a test, and the student passes if her score is 50 or more and fails if it is less than 50. A program can be written to *test* the *condition*

```
score >= 50
```

If it is true, the student passes; if it is false, the student fails. In Julia, we can write this as follows:

```
if score >= 50
    println("Pass")
else
    println("Fail")
end
```

When the computer gets to this statement, it compares the current value of score with 50. If the value is greater than or equal to 50, we say the condition score >= 50 is true. In this case the program prints Pass. If the value of score is less than 50, we say the condition score >= 50 is false. In this case, the program prints Fail.

In this chapter, we will see how Boolean expressions are used in if, if…else and if…elseif…else statements and, in Chapter 4, we will see how they are used in while statements.

3.2.1 AND, &&

With relational operators, we can create *simple* conditions. But sometimes, we need to ask if one thing is true AND another thing is true. We may also need to know if one of two things is true. For these situations, we need *compound* conditions. To create compound conditions, we use the *logical operators* AND, OR and NOT.

For example, suppose we want to know if the value of h lies between 1 and 99, inclusive. We want to know if h is greater than or equal to 1 AND if h is less than or equal to 99. In Julia, we can express this as follows:

```
(h >= 1) && (h <= 99)
```

The symbol for AND is &&.

Note the following:

- The variable h *must be repeated* in both conditions. It is tempting, but wrong, to write

    ```
    h >= 1 && <= 99 # this is wrong
    ```

- The brackets around h >= 1 and h <= 99 are not *required*, but it is not wrong to put them. This is so since && (and ||, see next) have *lower precedence* than the relational operators. Without the brackets,

```
h >= 1 && h <= 99
```

would be interpreted by Julia like this:

```
(h >= 1) && (h <= 99)
```

This is the same as with the brackets.

- Julia allows the condition to be written like this:

```
1 <= h <= 99 # this is more concise and, possibly, clearer
```

3.2.2 OR, ||

If n is an integer representing a month of the year, we can check if n is invalid by testing if n is less than 1 OR n is greater than 12. In Julia, we express this as follows:

```
(n < 1) || (n > 12)
```

The symbol for OR is ||. As discussed above, the brackets are not required and we could write the expression like this:

```
n < 1 || n > 12
```

This tests if n is invalid. Of course, we can test if n is valid by using this:

```
n >= 1 && n <= 12
```

The choice of which test to use depends on how *we* wish to express our logic. Sometimes it's convenient to use the valid test, sometimes the reverse.

3.2.3 NOT, !

If p is some Boolean expression, then NOT p reverses the truth value of p. In others words, if p is true then NOT p is false; if p is false, NOT p is true. In Julia, the symbol for NOT is the exclamation mark, !. Using the example above, since

```
n >= 1 && n <= 12
```

tests for valid n, the condition NOT (n >=1 && n <= 12) tests for invalid n, written in Julia like this:

```
!(n >= 1 && n <= 12)
```

This is equivalent to n < 1 || n > 12. Those familiar with de Morgan's laws will know that

```
not(a and b) ≡ (not a) or (not b)
```

and

```
not(a or b) ≡ (not a) and (not b)
```

In general, if p and q are Boolean expressions, we have the following:

- p && q is true when both p and q are true and false, otherwise
- p || q is true when either p or q is true and false only when both p and q are false
- !p is true when p is false and false when p is true

This is summarized in the following table (with T for true and F for false):

p	q	&&	||	!p
T	T	T	T	F
T	F	F	T	F
F	T	F	T	T
F	F	F	F	T

Most of the programs in this book will use simple conditions. A few will use compound conditions.

3.3 The type Bool

As we've seen, the value of a Boolean expression is true or false. In Julia, such expressions are said to be of type Bool. Therefore, a Bool variable is one which can take on one of two values—true or false.

If we assign a Boolean expression to a variable, it's as if we declared the variable to be of type Bool. Study the following:

```
julia> visited = true   # the type of visited becomes Bool
true
julia> typeof(visited)
Bool

julia> score = 73;
julia> rank = score >= 50
true
julia> typeof(rank)
Bool

julia> n = 13;
julia> validMonth = n >= 1 && n <= 12
false
julia> typeof(validMonth) # expression is false; its type is Bool
Bool
```

Caution: Some languages allow the use of a numeric expression (*n*, say) where a Boolean expression is expected. If *n* is non-zero, it is interpreted as true; if zero, it is false. Julia does *not* allow this. It is an error if the value of an expression (used as a *condition*) is anything but true or false. The following generates an error since b is an Int64 variable whose value (1) is neither true nor false.

```
julia> b = 1;
julia> if (b) println("true") end
ERROR: TypeError: non-boolean (Int64) used in boolean context
```

3.4 The if Statement

Let us write a program for the following problem:

> A computer repair shop charges $100 per hour for labour plus the cost of any parts used in the repair. However, the minimum charge for any job is $150. Prompt for the number of hours worked and the cost of parts (which could be $0) and print the charge for the job.

We will write the program so that it works as follows:

```
Hours worked? 2.5
Cost of parts? 20

Total charges: $270.00
```

or

```
Hours worked? 1
Cost of parts? 25

Total charges: $150.00
```

The following algorithm describes the steps required to solve the problem:

```
prompt for and read the hours worked
prompt for and read the cost of parts
calculate charge = hours worked * 100 + cost of parts
if (charge is less than 150) set charge to 150
print charge
```

This is another example of an algorithm written in *pseudocode*—an informal way of specifying programming logic.

The algorithm introduces a new statement—the if statement. The expression

```
charge is less than 150
```

is an example of a *condition*. If the condition is true, the statement which follows is executed; if it is false, the statement is *not* executed.

Program P3.1 shows how to express this algorithm as a Julia program.

```
# Program P3.1 - Job Charge
# print job charge based on hours worked and cost of parts
using Printf
function jobCharge()
    print("Hours worked? ")
    hours = parse(Float64, readline())
    print("Cost of parts? ")
    parts = parse(Float64, readline())
    jobCharge = hours * 100 + parts
    if jobCharge < 150
        jobCharge = 150
    end
    @printf("\nTotal charges: \$%0.2f\n", jobCharge)
end # jobCharge

jobCharge()
```

For this program, we use 3 variables—hours, parts and jobCharge.

It is very important that you make an extra effort to understand the if statement since it is one of the most important statements in programming. It is the if statement that can make a program appear to think.

The condition

```
charge is less than 150
```

of the pseudocode algorithm is expressed in our program as

```
jobCharge < 150
```

(If you wish, you may enclose the condition in brackets but it's not necessary.)

When the program is executed, the job charge is calculated in the normal way (hours*100 + parts). The if statement then tests if this value, jobCharge, is less than 150; if it is, then jobCharge is set to 150. If it is not less than 150, jobCharge remains as it is.

The following is an example of the if statement in Julia:

```
if jobCharge < 150
    jobCharge = 150
end
```

Terminology: We'll use the term **block** to refer to a set of one or more consecutive statements.

In general, the if statement takes the following form:

```
if <condition>
    <block>
end
```

The words if and end are required. You must supply <condition> and <block>.

<condition> is a Boolean expression: if true, <block> is executed; if false, <block> is *not* executed. In either case, the program continues with the statement, if any, after end.

In the program, <condition> is jobCharge < 150

and <block> is the one statement

```
jobCharge = 150
```

To give an example where <block> consists of more than one statement, suppose we want to exchange the values of two variables b and c but only if b is bigger than c. This can be done with the following assuming, as an example, that b = 15, c = 8:

```
if b > c
    h = b    # store b in h (hold); h becomes 15
    b = c    # store c in b; b becomes 8
    c = h    # store old value of b, 15,in c
end
```

Here, <block> consists of the 3 assignment statements. If b is greater than c, the block is executed (and the values are exchanged); if b is *not* greater than c, the block is *not* executed (and the values remain as they are).

We point out that exchanging the values of two variables requires *three* assignment statements; it *cannot* be done with *two*. If you are not convinced, try it.

It is also possible to exchange the values of two variables *without* using a third for interim storage. Can you figure out how to do it? *Hint*: you must still use three assignment statements.

It is good programming practice to *indent* the statements in the block. This makes it easy to see at a glance which statements are in the block. If we had written the above as follows, the structure of the block would not be so easy to see:

```
if b > c
h = b    # store b in h; h becomes 15
b = c    # store c in b; b becomes 8
c = h    # store old value of b, 15,in c
end
```

Caveat: The above assumes we are using simple assignment statements, with one variable on the left hand side. If we use the full power of Julia, we can exchange the values of b and c with this:

```
if b > c
    b, c = c, b
end
```

3.4.1 Find the Sum of Two Lengths

Suppose a length is given in meters and centimeters, for example, 3m 75cm. You are given two pairs of integers representing two lengths. Write a program to prompt for two lengths and print their sum such that the centimeter value is less than 100.

For example, the sum of 3m 25cm and 2m 15cm is 5m 40cm, but the sum of 3m 75cm and 5m 50cm is 9m 25cm.

Assume we want the program to work as follows:

```
Enter values for m and cm: 3 75
Enter values for m and cm: 5 50

Sum is 9m 25cm
```

Observe that the data must be entered with digits only. If, for instance, we type 3m 75cm we will get an error since 3m is not a valid integer constant. Our program will assume the first number entered is the meter value and the second number is the centimeter value.

We find the sum by adding the two meter values and adding the two centimeter values. If the centimeter value is less than 100, there is nothing more to do. But if it is not, we must subtract 100 from it and add 1 to the meter value. This logic is expressed as follows:

```
mSum = sum of metre values
cmSum = sum of centimetre values
if cmSum >= 100
    subtract 100 from cmSum
    add 1 to mSum
endif
```

For noting: endif is just a convention programmers use when writing pseudocode to indicate the end of an if statement. In a Julia program, it would be replaced by the reserved word end.

As a *boundary* case, we must check that our program works if cmSum is exactly 100. As an exercise, verify that it does.

Program P3.2 solves the problem as described. Note this statement:

```
m1, cm1 = [parse(Int, x) for x in split(readline())]
```

If the data entered was "3 75", split converts this into two values "3" and "75". Then parse converts each of these to an Int. It assigns the first (3) to m1 and the second (75) to cm1.

```
# Program P3.2
# find the sum of two lengths given in meters and centimeters
function sumLengths()
    print("Enter values for m and cm: ")
    m1, cm1 = [parse(Int, x) for x in split(readline())]
    print("Enter values for m and cm: ")
    m2, cm2 = [parse(Int, x) for x in split(readline())]
```

```
    mSum = m1 + m2        # add the meters
    cmSum = cm1 + cm2   # add the centimeters
    if cmSum >= 100
         cmSum = cmSum - 100
         mSum = mSum + 1
    end
    print("\nSum is $(mSum)m $(cmSum)cm\n")
end # sumLengths

sumLengths()
```

We use the variables m1 and cm1 for the first length, m2 and cm2 for the second length, and mSum and cmSum for the sum of the two lengths.

The program assumes that the centimeter part of the given lengths is less than 100 and it works correctly if this is so. But what if the lengths were 3m 150cm and 2m 200cm?

The program will print 6m 250cm. (As an exercise, follow the logic of the program to see why.) While this is correct, it is not in the correct format since we require the centimeter value to be less than 100. We can modify our program to work in these cases as well by using integer division (÷) and % (the *remainder* operator).

The following pseudocode shows how:

```
mSum = sum of meter values
cmSum = sum of centimeter values
if cmSum >= 100
     add cmSum ÷ 100 to mSum
     set cmSum to cmSum % 100
endif
```

Using the above example, mSum is first set to 5 and cmSum is set to 350. Since cmSum is greater than 100, we work out 350 ÷ 100 (this finds how many 100s there are in cmSum) which is 3; this is added to mSum, giving 8. The next line sets cmSum to 350 % 100 which is 50. So we get the answer 8m 50cm, which is correct *and* in the correct format.

Note that the statements in the if block *must* be written in the order shown. We must use the (original) value of cmSum to work out cmSum ÷ 100 *before* changing it to cmSum % 100. As an exercise, work out what value will be computed for the sum if these statements are reversed. (The answer will be 5m 50cm, which is *wrong*. Can you see why we get this answer?)

These changes are reflected in Program P3.3.

```
# Program P3.3 - Sum of two lengths

# Find the sum of two lengths given in meters and centimeters
# Modified to cater for cm input values > 100

function sumLengths()
    print("Enter values for m and cm: ")
    m1, cm1 = [parse(Int, x) for x in split(readline())]
    print("Enter values for m and cm: ")
    m2, cm2 = [parse(Int, x) for x in split(readline())]
    mSum = m1 + m2        # add the meters
    cmSum = cm1 + cm2   # add the centimeters
    if cmSum >= 100
         mSum = mSum + cmSum ÷ 100
         cmSum = cmSum % 100
    end
    print("\nSum is $(mSum)m $(cmSum)cm\n")
end # sumLengths
sumLengths()
```

The following is a sample run of this program:

```
Enter values for m and cm: 3 150
Enter values for m and cm: 2 200

Sum is 8m 50cm
```

The astute reader may recognize that we do not even need the if statement.

Consider this:

```
mSum = m1 + m2        # add the meters
cmSum = cm1 + cm2;    # add the centimeters
mSum = mSum + cmSum ÷ 100
cmSum = cmSum % 100
```

The last two statements come from the if statement.

So we know that this will work if cmSum is greater than or equal to 100 since, when that is the case, these four statements are executed.

What if cmSum is less than 100? Originally, the last two statements would not have been executed since the if condition would have been false. *Now* they are executed. Let us see what happens. Using the example of 3m 25cm and 2m 15cm, we get mSum as 5 and cmSum as 40.

In the next statement 40 ÷ 100 is 0 so mSum does not change and in the last statement 40 % 100 is 40 so cmSum does not change. The answer will be printed correctly as

```
Sum is 5m 40cm
```

You should begin to realize by now that there is usually more than one way to express the logic of a program. With experience and study, you will learn which ways are better and why.

3.5 The if...else Statement

Let us write a program for the following problem:

A student is given 3 tests, each marked out of 100. The student passes if his average mark is greater than or equal to 50 and fails if his average mark is less than 50. Prompt for the 3 marks and print Pass if the student passes and Fail if he fails.

We will write the program assuming it works as follows:

```
Enter 3 marks: 60 40 56

Average is 52.0 Pass
```

or

```
Enter 3 marks: 40 60 36

Average is 45.3 Fail
```

The following pseudocode algorithm describes the steps required to solve the problem:

```
prompt for the 3 marks
calculate the average
if average is greater than or equal to 50
```

```
      print "Pass"
  else
      print "Fail"
  endif
```

The part from `if` to `endif` is an example of the `if...else` statement (we sometimes say the if...else *construct*).

The condition

```
  average is greater than or equal to 50
```

is another example of a relational expression. If it is `true`, the statement immediately following (the *if block*) is executed; if it is `false`, the statement after `else` (the *else block*) is executed.

The entire statement is terminated with `endif`.

When you write pseudocode, what is important is that the logic intended is unmistakably clear. Indentation can help by making it easy to identify the `if` and `else` blocks.

In the end, though, you must express the code in some programming language for it to be run on a computer. Program P3.4 shows how to do this in Julia for the above algorithm.

```
# Program P3.4 - Pass/Fail?
# request 3 marks; print their average and Pass/Fail
function PassFail()
    print("Enter 3 marks: ")
    m1, m2, m3 = [parse(Int, x) for x in split(readline())]
    average = round((m1 + m2 + m3)/3,digits=1)
    print("\nAverage is $average ")
    if average >= 50
        println("Pass")
    else
        println("Fail")
    end
end # Pass/Fail

PassFail()
```

Study carefully the `if...else` statement in the program. It reflects the logic expressed on the previous page.

In general, the `if...else` statement takes the form shown below.

```
  if <condition>
      <block1>
  else
      <block2>
  end
```

The words `if`, `else` and `end` are required. You must supply `<condition>`, `<block1>` and `<block2>`.

If `<condition>` is true, `<block1>` is executed and `<block2>` is skipped; if `<condition>` is false, `<block1>` is skipped and `<block2>` is executed.

When the if statement is executed, *either* `<block1>` *or* `<block2>` is executed, but not both. In either case, the program continues with the statement, if any, after `end`.

3.5.1 Calculate Pay

For an example that requires blocks of more than one statement, suppose we have values for hours worked and rate of pay (the amount paid per hour) and wish to calculate a person's regular pay, overtime pay and gross pay based on the following:

If hours worked is less than or equal to 40, regular pay is calculated by multiplying hours worked by rate of pay, and overtime pay is 0. If hours worked is greater than 40, regular pay is calculated by multiplying 40 by the rate of pay, and overtime pay is calculated by multiplying the hours *in excess of* 40 by the rate of pay by 1.5. Gross pay is calculated by adding regular pay and overtime pay.

For example, if hours is 36 and rate is 20 dollars per hour, regular pay is $720 (36 times 20) and overtime pay is $0. Gross pay is $720.

And if hours is 50 and rate is 12 dollars per hour, regular pay is $480 (40 times 12) and overtime pay is $180 (excess hours 10 times 12 times 1.5). Gross pay is $660 (480 + 180).

The above description could be expressed in pseudocode as follows:

```
if hours is less than or equal to 40
    set regular pay to hours x rate
    set overtime pay to 0
else
    set regular pay to 40 x rate
    set overtime pay to (hours - 40) x rate x 1.5
endif
set gross pay to regular pay + overtime pay
```

We use indentation to highlight the statements to be executed if the condition "hours is less than or equal to 40" is true and those to be executed if the condition is false. The entire statement is terminated with `endif`.

The next step is to convert the pseudocode to Julia. When we do, we have to make sure that we stick to Julia's rules for writing an `if...else` statement.

Using the variables `hours` (hours worked), `rate` (rate of pay), `regPay` (regular pay), `ovtPay` (overtime pay) and `grossPay` (gross pay), we write the code like this:

```
if hours <= 40
    regPay = hours * rate
    ovtPay = 0
else
    regPay = 40 * rate
    ovtPay = (hours - 40) * rate * 1.5
end
grossPay = regPay + ovtPay
```

Problem: Write a program to prompt for hours worked and rate of pay. The program then calculates and prints regular pay, overtime pay and gross pay, based on the above description.

The following algorithm outlines the overall logic of the solution:

```
prompt for hours worked and rate of pay
if hours is less than or equal to 40
    set regular pay to hours x rate
    set overtime pay to 0
else
    set regular pay to 40 x rate
    set overtime pay to (hours - 40) x rate x 1.5
endif
```

```
        set gross pay to regular pay + overtime pay
        print regular pay, overtime pay and gross pay
```

This algorithm is implemented as Program P3.5.

```
# Program P3.5 - Calculate pay
using Printf
function calculatePay()
    print("Hours worked? ")
    hours = parse(Float64, readline())
    print("Rate of pay? ")
    rate = parse(Float64, readline())

    if hours <= 40
        regPay = hours * rate
        ovtPay = 0
    else
        regPay = 40 * rate
        ovtPay = (hours - 40) * rate * 1.5
    end
    grossPay = regPay + ovtPay
    @printf("\nRegular pay: \$%0.2f\n", regPay)
    @printf("Overtime pay: \$%03.2f\n", ovtPay)
    @printf("Gross pay: \$%0.2f\n", grossPay)
end # calculatePay

calculatePay()}
```

Here's a sample run of this program:

```
Hours worked? 50
Rate of pay? 12

Regular pay: $480.00
Overtime pay: $180.00
Gross pay: $660.00
```

You should verify that the results are indeed correct.

3.6 On Program Testing

When we write a program we should test it thoroughly to ensure that it is working correctly. As a minimum, we should test *all paths* through the program. This means that our *test data* must be chosen so that each statement in the program is executed at least once.

For P3.5, the sample run tests only when hours > 40. Based on this test alone, we cannot be sure the program will work correctly if hours <= 40. To be sure, we must run another test in which hours <= 40. The following is such a sample run:

```
Hours worked? 36
Rate of pay? 20

Regular pay: $720.00
Overtime pay: $0.00
Gross pay: $720.00
```

These results are correct which gives us greater assurance that our program is correct. We should also run a test when the hours is exactly 40; we must always test a program at its 'boundaries'. For this program, 40 is a boundary—it is the value at which overtime begins to be paid.

What if the results are incorrect? For example, suppose overtime pay is wrong. We say the program contains a *bug* (an error), and we must *debug* (remove the error from) the program. In this case, we can look at the statement(s) which calculate the overtime pay to see if we have specified the calculation correctly. If this fails to uncover the error, we must painstakingly 'execute' the program by hand using the test data which produced the error. If done properly, this will usually reveal the cause of the error.

3.7 Symbolic Constants

In Program 3.1, we used two constants—100 and 150—denoting the labour charge per hour and the minimum job cost, respectively. What if these values change after the program has been written? We would have to find all occurrences of them in the program and change them to the new values.

This program is fairly short so this would not be too difficult to do. But imagine what the task would be like if the program contained hundreds or even thousands of lines of code. It would be difficult, time-consuming and error-prone to make all the required changes.

We can make life a little easier by using *symbolic constants* (also called *manifest* or *named* constants)—identifiers which we set to the required constants in one place. If we need to change the value of a constant, the change would have to be made in one place only. For example, in Program P3.1, we could have used the symbolic constants ChargePerHour and MinJobCost. We would set ChargePerHour to 100 and MinJobCost to 150.

In Julia, we use the const declaration to define symbolic constants (among other things). We show how by rewriting Program P3.1 as Program P3.6.

```
# Program P3.6 - Job charge, const declaration
# This program illustrates the use of symbolic constants
# Print job charge based on hours worked and cost of parts
using Printf
const ChargePerHour = 100
const MinJobCost = 150

function jobCharge()
    print("Hours worked? ")
    hours = parse(Float64, readline())
    print("Cost of parts? ")
    parts = parse(Float64, readline())

    jobCharge = hours * ChargePerHour + parts
    if jobCharge < MinJobCost
        jobCharge = MinJobCost
    end
    @printf("\nTotal charges: \$%0.2f\n", jobCharge)
end # jobCharge

jobCharge()
```

The identifier const is used to declare global variables (outside of any function) whose values will not change during the execution of the program. It allows us to declare an identifier as a symbolic constant.

In this program, we declared ChargePerHour and MinJobCost using separate declarations. However, Julia allows us to declare more than one constant in the same declaration. Here, we could have used this:

```
const ChargePerHour, MinJobCost = 100, 150
```

In this book, we will use the *convention* of starting a symbolic constant identifier with an uppercase letter. Note, however, that Julia lets you use any valid identifier.

Consider, again, Program 3.5. There, we used two constants—40 and 1.5—denoting the maximum regular hours and the overtime rate factor, respectively. We rewrite program P3.5 as program P3.7 using the symbolic constants MaxRegularHours (set to 40) and OvertimeFactor (set to 1.5).

```julia
# Program P3.7 - Calculate pay with symbolic constants
using Printf
const MaxRegularHours = 40
const OvertimeFactor = 1.5

function calculatePay()
    print("Hours worked? ")
    hours = parse(Float64, readline())
    print("Rate of pay? ")
    rate = parse(Float64, readline())

    if hours <= MaxRegularHours
        regPay = hours*rate
        ovtPay = 0
    else
        regPay = MaxRegularHours*rate
        ovtPay = (hours-MaxRegularHours)*rate*OvertimeFactor
    end
    grossPay = regPay + ovtPay
    @printf("\nRegular pay: \$%0.2f\n", regPay)
    @printf("Overtime pay: \$%03.2f\n", ovtPay)
    @printf("Gross pay: \$%0.2f\n", grossPay)
end # calculatePay

calculatePay()
```

Suppose, for instance, the maximum regular hours changes from 40 to 35. Program P3.7 would be easier to change than Program P3.5, since we would need to change the value in the const declaration only, like this:

```julia
const MaxRegularHours = 35
```

No other changes would be needed.

The numbers 40 and 1.5 used in Program P3.5 are referred to as *magic numbers*—they appear in the program for no apparent reason, as if by magic. Magic numbers are a good sign that a program may be restrictive, tied to those numbers. As far as possible, we must write our programs without magic numbers. Using symbolic constants can help to make our programs more flexible and easier to maintain.

3.8 The if…elseif…else Statement

In expressing the logic of our program, we use the if statement when there is only one option. We use the if…else statement when there are two. But when there are three or more we use the if…elseif…else statement.

To illustrate, we write programs to solve two problems. In the sample runs, the underlined items are typed by the user; everything else is printed by the computer.

3.8.1 Print a Letter Grade

Write a program to request a score in a test and print a letter grade based on the following:

```
F: score < 50
B: 50 <= score < 75
A: score >= 75
```

The program should work as follows:

```
Enter a score: 70

Grade B
```

```
Enter a score: 99

Grade A
```

```
Enter a score: 42

Grade F
```

To make sure the program is correct, we run it with at least 3 different scores (e.g. 70, 99, 42) to verify that each of the 3 grades is printed correctly. You should also test it at the 'boundary' numbers, 50 and 75.

A solution to this problem is shown as Program P3.8.

```
# Program P3.8 - Request a score; print letter grade
const Flimit = 50
const Blimit = 75

function letterGrade()
    print("Enter a score: ")
    score = parse(Int64, readline())

    if score < Flimit
        println("Grade F")
    elseif score < Blimit
        println("Grade B")
    else
        println("Grade A")
    end
end # letterGrade

letterGrade()
```

The if...elseif...else statement takes this form:

```
if <cond1>
    <block1>
elseif <cond2>
    <block2>
elseif <cond3>
    <block3>
.
else
    <block>
end
```

The `if` part is followed by one or more `elseif` parts followed by the `else` part. Each of the `if` and `elseif` parts consists of *a condition* and *a block* to be executed if the condition is true. The `else` block is executed if none of the conditions is true. The entire construct is terminated by `end`.

`<cond1>`, `<cond2>`, etc. are *conditions* (`true` or `false`); `<block1>`, `<block2>`, etc. are blocks (one or more statements).

If `<cond1>` is true, `<block1>` is executed and the rest of the construct is skipped. If `<cond1>` is false, `<cond2>` is tested; if true, `<block2>` is executed and the rest of the construct is skipped; if false, `<cond3>` is tested...

We proceed in this manner until one of the conditions is true. When that happens, the corresponding block is executed and the rest of the construct is skipped. If none of the conditions is true, the `else` block is executed and the program continues with the next statement.

As an exercise, modify the program to print the correct grade based on the following:

```
F: score < 50
C: 50 <= score < 65
B: 65 <= score < 80
A: score >= 80
```

3.8.2 Classify a Triangle

Given three integer values representing the sides of a triangle, print:

- `Not a triangle` if the values cannot be the sides of any triangle. This is so if any value is negative or zero, or if the length of any side is greater than or equal to the sum of the other two;
- `Scalene` if the triangle is scalene (all sides different);
- `Right-angled` if the triangle is right-angled;
- `Isosceles` if the triangle is isosceles (two sides equal);
- `Equilateral` if the triangle is equilateral (three sides equal).

The program should work as follows:

```
Enter 3 sides of a triangle: 7 4 7

Isosceles
```

```
Enter 3 sides of a triangle: 5 13 12

Right-angled
```

A solution is shown as Program P3.9.

```
# Program P3.9 - Given three sides, classify the triangle, if any
# Request 3 sides; determine type of triangle
function classifyTriangle()
    print("Enter 3 sides of a triangle: ")
    a, b, c = [parse(Int, x) for x in split(readline())]

    if a <= 0 || b <= 0 || c <= 0
        print("\nNot a triangle\n")
```

```
    elseif a >= b + c || b >= c + a || c >= a + b
        print("\nNot a triangle\n")
    elseif a^2==b^2+c^2 || b^2==c^2+a^2 || c^2==a^2+b^2
        print("\nRight-angled\n")
    elseif a == b && b == c
        print("\nEquilateral\n")
    elseif a == b || b == c || c == a
        print("\nIsosceles\n")
    else
        print("\nScalene\n")
    end
end # classifyTriangle

classifyTriangle()
```

The first task is to establish that the three numbers given can be the sides of a valid triangle. The first `if` checks if any of the sides is negative or zero. If so, `Not a triangle` is printed.

If they are all positive, we go to the first `elseif` part which checks if any one side is greater than or equal to the sum of the other two. If so, `Not a triangle` is printed. If not, we have a valid triangle and must determine its type by executing the second `elseif` part. This checks if the triangle is right-angled.

The next `elseif` part checks if it is equilateral. If two different *pairs of sides* are equal—`a == b && b == c`—then all three are equal and we have an equilateral triangle.

If it is not equilateral, we check if it is isosceles. If any two sides are equal—`a == b || b == c || c == a`—we have an isosceles triangle.

If it is neither equilateral nor isosceles, then it must be scalene.

You should test the program to ensure that it prints the correct answer in all cases.

EXERCISES 3

1. An auto repair shop charges as follows. Inspecting the vehicle costs $75. If no work needs to be done, there is no further charge. Otherwise, the charge is $75 per hour for labour plus the cost of parts, with a minimum charge of $120. If any work is done, there is no charge for inspecting the vehicle.

   Write a program to read values for hours worked and cost of parts (either of which could be 0) and print the charge for the job.

2. Write a program which requests two weights in kilograms and grams and prints the sum of the weights. For example, if the weights are 3kg 500g and 4kg 700g, your program should print 8kg 200g.

3. Write a program which requests two lengths in feet and inches and prints the sum of the lengths. For example, if the lengths are 5ft 4in and 8ft 11in, your program should print 14ft 3in. (1 ft = 12 in)

4. A variety store gives a 15% discount on sales totalling $300 or more. Write a program to request the cost of 3 items and print the amount the customer must pay.

5. Write a program to read two pairs of integers. Each pair represents a fraction. For example, the pair 3 5 represents the fraction 3/5. Your program should print the sum of the given fractions. For example, given the pairs 3 5 and 2 3, your program should print 19/15.

Modify the program so that it prints the sum with the fraction reduced to a proper fraction; for this example, your program should print 1 4/15.

6. Write a program to read a person's name, hours worked, hourly rate of pay and tax rate (a number representing a percentage, e.g. 25 means 25%). The program must print the name, gross pay, tax deducted and net pay.

Gross pay is calculated as described in Section 3.5.1. The tax to be deducted is calculated by applying the tax rate to 80% of gross pay. And the net pay is calculated by subtracting the tax deducted from the gross pay.

For example, if the person works 50 hours at $20/hour and the tax rate is 25%, his gross pay would be (40 x 20) + (10 x 20 x 1.5) = $1100. He pays 25% tax on 80% of $1100, that is, 25% of $880 = $220. His net pay is 1100 - 220 = $880.

7. Write a program to read integer values for month and year and print the number of days in the month. For example, 4 2005 (April 2005) should print 30; 2 2004 (February 2004) should print 29; and 2 1900 (February 1900) should print 28.

A leap year, n, is divisible by 4; however, if n is divisible by 100 then it is a leap year only if it is also divisible by 400. So 1900 is not a leap year but 2000 is.

8. In an English class, a student is given 3 term tests (marked out of 25) and an end-of-term test (marked out of 100). The end-of-term test carries the same weight as all 3 term tests (50% each) in determining the final mark (out of 100).

Write a program to read marks for the 3 term tests followed by the mark for the end-of-term test. The program then prints the final mark and an indication of whether the student passes or fails. To pass, the final mark must be 50 or more.

For example, given the data 20 10 15 56, the final mark is calculated by this: (20+10+15)/75*50 + 56/100*50 = 58

9. Write a program to request two times given in 24-hour clock format and find the time (in hours and minutes) that has elapsed between the first time and the second time. You may assume that the second time is later than the first time. Each time is represented by two numbers: e.g. 16 45 means the time 16:45, that is, 4:45 p.m.

For example, if the two given times are 16 45 and 23 25 your answer should be 6 hours 40 minutes.

Modify the program so it works as follows: if the second time is sooner than the first time, take it to mean a time for the *next* day. For example, given the times 20:30 and 6:15, take this to mean 8.30 p.m. to 6.15 a.m. of the next day. Your answer should be 9 hours 45 minutes.

10. A fictitious bank pays interest based on the amount of money deposited. If the amount is less than $5,000, the interest is 4% per annum. If the amount is $5,000 or more but less than $10,000, the interest is 5% per annum. If the amount is $10,000 or more but less than $20,000, the interest is 6% per annum. If the amount is $20,000 or more, the interest is 7% per annum.

Write a program to request the amount deposited and print the interest earned for one year.

11. Write a program to prompt for the name of an item, its previous price and its current price. Print the percentage increase or decrease in the price. For example, if the previous price is $80 and the current price is $100, you should print increase of 25%; if the previous price is $100 and the current price is $80, you should print decrease of 20%.

12. A country charges income tax as follows based on one's gross salary. No tax is charged on the first 20% of salary. The remaining 80% is called *taxable income*. Tax is paid as follows:

   - 10% on the first $15,000 of taxable income;
   - 20% on the next $20,000 of taxable income;
   - 25% on all taxable income in excess of $35,000;

   Write a program to read a value for a person's salary and print the amount of tax to be paid. Also print the *average tax rate*, that is, the percentage of salary that is paid in tax.

   For example, on a salary of $20,000, a person pays $1700 in tax.

   The average tax rate is `1700/20000*100 = 8.5%`.

13. For any `year` between 1900 and 2099, inclusive, the `month` and `day` on which Easter Sunday falls can be determined by the following algorithm:

```
set a to year minus 1900
set b to the remainder when a is divided by 19
set c to the integer quotient when 7b + 1 is divided by 19
set d to the remainder when 11b + 4 - c is divided by 29
set e to the integer quotient when a is divided by 4
set f to the remainder when a + e + 31 - d is divided by 7
set g to 25 minus the sum of d and f
if g is less than or equal to 0 then
    set month to 'March'
    set day to 31 + g
else
    set month to 'April'
    set day to g
endif
```

   Write a program which requests a year between 1900 and 2099, inclusive, and checks if the year is valid. If it is, print the day on which Easter Sunday falls in that year. For example, if the year is `1999`, your program should print `April 4`.

CHAPTER 4

The `for` and `while` Statements

In this chapter, we will explain the following:

- How to use the `while` statement to perform 'looping' in a program
- How to find the `gcd` (also called `hcf`) of two numbers
- How to find the sum and average of an arbitrary set of numbers
- How to read data until there's no more
- How to find the largest and smallest of an arbitrary set of numbers
- How to fetch (read) data from a file
- How to send (write) output to a file
- How to use the `for` statement to perform 'looping' in a program
- How to produce tables using `for`
- How to use `break`/`continue` in `while`/`for` statements
- Nested `for` statements

4.1 Introduction

In Chapter 2, we showed you how to write programs using *sequence* logic—programs whose statements are executed "in sequence" from the first to the last. In Chapter 3, we showed you how to write programs for problems which require *selection* logic. These programs used the `if`, `if…else` and `if…elseif…else` statements.

In this chapter, we discuss problems which require *repetition* logic. The idea is to write statements once and get the computer to execute them repeatedly for a specified number of times or as long as some condition is true. We will see how to express repetition logic using the `for` and `while` statements.

4.2 The `for` Statement

Traditionally, the `for` statement has been used in programming languages for *counting*, to perform an action (or actions) a specified number of times. We speak of *performing (executing) a for loop*. We say things like "perform the loop 10 times" or "get a value for *n*, and perform the loop *n* times".

The `for` statement in Julia can do all that, and much, much more. It's one of the most powerful and versatile statements in Julia, with features most other languages lack. We start with the basic uses.

© The Author(s), under exclusive license to Springer Nature Switzerland AG 2021
N. Kalicharan, *Julia - Bit by Bit*, Undergraduate Topics in Computer Science,
https://doi.org/10.1007/978-3-030-73936-2_4

Consider the following:

```
for h = 1 : 4
    println("I must ask questions in class")
end
```

This says to execute the `println` statement 4 times, with h assuming the values 1, 2, 3 and 4, one value for each of the 4 times. The effect is to print this:

```
I must ask questions in class
I must ask questions in class
I must ask questions in class
I must ask questions in class
```

The loop consists of:

- the word `for`
- the *loop variable* (h, in the example)
- `=`
- the *initial* value (1, in the example)
- a colon (`:`)
- the *final* value (4, in the example)
- one or more statements to be executed each time through the loop; these statements make up the *body* of the loop. Here, the body has one `println` statement.
- the word `end`, indicating the end of the loop

To highlight the structure of the loop and make it more readable, we line up `for` and `end`, and indent the statement(s) in the body.

The initial and final values in the `for` statement do not have to be constants; they can be variables or expressions. For example, consider this:

```
for h = 1 : n
```

When this statement is encountered, if n is 7, the body would be executed 7 times.

This means that *before* the computer gets to the `for` statement, n must have been assigned some value and it is *this* value which determines how many times the loop is executed. If a value has not been assigned to n, the `for` statement would not make sense and the program will crash (or, at best, give some nonsensical output).

To illustrate, we can modify the code above to ask the user how many lines she wants to print. The number entered is then used to control how many times the loop is executed and, hence, how many lines are printed.

The changes are shown in Program P4.1.

```
# Program P4.1 - Print Lines
function printLines()
    print("How many lines? ")
    n = parse(Int, readline())
    for h = 1 : n    # the spaces around : are optional
        println("I must ask questions in class")
    end
end

printLines()
```

The following is a sample run:

```
How many lines? 3
I must ask questions in class
I must ask questions in class
I must ask questions in class
```

This program is more flexible in that it lets the user say how many lines she wants printed.

Need to know: The loop variable h is *local* to the for statement; its *scope* is limited to the body of the for. If, for instance, we tried to print it outside the for loop, we would get a message to the effect that h is not defined.

In the example, we did not use the value of the loop variable, h. But it's available inside the loop and can be used in any way we want. The next example uses it to number the lines.

```
# Program P4.2 - Print Lines, Number Them

function printLines()
    print("How many lines? ")
    n = parse(Int, readline())
    for h = 1 : n   # the spaces around : are optional
        println("$h. I must ask questions in class")
    end
end

printLines()
```

The following is a sample run:

```
How many lines? 3
1. I must ask questions in class
2. I must ask questions in class
3. I must ask questions in class
```

To further expand on the scope of h, consider this:

```
# Program P4.2x - Print Lines, Scope Rule

# Show how scope rule works
function printLines()
    print("How many lines? ")
    n = parse(Int, readline())
    h = 99
    for h = 1 : n
        println("$h. I must ask questions in class")
    end
    println("\nValue of h after loop: $h")
end

printLines()
```

Here's a run:

```
How many lines? 3
1. I must ask questions in class
2. I must ask questions in class
3. I must ask questions in class
```

```
Value of h after loop: 99
```

We set h to 99 before the for loop. In the loop, it takes on the values 1, 2, 3. On exit from the loop, it reverts to its original value, 99. In reality, the loop variable h is a different variable from the one outside the loop; it just happens to have the same name. But there should be no confusion once we understand the scope rule.

4.2.1 Multiplication Tables

The for statement is handy for producing tables, especially multiplication tables. We write a program to produce a "2-times" table from 1 to 12. The following should be printed by the program:

```
 1 x 2 =  2
 2 x 2 =  4
 3 x 2 =  6
 4 x 2 =  8
 5 x 2 = 10
 6 x 2 = 12
 7 x 2 = 14
 8 x 2 = 16
 9 x 2 = 18
10 x 2 = 20
11 x 2 = 22
12 x 2 = 24
```

Program P4.3 shows how to produce the table.

```
# Program P4.3 - Print 2-times table
using Printf
function twoTimesTable()
    for h = 1 : 12
        @printf("%2d x 2 = %2d\n", h, h*2)
    end
end # twoTimesTable

twoTimesTable()
```

The specifications %2d in @printf ensures the numbers line up neatly as shown above.

What if we want to print a "7-times" table? What changes would be needed? We would just need to change the @printf statement to this:

```
@printf("%2d x 7 = %2d\n", h, h*7)
```

Similarly, if we want a "9 times" table, we would have to change the 7s to 9s. Also, since the 9 times table would contain a 3-digit number (108) we would have to change the second %2d to %3d for the table to look neat. And we would have to keep changing the program for each table that we want.

A better approach is to let the user tell the computer which table he wants. The program will then use this information to produce the table requested. Now when the program is run, it will prompt:

```
Enter type of table:
```

If the user wants a "9 times" table, he will enter 9. The program will then go ahead and produce a "9 times" table. Program P4.4 shows how.

```
# Program P4.4 - Print any times table
using Printf
function anyTimesTable()
     print("Type of table? ")
     tt = parse(Int, readline())
     println()
     for h = 1 : 12
          @printf("%2d x %d = %3d\n", h, tt, h*tt)
     end
end

anyTimesTable()
```

Here's a run of Program P4.4:

```
Type of table? 9

 1 x 9 =    9
 2 x 9 =   18
 3 x 9 =   27
 4 x 9 =   36
 5 x 9 =   45
 6 x 9 =   54
 7 x 9 =   63
 8 x 9 =   72
 9 x 9 =   81
10 x 9 =   90
11 x 9 =   99
12 x 9 =  108
```

We now have a program which can produce any multiplication table from 1 to 12. But there is nothing sacred about the range 1 to 12 (special, maybe, since that's what we learnt in school).

How can we *generalize* the program to produce *any* table in any range? We must let the user tell the program what type of table and what range he wants. And in the program, we will need to replace the numbers 1 and 12 by variables, (first and last, say).

These changes are reflected in Program P4.5.

```
# Program P4.5 - Print any range times table
using Printf
function anyRangeTimesTable()
     print("Type of table? ")
     tt = parse(Int, readline())
     print("From? ")
     first = parse(Int, readline())
     print("To? ")
     last = parse(Int, readline())
     println()

     for h = first : last
          @printf("%2d x %d = %3d\n", h, tt, h*tt)
     end
end # anyRangeTimesTable

anyRangeTimesTable()
```

Here's a sample run:

```
Type of table? 13
From? 8
To? 14

 8 x 13 = 104
 9 x 13 = 117
10 x 13 = 130
11 x 13 = 143
12 x 13 = 156
13 x 13 = 169
14 x 13 = 182
```

The program assumes that `first` is less than or equal to `last`. What if this is not so? For example, suppose the user enters 15 for `first` and 11 for `last`. The `for` statement becomes this:

```
for h = 15 : 11
```

`h` is set to 15; since this value is immediately bigger than the final value 11, the body is not executed at all and the program ends with nothing printed.

To cater for this possibility, we can let the program *validate* the values of `first` and `last` to ensure the *From* value is less than or equal to the *To* value. One way to do this is as follows:

```
if first > last
    println("Invalid data: From value bigger than To value")
else
    for h = first : last
        @printf("%2d x %d = %3d\n", h, tt, h*tt)
    end
end
```

Validating data entered is yet another example of *defensive programming*. Also, it is better to print a message informing the user of the error rather than have the program do nothing. This makes the program more *user-friendly*.

Another option here is *not* to treat a bigger `first` value as an error but simply print the table in descending order, going from the bigger `first` value to the smaller `last` value. Yet another possibility is to swap `first` and `last` and print the table in the normal way. We will discuss the first option and leave the second as an exercise.

The question is, what should the program do if, for instance, the user enters 15 for `first` and 11 for `last`? If it's a 7 times table, one possibility is to print the following:

```
15 x 7 = 105
14 x 7 =  98
13 x 7 =  91
12 x 7 =  84
11 x 7 =  77
```

All we need to do is change the above `if...else` statement to this:

```
if first <= last
    for h = first : last
        @printf("%2d x %d = %3d\n", h, tt, h*tt)
    end
else
    for h = first : -1 : last
        @printf("%2d x %d = %3d\n", h, tt, h*tt)
    end
end
```

The second `for` statement is a bit different from those we have seen so far:

```
for h = first : -1 : last
```

If `first` is 15 and `last` is 11, `h` will take on values from 15 to 11 *in steps of* -1. In other words, `for` lets us specify an *increment* option (`incr`, say). Each time through the loop, `incr` is added to `h`. Here, `incr` is -1.

For comparison and consistency, we *could* have written the first `for` like this:

```
for h = first : 1 : last
```

In the following, `h` will take on the values 1, 4, 7, 10, 13 (incr = 3):

```
for h = 1 : 3 : 15     # increment is 3
```

The next value of `h` (16) exceeds 15 so the program exits the loop.

And, in the following, `h` will take on the values 15, 11, 7, 3 (incr = -4):

```
for h = 15 : -4 : 1
```

Before we close this example, we point out a more concise way of writing the above `if..else` statement.

```
first <= last ? incr = 1 : incr = -1
for h = first : incr : last
    @printf("%2d x %d = %3d\n", h, tt, h*tt)
end
```

The first statement sets `incr` to 1 if `first` is less than or equal to `last`, and sets it to -1 if `first` is bigger. The `for` loop uses this value to print the appropriate table (increasing or decreasing).

Tip: Consider this: `for h = first : incr : last`

If `incr > 0`, the loop ends when `h` first *exceeds* `last`. The following prints nothing since the first value of `h` (3) is immediately bigger than `last` (1).

```
for h = 3 : 1: 1 println(h) end
```

If `incr < 0`, the loop ends when `h` first becomes *less than* `last`. The following prints nothing since the first value of `h` (1) is immediately less than `last` (3).

```
for h = 1 : -1 : 3 println(h) end
```

If `incr = 0`, Julia reports an error.

4.2.2 Temperature Conversion

Some countries use the Celsius scale for measuring temperature while others use the Fahrenheit scale. Suppose we want to print a table of temperature conversions from Celsius to Fahrenheit. The table runs from 0 degrees C to 100 degrees C in steps of 10, like this:

```
Celsius  Fahrenheit
     0         32
    10         50
    20         68
    30         86
    40        104
    50        122
    60        140
    70        158
    80        176
```

90	194
100	212

For a Celsius temperature, C, the Fahrenheit equivalent is 32 + 9C/5.

If we use c to hold the Celsius temperature, we can write a for statement in which c takes on the values 0, 10, 20, ..., up to 100:

```
for c = 0 : 10 : 100   # start at 0, in steps of 10, up to 100
```

Each time the loop is executed, c is incremented by 10. Using this, we write Program P4.6 to produce the table.

```
# Program P4.6 - Print Celsius to Fahrenheit Table
using Printf

function CelsiusToFahrenheit()
    println("Celsius  Fahrenheit\n")
    for c = 0 : 10 : 100   # start at 0, in steps of 10, up to 100
        f = 32 + 9c/5       # In Julia, 9c is valid and means 9*c
        @printf("%5.0f %9.0f\n", c, f)
    end
end

CelsiusToFahrenheit()
```

An interesting part of the program are the print statements. In order to get the temperatures centred under the heading, we need to do some counting. Consider the heading

```
Celsius  Fahrenheit
```

with the C in column 1, and 2 spaces between s and F.

Assume we want the Celsius temperatures lined up under i and the Fahrenheit temperatures lined up under n (see output above).

By counting, we find that i is in column 5 and n is in column 15.

From this, we can figure out that the value of c must be printed in a field width of 5 (the first 5 columns) and the value of f must be printed in the next 10 columns. We use a field width of 9 for f since there is already one space between f and % in @printf(...).

We print c and f without a decimal point using 0 as the number of decimal places in the format specification. If any temperature is not a whole number, the 0 specification will print it *rounded* to the nearest whole number, as in the table below.

```
Celsius  Fahrenheit

   20        68
   22        72
   24        75
   26        79
   28        82
   30        86
   32        90
```

As an exercise, re-write Program P4.6 so it requests three values for first, last and incr and produces a table as above; Celsius temperatures go from first to last in steps of incr.

Follow the ideas of the previous section for producing any multiplication table. For example, if first is 20, last is 32 and incr is 2, the program should produce the table above (with Fahrenheit temperatures rounded to the nearest whole number).

As another exercise, write a program which produces a table from Fahrenheit to Celsius. For a Fahrenheit temperature, F, the Celsius equivalent is

```
5(F - 32)/9
```

Point of interest: Julia lets you specify the calculation exactly as shown:

```
C = 5(F - 32)/9
```

4.3 The Expressive Power of for

So far, we have seen several examples of how the for statement can be used to *iterate* through a set of numbers, upwards or downwards, in steps of one or more. But it can do much more than that. For instance, it can iterate through strings and files. (Later, we will show how to iterate through *tuples* and *arrays*.)

Terminology: The symbols = and ∈, and the word in are synonyms of each other. They can be used interchangeably. For example, the following all mean the same thing:

```
for n = 1:4
for n in 1:4
for n ∈ 1:4
```

So why do we need three operators all meaning the same thing? It's just that in some situations, one might be more natural to use than the others. In the examples with numbers we saw before, = was probably the most appropriate to use; but it is more natural to talk about characters *in* a string or elements belonging to (∈) a set.

We now look at several examples that illustrate the versatile nature of the for statement. They will take the following form:

```
for <iterator> in <source>
    <body>
end
```

<iterator> is a variable which will be set to each of the values in <source>.

Here are some examples:

For each number in a range of numbers:

```
for t in lo : hi
    <body>
end
```

t is set to each value from lo to hi, inclusive, and, for each, <body> is executed.

```
Example 1:
function forSum()
    sum = 0
    for t in 1 : 7
        sum += t        # each value of t is added to sum
    end
    println(sum)
end # forSum

forSum()

Output
```

```
28
```

Example 2:

```
function forSum()
    sum = 0
    for t in 1 : 2 : 7  # t = 1, 3, 5, 7
        sum += t
    end
    println(sum)
end # forSum

forSum()
```

Output

```
16
```

For each character in a *String*:

```
str = "Sample String"
for c in str
    <body>
end
```

c is set to each character in str, and, for each, <body> is executed.

Example 1:

```
function forString()
    S = "Flowers"
    for s in S          # s is set to each character in S
        print("$s ")    # print character followed by a space
    end
    println()
end

forString()
```

Output

```
F l o w e r s
```

Example 2:

```
function forString()
    for s in "HAL"
        print("$(s+1) ")  # print the letter that comes after s
    end
    println()
end

forString()
```

Output

```
I B M
```

For each line in a file:

```
for line in eachline(file)
    <body>
end
```

line is set to each line in the file designated by file, and, for each, <body> is executed.

```
function forFile()
    n = 0
    for ln in eachline("words.txt")  # ln is set to each line of the file words.txt
        println("$(n+=1). $ln")
    end
end
forFile()
```

Suppose the file `words.txt` contains the following:

```
Where the mind is without fear
And the head is held high
Where knowledge is free
```

When run, the function prints this:

```
1. Where the mind is without fear
2. And the head is held high
3. Where knowledge is free
```

We'll elaborate on this way of reading from a file in Section 4.5.

4.4 break/continue in for

We start with an example to illustrate how the break and continue statements work. Suppose we want to find the sum of the numbers from 1 to 10 *except* 7. We can do it as follows:

```
function forAllBut7()
    sum = 0
    for h = 1 : 10
        if h == 7 continue end
        sum += h
    end
    println("Sum is $sum")
end

forAllBut7()
```

When used in a for loop, continue causes the *current iteration* of the loop to cease; control goes to the top of the loop to prepare for the next iteration, if any (increment and test the loop variable).

When h is 7, the statement that adds h to sum is skipped. When run, the program prints this:

```
Sum is 48
```

Next, suppose we replace continue with break in the if statement:

```
if h == 7 break end
```

When run, the program prints this:

```
Sum is 21
```

When h is 7, break causes control to break out of the for loop entirely; execution continues with the println statement after the loop. 7 is not added to the sum, so 21 (sum from 1 to 6) is printed.

Let's write a program to solve this problem:

An amount of money P (for principal) is put into an account which earns interest at r% per annum. So, at the end of one year, the amount becomes P + P×r/100. This becomes the principal for the next year. Write a program to print the amount at the end of each year for the next 10 years. However, if the amount ever exceeds 2P, stop any further printing. Your program should prompt for the values of P and r.

Here are two sample runs:

```
Principal? 1000
Interest Rate? 5.5
Year  Amount
   1  1055.00
```

```
 2   1113.03
 3   1174.24
 4   1238.82
 5   1306.96
 6   1378.84
 7   1454.68
 8   1534.69
 9   1619.09
10   1708.14
```

```
Principal? 1000
Interest Rate? 15
Year  Amount
 1   1150.00
 2   1322.50
 3   1520.88
 4   1749.01
 5   2011.36
```

Program P4.7 shows how we can get these outputs. After prompting for the principal and interest rate, we use a for loop in which we calculate the new amount for each year. We break out of the loop if the year-end amount ever exceeds twice the principal.

```
# Program P4.7 Calculate Interest
using Printf
function calcInterest()
    print("Principal? ")
    P = parse(Int64, readline())
    print("Interest Rate? ")
    r = parse(Float64, readline())

    println("Year  Amount")
    amt = P
    for y = 1 : 10
        amt += amt*r/100
        @printf("%3d %8.2f\n", y, amt)
        if amt > 2P break end
    end
end # calcInterest

calcInterest()
```

4.5 Read Data From File

Except for one example, we have written our programs assuming that data to be supplied is typed at the keyboard. We have fetched the data using readline() and converted it to the appropriate type using parse().

Typically, the program issues a prompt and waits for the user to type the data. When the data is typed, the program reads it, stores it in a variable (or variables) and continues with its execution. This mode of supplying data is called *interactive* since the user is interacting with the program.

We say we have been reading data from the "standard input". Similarly, we have been writing (printing) our output to the "standard output", the screen.

We can also supply data to a program by storing the data in a file. When the program needs data, it fetches it directly from the file, without user intervention. Of course, we have to ensure that the appropriate data has been stored in the file in the correct order and format.

This mode of supplying data is normally referred to as *batch* mode. (The term batch is historical and comes from the old days when data had to be 'batched' before being submitted for processing.)

For example, suppose we need to supply an item number (integer) and a price (floating-point) for some items. If the program is written assuming that the data file contains several pairs of numbers (an `Int64` followed by a `Float64`) then we must ensure the data in the file conforms to this.

Suppose we create a file called `input.txt` and *type* data in it. This is a *file of characters* or a *text* file. How can we get a program to read this data? There are a few ways.

Perhaps the simplest is what we met in Section 4.3. We will use that method for the next few sections and discuss other ways in Section 4.7.

In Section 4.3, we saw how to read data from a file, one line at a time, with this:

```
for line in eachline(file)
```

Let's write a program to read some numbers from a file, one per line, and find their sum. Here is the pseudocode:

```
# Algorithm for finding sum
set sum to 0
for each line in the file
    num = line converted to a number
    add num to sum
end
print sum
```

To find the sum, we need to:

- Choose a variable to hold the sum; we use `sum`.
- Initialize `sum` to `0` (before the `for` loop).
- Each line in the file has a number `num`; fetch it and add it to `sum`.

On exit from the `for` loop, `sum` contains the sum of all the numbers in the file; print `sum`.

We assume the data is stored in a file `input.txt`, like this:

```
24
13
32
17
```

The statement `for snum in eachline("input.txt")` will store each number, in turn, in `snum` as a string. We convert it to an integer using `num = parse(Int64, snum)`.

The program is shown as P4.8.

```
# Program P4.8 - Find the sum of numbers stored in a file
function sumNumbers()
    sum = 0
    for snum in eachline("input.txt")
        num = parse(Int64, snum)
        sum = sum + num
    end
    println("The sum is $sum")
end # sumNumbers

sumNumbers()
```

When run with the above data, the program prints this:

```
The sum is 86
```

4.5.1 Keep a Count

Program P4.8 finds the sum of the numbers in the file. Suppose we want to *count* how many numbers were added. We could use an integer variable n to hold the count. To get the program to keep a count, we need to do the following:

- Choose a variable to hold the count; we choose n.
- Initialize n to 0, *before* the for loop
- Add 1 to n *inside* the loop. Here, we must add 1 to n each time we fetch a number from the file, in other words, each time we execute the body of the loop. The statement n += 1 (which adds 1 to n) must be placed *inside* the loop.
- Print n, *after* the loop.

Program P4.9 is the modified program for counting the numbers.

```
# Program P4.9 - Sum and count numbers in a file
function sumCountNumbers()
    sum = 0
    n = 0
    for snum in eachline("input.txt")
        n += 1
        num = parse(Int64, snum)
        sum += num
    end
    println("$n number(s) entered")
    println("Sum is $sum")
end # sumCountNumbers

sumCountNumbers()
```

When run with the above data in "input.txt", the program prints this:

```
4 number(s) entered
Sum is 86
```

4.5.2 Find Average

Program P4.9 can be easily modified to find the average of the numbers entered. As we saw above, on exit from the for loop, we know the sum (sum) and how many numbers were entered (n). We can add a statement to print the average to 1 decimal place, say, like this:

```
println("Average is $(round(sum/n,digits=1))")
```

The following is a sample run of the modified program:

```
4 number(s) entered
Sum is 86
Average is 21.5
```

However, there is still a problem. If the file is empty, execution will reach the above println statement with sum and n both having the value 0. The program will attempt to divide 0 by 0.

In most languages, this will give an error: "Attempt to divide by 0". However, Julia prints this:

```
Average is NaN
```

NaN stands for "Not a Number". While this is better than the program crashing and reporting an *execution error*, it is better for us to anticipate this possibility and cater for it. We could do so by writing the following after the for loop:

```
if n == 0
    println("No numbers entered")
else
    println("$n number(s) entered")
    println("Sum is $sum")
    println("Average is $(round(sum/n,digits=1))")
end
```

The moral of the story is, whenever possible, you should try to anticipate the ways in which your program might fail and cater for them—another example of *defensive programming*.

4.6 Find Largest Number

We want to write a program which reads numbers from a file input.txt and finds the largest. Suppose the file contains this data:

```
36
17
52
43
```

The program should print this:

```
Largest is 52
```

Finding the largest number involves the following steps:

- Choose a variable to hold the largest number; we choose bigNum.
- Initialize bigNum to a very small value. The value chosen should be such that no matter what number is read, it would be bigger than this initial value. We set bigNum to typemin(Int64), the smallest 64-bit integer in Julia. It is -9223372036854775808.
- Each number in the file is read as a string snum. This is converted to the integer num which is compared with bigNum; if num is bigger, we set bigNum to this new number.
- When all the numbers have been read and checked, bigNum will contain the largest one.

These ideas are expressed in the following algorithm:

```
set bigNum to typemin(Int64)
for each line in the file
    num = line converted to a number
    if num > bigNum set bigNum to num
end
print bigNum
```

We implement the algorithm as shown in Program P4.10.

```
# Program P4.10 - Find Largest Number
# Print the largest of a set of numbers
function findLargest()
    bigNum = typemin(Int64)

    for snum in eachline("input.txt")
        num = parse(Int64, snum)
        if num > bigNum
```

```
            bigNum = num
        end
    end
    println("Largest is $bigNum")
end # findLargest

findLargest()
```

Let us 'step through' this program using the sample data above. For easy reference, the data was supplied in this order:

```
36   17   52   43
```

Initially, bigNum is -9223372036854775808:

bigNum	-9223372036854775808

"36" is read; it is converted to 36 (by parse) and stored in num;
num (36) is compared with bigNum (-9223372036854775808);
36 is bigger so bigNum is set to 36, giving this:

num	36		bigNum	36

"17" is read; it is converted to 17 and stored in num;
num (17) is compared with bigNum (36);
17 is not bigger so bigNum remains at 36, giving this:

num	17		bigNum	36

"52" is read; it is converted to 52 and stored in num;
num (52) is compared with bigNum (36);
52 is bigger so bigNum is set to 52, giving this:

num	52		bigNum	52

"43" is read; it is converted to 43 and stored in num;
num (43) is compared with bigNum (52);
43 is not bigger so bigNum remains at 52, giving this:

num	43		bigNum	52

All the numbers have been processed; we exit the for loop and println prints this:

```
Largest is 52
```

The program gives the correct answer. It would do so, regardless of whether the numbers supplied are positive, negative or a combination of both. Suppose input.txt contains this:

```
-7
-9
-3
-6
```

When run, the program prints

```
Largest is -3
```

4.6.1 Find 'Largest' Word

Suppose, instead of numbers, each line of the input file contained a word. We could find the 'largest' using the same algorithm above. However, note that when applied to words, 'largest' means latest in alphabetical order.

Program P4.11 reads words from the file input.txt and finds the last in alphabetical order.

```
# Program P4.11 - Find Last Word (Alphabetical Order)
function findLastWord()
    lastWord = ""
    for word in eachline("input.txt")
        if word > lastWord
            lastWord = word
        end
    end
    println("Last word is $lastWord")
end # findLastWord

findLastWord()
```

Hey, it's even easier than finding the largest number since no conversion to a number is necessary. We just read a word and compare it to the largest so far.

We initialize lastWord to the empty string; *any* word would be 'larger' than this. Assume input.txt contains these words:

```
wish
you
were
here
```

When run, program P4.11 prints this:

```
Last word is you
```

But if the file contained this:

```
Wish
You
Were
here
```

the program will print this:

```
Last word is here
```

This is so since lowercase letters come *after* uppercase ones in the ASCII character set. So h comes after W and Y.

If we want true alphabetical order, regardless of case, we must change

```
if word > lastWord
```

to this:

```
if lowercase(word) > lowercase(lastWord)
```

or this:

```
if uppercase(word) > uppercase(lastWord)
```

We convert both words to the same case before comparing them.

With either of these changes, and the data above, the program will print this:

```
Last word is You
```

4.6.2 Find Longest Word

What if we wanted to find the longest word—the one with the most letters? This is just the same as finding the largest of a set of numbers. Here, each number is the length of a word.

However, since we need to know *which* word is the longest, each time we get a bigger length, we must save the bigger length *and* the word with that length. We show how to do this in Program P4.12. The standard Julia function length is used to return the length of a word.

```julia
# Program P4.12 - Find Longest Word
function findLongestWord()
    longest = 0
    longWord = ""
    for word in eachline("input.txt")
        if (len = length(word)) > longest
            longest = len
            longWord = word
        end
    end
    println("Longest word is $longWord, Length: $longest")
end # findLongestWord

findLongestWord()
```

Suppose input.txt contains this:

```
Abecedarian
Parliamentarian
Contrarian
Humanitarian
```

When run, the program prints this:

```
Longest word is Parliamentarian, Length: 15
```

If two or more words have the same longest length, the one that comes first in the file is printed.

4.6.3 Find Smallest Number

The *process* of finding the smallest number is the same as that for finding the largest. But whereas earlier we initialized bigNum to a very small number, now we will initialize smallNum to a very big number. We will use typemax(Int64). It's value is 9223372036854775807.

With largest, we saved the new number if it was bigger. Now we save it if it is smaller.

Finding the smallest involves the following steps:

- Choose a variable to hold the smallest number; we choose smallNum.
- Initialize smallNum to a very big value. The value chosen should be such that no matter what number is read, its value would be smaller than this initial value. We let Julia tell us this "biggest" value: typemax(Int64).

- Each number in the file is read as a string snum. This is converted to the integer num which is compared with smallNum; if num is smaller, we set smallNum to this new number.
- When all the numbers have been read and checked, smallNum will contain the smallest.

These ideas are expressed in the following algorithm:

```
set smallNum to typemax(Int64)
for each line in the file
    num = line converted to a number
    if num < smallNum set smallNum to num
end
print smallNum
```

We implement the algorithm as shown in Program P4.13.

```
# Program P4.13 - Find Smallest Number
# Print the smallest of a set of numbers
function findSmallest()
    smallNum = typemax(Int64)
    for snum in eachline("input.txt")
        num = parse(Int64, snum)

        if num < smallNum
            smallNum = num
        end
    end
    println("Smallest is $smallNum")
end # findSmallest

findSmallest()
```

Suppose input.txt contains the following:

```
36
4
-7
23
```

When run, program P4.13 prints this:

```
Smallest is -7
```

Exercise: Finding the first word in alphabetical order is similar to finding the last word in alphabetical order. And finding the shortest word is similar to finding the longest word. All it takes is a change of variable names and replacing > with <. We leave these as exercises.

4.7 Nested for Statement

Consider the following:

```
for i = 1 : 3
    for j = 1 : 5
        print("($i,$j) ")
    end
    println()
end
```

This is an example of a for statement *nested* within another; we say a *nested for loop* or just *nested loop*. We refer to the i loop as the *outer loop* and the j loop as the *inner loop*. The code is executed as follows:

- i is set to 1: the inner loop is executed with j going from 1 to 5. This will be printed: (1,1) (1,2) (1,3) (1,4) (1,5); println() ends the line so subsequent output will start at the left margin of the next line.
- i is set to 2: the inner loop is executed with j again going from 1 to 5. This will be printed: (2,1) (2,2) (2,3) (2,4) (2,5); println() ends the line so subsequent output will start at the left margin of the next line.
- i is set to 3: the inner loop is executed with j again going from 1 to 5. This will be printed: (3,1) (3,2) (3,3) (3,4) (3,5); println() ends the line so subsequent output will start at the left margin of the next line.

At the end, the following would have been printed:

```
(1,1) (1,2) (1,3) (1,4) (1,5)
(2,1) (2,2) (2,3) (2,4) (2,5)
(3,1) (3,2) (3,3) (3,4) (3,5)
```

It is sometimes helpful to think that, here, the body of the i loop consists of two statements. One of them just happens to be the j loop and the other println(). Thinking this way may help reduce some confusion about nested loops.

We can achieve the same effect with this (only one for statement):

```
for i = 1:3, j = 1:5
    print("($i,$j) ")
    if j == 5 println() end
end
```

i is set to 1: the loop is executed with j assuming the values 1, 2, 3, 4, 5. When j = 5, println() terminates the line. The following is printed:

```
(1,1) (1,2) (1,3) (1,4) (1,5)
```

i is set to 2: the loop is executed with j assuming the values 1, 2, 3, 4, 5. When j = 5, println() terminates the line. The following is printed:

```
(2,1) (2,2) (2,3) (2,4) (2,5)
```

i is set to 3: the loop is executed with j assuming the values 1, 2, 3, 4, 5. When j = 5, println() terminates the line. The following is printed:

```
(3,1) (3,2) (3,3) (3,4) (3,5)
```

In this example, the result is the same in both versions but that may not always be so; it depends on what is done inside the loop. However, once you understand *how* the execution is performed, you should be able to tell if the code does what you expect.

More generally, consider this for loop, rewritten using in:

```
for i1 in <source1>, i2 in <source2>
    <body>
end
```

i1 is set to the *first* element of <source1>; with this value of i1, and for *each* value i2 in <source2>, <body> is executed.

i1 is then set to the *second* element, if any, of <source1>; with this value of i1, and for *each* value i2 in <source2>, <body> is executed.

i1 is then set to the *third* element, if any, of <source1>; with this value of i1, and for *each* value i2 in <source2>, <body> is executed.

And so on, until…

i1 is set to the *last* element of <source1>; with this value of i1, and for *each* value i2 in <source2>, <body> is executed.

At this point, the execution of the for loop is completed and the program continues with the statement, if any, after end.

We illustrate with this example:

```
for n in [1,5,7], U in "ADEL"
    print("($n,$U) ")
    if U == 'L' println() end
end

(1,A) (1,D) (1,E) (1,L)
(5,A) (5,D) (5,E) (5,L)
(7,A) (7,D) (7,E) (7,L)
```

Nested for statements are particularly useful for working with two-dimensional arrays and matrices.

4.8 Read Data From File, Cont'd

So far, we have read from a file a line at a time using this:

```
for line in eachline("input.txt")
```

Each time through the for loop, we get to work with the next line of data which, until now, has consisted of a single number/word. But what if each line may have several numbers or words that we want to pick off individually?

For example, consider a file with data like this:

```
36 17 52 43
21   14   64
10 41 39 50 44
```

How can we read and process the numbers one at a time? We can use the following idea:

```
for each line in the data
    for each number in line
        <process number>
    end
end
```

Consider this:

```
function getData()
    for line in eachline("input.txt")
        for snum in split(line)
            print("$snum ")
        end
    end
    println()
end
```

When run with the above data, the program prints this:

```
36 17 52 43 21 14 64 10 41 39 50 44
```

Note that while they may *look* like numbers, they are numeric strings stored one at a time in snum. If we want to *process* them as numbers (add them, say), we would have to convert them with parse, like here:

```
function addData()
    sum = 0
```

```
        for line in eachline("input.txt")
            for snum in split(line)
                sum += parse(Int64, snum)
            end
        end
        println("Sum is $sum")
    end
```

If `addData()` is called with the above data, it prints this, the sum of all the numbers in the file:

```
Sum is 431
```

As we've seen, `for line in eachline("input.txt")` lets us do many things, but it has its limitations. For instance, what if we want one function to read one line of data and another function read the second line. More generally, we may want one function to continue reading from where another left off.

If we use `for line in eachline("input.txt")` in both functions, each will start reading from the beginning, and read the whole file.

While we can't use `for line in eachline(..)` in this situation, it's no trouble. Julia provides the tools we need to handle this and most other file-handling problems.

File Pointer

Assume we want to read data from the file `input.txt`. The first thing we need to do is declare an identifier called a "file pointer" and associate it with the file. We can do so with this statement:

```
inn = open("input.txt", "r")
```

We have used the identifier `inn`; any other will do, such as `f`, `inf`, `infile`, `inputFile`, `payData`. (We choose to use `inn` rather than `in` since the latter, though not a reserved word, is used for special purposes, like in the `for` statement, as we've seen. Also, it has the same number of letters as `out`, which we'll use for output files.)

This tells Julia to "open the file `input.txt` for reading": `"r"` indicates reading. (We use `"w"` if we want the file to be opened for "writing", that is, to receive output.) The *type* of `inn` is `IOStream`:

```
julia> inn = open("input.txt", "r")
IOStream(<file input.txt>)
```

Once this is done, Julia will position a *data pointer* at the beginning of the file. As we read data from the file, the pointer will move, keeping track of where we've reached in the file.

eof: If we need to, we can check if the pointer has reached the end of the file associated with `inn`; `eof(inn)` returns `true` if the pointer has reached end-of-file and `false`, if it has not.

Having declared `inn`, we can read data from the file, `input.txt`. We will see how shortly.

Caution: It is up to us to ensure that the file exists and contains the appropriate data. If not, we will get an error message such as "File not found".

If needed, we can specify the *path* to the file. Suppose the file is located at `C:\testdata\input.txt`.

We can tell Julia we will be reading data from the file with this:

```
inn = open("C:\\testdata\\input.txt", "r")
```

Recall that the escape sequence \\ is used to represent \ within a string. If the file is on a flash drive with assigned letter E, we can use this:

```
inn = open("E:\\input.txt", "r")
```

Tip: If the data file is in the *current working directory*, we don't need to specify the full path; we can simply use the file name, e.g. input.txt. To find out the current working directory, type pwd() (**p**rint **w**orking **d**irectory):

```
julia> pwd()
"C:\\Julia Programming\\Julia Programs"
```

If this wasn't the current directory, we could *change* to it with this:

```
julia> cd("C:\\Julia Programming\\Julia Programs")
```

Suppose we have opened the file input.txt with this:

```
inn = open("input.txt", "r")
```

Once opened *for reading*, we can read one line of input with this statement:

```
inp = readline(inn)
```

The argument to readline is the file pointer, inn. This statement will fetch the first line of data from input.txt and store it in the variable inp. We can read the first two lines of data and print them with this:

```
inp = readline(inn)     # read first line
println(inp)
inp = readline(inn)     # read second line
println(inp)
```

Any subsequent reading from inn will start from the third line.

We can do more. We can have three different functions, each reading a different line from the file. However, we must tell the functions from which file to read by calling each with inn as an argument. To illustrate:

```
function print3lines()
    inn = open("input.txt", "r")
    print1(inn)        # read and print first line
    print2(inn)        # read and print second line
    print3(inn)        # read and print third line
end
function print1(in1)
    println(readline(in1))
end
function print2(in2)
    println(readline(in2))
end
function print3(in3)
    println(readline(in3))
end
```

print1 is written with argument in1, print2 with argument in2 and print3 with argument in3. However, when for instance, we make the call print1(inn), in1 becomes associated with inn, the file input.txt.

Suppose `input.txt` contains this:

```
If you can keep your head
When all about you
Are losing theirs
And blaming it on you
```

The call `print3lines()` will print the following, one line printed by each of `print1`, `print2` and `print3`:

```
If you can keep your head
When all about you
Are losing theirs
```

When called with argument `inn`, each function reads from the position reached in the file designated by `inn`.

As another example, suppose we needed to read and process the first five lines from the file designated by `inn`. We could use something like this:

```
for h = 1 : 5
    inp = readline(inn)
    <do something with inp>
end
```

If `inn` has less than five lines, the empty string is stored in `inp` for the missing lines.

Shortly, we will show how to read and process data from a file as long as we haven't reached the "end of file". We do so after we introduce the `while` statement.

4.9 The while Statement

In Julia, the `while` statement takes the following form:

```
while <condition>
    <body>
end
```

`<body>` consists of one or more statements; it is executed as long as `<condition>` is `true`. We normally refer to the whole construct as a `while` loop.

The loop is executed as follows:

1. `<condition>` is tested.
2. If `true`, `<body>` is executed and we go back to step 1; if `false`, we *exit the loop* and continue with the statement, if any, after `end`.

Consider the following code which reads data, line by line, from a file `input.txt` and prints it:

```
inn = open("input.txt", "r")
inp = readline(inn)
while inp != ""
    println(inp)
    inp = readline(inn)
end
```

Here, `<condition>` is `inp != ""`. In order for this condition to make sense the first time, `inp` is assigned a value *before* we enter the loop. The loop condition would have no meaning if `inp` had no value.

If `inp` is *not* the empty string, `<body>` is executed; it consists of two statements. The first prints the line just read and the second reads the next line. After execution of `<body>`, control goes back to <condition>; if true (inp is *not* the empty string), we enter the loop again and repeat this process.

Execution ends when readline stores the empty string in inp, that is, when a blank (empty) line is in the input or the end-of-file has been reached. In that case, inp != "" is false so we exit (*drop out of*) the while loop.

Caution: If the end-of-file is reached, readline will store the empty string in inp. However, a blank (empty) line in the input will also store the empty string in inp. So inp=="" should *not* be used to test for end-of-file. Use eof(inn), discussed later.

We wrote the code as we did in order to simplify the explanation. But since Julia lets us read a value, assign *and* test it in the while condition, we could write it like this:

```
inn = open("input.txt", "r")
while (inp = readline(inn)) != ""    # all brackets required
    println(inp)
end
```

To add a little variation, let's read the file and print it with the lines numbered.

For instance, suppose the file input.txt contains this:

```
If you can keep your head
When all about you
Are losing theirs
And blaming it on you
```

We want our program to print the lines numbered, like this:

```
1. If you can keep your head
2. When all about you
3. Are losing theirs
4. And blaming it on you
```

Program P4.14 will do the job.

```
# Program P4.14 - Read Data, Number Lines
# Read data, print the lines numbered

function readDataNumberLines()
    inn = open("input.txt", "r")
    line = 0
    while (inp = readline(inn)) != ""
        println("$(line+=1). $inp")
    end
    close(inn)
end

readDataNumberLines()
```

When we are finished reading data from the file, we should *close* it, like this:

```
close(inn)
```

There is one argument, the file pointer (*not* the name of the file). This statement breaks the association of the file pointer inn with the file input.txt. If we want to, we could now associate inn with another file (paydata.txt, say) using this:

```
inn = open("paydata.txt", "r")
```

Subsequent readline(inn) statements will read data from paydata.txt.

4.9.1 Sum of Numbers (Prompt)

Next, consider the problem of writing a program to find the sum of some numbers (we'll use integers) which the user enters one at a time. The program will prompt the user to enter numbers as follows:

```
Enter a number: 24
Enter a number: 13
Enter a number: 32
```

and so on. We want to let the user enter as many numbers as he wishes.

Since we can have no idea how many that will be, and the amount could vary from one run of the program to the next, we must let the user 'tell' us when he wishes to stop entering numbers.

How does he 'tell' us? Well, the only time the user 'talks' to the program is when he types a number in response to the prompt. To tell the program he is finished, he can enter some 'agreed upon' value; when the program reads this value, it will know the user wishes to stop.

Typically, programmers use 0 or -1 as the *end-of-data* value. But a problem arises if these can be valid data values.

Fortunately, Julia gives us a better, more flexible option. If the user hits Enter/Return in response to the prompt, the empty string (instead of a number) is stored in the variable used to hold the input. And we can test for this, similar to how we did above. The only difference is since we are now reading from the keyboard instead of a file, we use readline() instead of readline(inn):

```
while (snum = readline()) != ""
```

We will use this in our next program.

Tip: readline(stdin) is a synonym for readline().

The logic for solving the problem posed can be expressed as follows:

```
# Algorithm for finding sum
set sum to 0
prompt for a number; fetch it as a string, snum
while snum is not ""
    convert snum to a number, num
    add num to sum
    prompt for a number; fetch it as a string, snum
endwhile
print sum
```

As long as a number is entered, it is converted to a number which is added to sum. When the user presses Enter/Return only, it's the signal that there's no more data. The program exits the while loop and prints sum.

This logic is implemented as program P4.15.

```
# Program P4.15 - Sum Numbers (Interactive)
# Find and print the sum of several numbers entered by a user
function sumNumbers()
    sum = 0
    print("Enter a number: ")
    while (snum = readline()) != ""
        sum += parse(Int64, snum)
        print("Enter a number: ")
    end
```

```
    println("\nSum is $sum")
end # sumNumbers

sumNumbers()
```

Here's a sample run:

```
Enter a number: 24
Enter a number: 13
Enter a number: 32
Enter a number: 17
Enter a number:

Sum is 86
```

When the program is run, what would happen if the user hits Enter/Return immediately? Since snum *is* the empty string, the while condition is immediately false so we drop out of the while loop and continue with the println statement. The program prints the correct answer:

```
The sum is 0
```

In general, if the while condition is false the first time it is tested, the body is not executed at all.

4.9.2 Sum, Count, Average (Prompt)

In Section 4.5, we wrote programs to read numbers from a file, count them, add them up, and find their average. We now modify Program P4.15 to do the same things, prompting the user for the numbers. We name it P4.16.

```
# Program P4.16 - Sum, Count, Average (Prompt)
# Print the sum, count and average of numbers entered
function sumCountAverage()
    n = 0
    sum = 0
    print("Enter a number: ")
    while (snum = readline()) != ""
        n += 1
        sum += parse(Int64, snum)
        print("Enter a number: ")
    end
    if n == 0
        println("\nNo numbers entered")
    else
        println("\n$n number(s) entered")
        println("Sum is $sum")
        println("Average is $(round(sum/n,digits=1))")
    end
end # sumCountAverage

sumCountAverage()
```

Here's a sample run:

```
Enter a number: 24
Enter a number: 13
Enter a number: 32
Enter a number: 17
Enter a number:

4 numbers entered
```

```
Their sum is 86
Their average is 21.5
```

4.9.3 Greatest Common Divisor

The *greatest common divisor*, GCD, (also called the *highest common factor*, HCF) of two number is the biggest number that's a factor of both. We want to write a program that will run as follows:

```
Enter two numbers: 42 24
GCD is 6
```

We will use Euclid's algorithm for finding the GCD of two integers, m and n. The algorithm follows:

```
1. if n is 0, the GCD is m; stop
2. set r to the remainder when m is divided by n
3. set m to n
4. set n to r
5. go to step 1
```

Using m as 42 and n as 24, step through the algorithm; verify that it gives the correct answer, 6.

Steps 2, 3 and 4 are executed as long as n is *not* 0. Hence, this algorithm can be expressed using a while loop as follows:

```
while n is not 0 do
    set r to m % n
    set m to n
    set n to r
endwhile
GCD is m
```

We can now write Program P4.17 which finds the GCD of two numbers entered.

 # Program P4.17 - Find GCD

```
# Find the GCD of two numbers entered by a user
function findGCD()
    print("Enter two numbers: ")
    m, n = [parse(Int, x) for x in split(readline())]
    while n != 0
        r = m % n
        m = n
        n = r
    end
    println("\nGCD is $m")
end # findGCD

findGCD()
```

Note that the while condition is n != 0 and the while body is this 3-statement block

```
r = m % n
m = n
n = r
```

The algorithm and, hence, the program, works whether m is bigger than n or not. Using the example above, if m is 24 and n is 42, when the loop is executed the first time, it will set m to 42 and n to 24.

In general, if m is smaller than n, the first thing the algorithm does is swap their values.

Tip: Julia provides the standard function gcd(m,n) which returns the *greatest common divisor* of m and n.

4.10 Send Output to a File

So far, our programs have read data from the standard input (the keyboard) and a file, and sent results to the standard output (the screen). We now show you how you can send output to a file.

This is important to know because when we send output to the screen, it is lost when we exit the program or when we switch off the computer. If we need to save our output, we must write it to a file. Then the output is available as long as we wish to keep the file.

The *process* is similar to reading from a file. We must declare a "file pointer" (we use out) and associate it with the actual file (output.txt, say) using open. We can do it like this:

```
out = open("output.txt", "w")
```

This tells Julia to "open the file output.txt for writing"; "w" indicates writing. When this statement is executed, the file output.txt is created if it does not already exist. If it exists, its contents are destroyed. In other words, whatever you write to the file will replace its original contents.

Caution: Be careful that you do not open "for writing" a file whose contents you wish to keep.

Having opened a file to receive output, we can use the familiar print/println statements with one modification. Previously, we used the following to send a line of output to the screen:

```
println("Sum is $sum")
```

Now we use the following to send the same line of output to a file designated by out:

```
println(out, "Sum is $sum")
```

We just include out as the first argument to println.

We write a program (P4.18) to find the average of some numbers supplied in a file input.txt. However, unlike the one we wrote before, this one sends its output to the file output.txt.

```
# Program P4.18 - Average - Output to File
# Read numbers from a file; find their average; write to file
function readWriteFileAverage()
    inn = open("input.txt", "r")
    out = open("output.txt", "w")
    n = 0
    sum = 0
    while (snum = readline(inn)) != ""
        n += 1
        sum += parse(Int64, snum)
    end
    close(inn)

    if n == 0
        println(out, "No numbers supplied")
    else
        println(out, "$n number(s) supplied")
        println(out, "Sum is $sum")
        println(out, "Average is $(round(sum/n,digits=1))")
```

```
      end
      close(out)   # This is important to flush all pending output
  end # readWriteFileAverage

  readWriteFileAverage()
```

Assume the file `input.txt` contains the following:

```
24
13
-6
19
```

When run, Program P4.18 sends the following to the file `output.txt`:

```
4 number(s) supplied
Sum is 50
Average is 12.5
```

Tip: When you run the program, it appears as if nothing has happened. If the program is stored in the file *P4.18ReadWriteFileAverage.jl*, the interaction with Julia looks as follows:

```
julia> include("P4.18ReadWriteFileAverage.jl")
julia>
```

Nothing. That's because you don't have to enter any input and no output is printed on the screen. However, you must open the file `output.txt` to view your results.

close(out)

It is very important that you close the output file with `close(out)`. If you do not, it is possible that some of your output would be missing. Julia does not send output directly to your file every time you issue a `print/println` statement. Writing to a disk is time-consuming compared to writing to memory.

For faster performance, Julia *buffers* your output (stores it in a temporary place in memory) and only writes to the file when the buffer is full or you close the file. When the program executes `close(out)`, all pending output is sent to the file before it is closed.

4.11 Payroll

We want to write a program to prepare the payroll of a small company. The data for each employee consists of a first name, a last name, the number of hours worked and the rate of pay. The data is stored in a file `paydata.txt` and output will be sent to the file `payroll.txt`.

We assume the data is stored in the file as follows:

```
Glen Reyes 50 12.00
Akira Kanda 40 15.00
Nigel Singh 48 20.00
Zara Barath 30 18.00
```

We will not use an end-of-data marker. The program will detect when there is no more data to be read. Pay is calculated as follows:

If hours worked is less than or equal to 40, we calculate regular pay by multiplying hours worked by rate of pay, and overtime pay is 0. If hours worked is greater than 40, we calculate regular pay by multiplying 40 by the rate of pay, and overtime pay by this: hours *in excess of* 40 × the rate of pay × 1.5. Gross pay is calculated by adding regular pay and overtime pay.

The employee name, hours worked, rate of pay, regular pay, overtime pay and gross pay are printed under a suitable heading. In addition, we will write the program to do the following:

- Count how many employees are processed.
- Calculate the total wage bill (total gross pay for all employees).
- Determine which employee earned the highest pay and how much. Ignore the possibility of a tie.

For the sample data, the output should look like this:

```
Name          Hours   Rate Regular  Overtime   Gross

Glen Reyes    50.0   12.00  480.00    180.00  660.00
Akira Kanda   40.0   15.00  600.00      0.00  600.00
Nigel Singh   48.0   20.00  800.00    240.00 1040.00
Zara Barath   30.0   18.00  540.00      0.00  540.00

Number of employees: 4
Total wage bill: $2840.00
Nigel Singh earned the most pay of $1040.00
```

An outline of the algorithm for reading the data is as follows:

```
while (eData = next line of data) != ""
    extract firstName, lastName, hours, rate
    do the calculations
    print results for this employee
endwhile
```

Because the name is supplied as two separate words, we will need to read the first and last names separately. However, in order to get the output to line up neatly as shown above, it would be more convenient to have the entire name stored in one variable (name, say). Suppose Robin is stored in firstName and Hood is stored in lastName. We will set name to Robin Hood as follows:

```
name = firstName * " " * lastName
```

We will use the specification %-13s to print name. This will print name *left-justified* in a field width of 13. In other words, all names will be printed using the same field width. This is necessary for the output to line up neatly. To cater for longer names, just increase the field width.

When faced with a program which requires so many things to be done, it is best to start by working on part of the problem, getting it right and then tackling the other parts.

For this problem, we can start by getting the program to read and process the data without counting, finding the total or finding the highest-paid employee. Program P4.19 just reads the data and calculates the gross pay for each employee.

```
# Program P4.19 - Calculate Pay Basic
using Printf
const MaxRegularHours = 40
const OvertimeFactor = 1.5

function calculatePay()
    inn = open("paydata.txt", "r")
    out = open("payroll.txt", "w")

    print(out,"Name            Hours   Rate Regular  Overtime     Net\n\n")
    while (eData = readline(inn)) != ""
```

```
            eData = split(eData) # eData[1]=first, eData[2]=last, eData[3]=hours...
            name = eData[1] * " " * eData[2] # make one name
            hours = parse(Float64, eData[3])
            rate = parse(Float64, eData[4])
            if hours <= MaxRegularHours
                regPay = hours * rate
                ovtPay = 0.0
            else
                regPay = MaxRegularHours * rate
                ovtPay = (hours - MaxRegularHours) * rate * OvertimeFactor
            end
            grossPay = regPay + ovtPay
            @printf(out, "%-13s %4.1f %6.2f", name, hours, rate)
            @printf(out, "%9.2f %9.2f %7.2f\n", regPay, ovtPay, grossPay)
        end #while
        close(inn)
        close(out)
    end

calculatePay()
```

When run with the sample data, above, it produces the following output:

```
Name          Hours   Rate  Regular  Overtime   Gross

Glen Reyes    50.0  12.00   480.00    180.00  660.00
Akira Kanda   40.0  15.00   600.00      0.00  600.00
Nigel Singh   48.0  20.00   800.00    240.00 1040.00
Zara Barath   30.0  18.00   540.00      0.00  540.00
```

Comments on Program P4.19

- We use the file pointer `inn` to read data from `paydata.txt` and file pointer `out` to send output to `payroll.txt`.
- Since data are being read from a file, prompts are not required.
- We use `readline(inn)` to read one line of data, `split` to break it up into four parts and store them in a string array `eData`.
- `eData[1]` contains the first name, `eData[2]` contains the last name, `eData[3]` contains the hours worked and `eData[4]` contains the rate of pay.
- We use `parse` to convert the hours worked and rate of pay from string to number.
- We print a heading with the following statement:
  `print(out,"Name       Hours Rate  Regular  Overtime  Gross\n\n")`
- To get the output to line up nicely, you will need to fiddle with the spaces between the words and the field widths in the statements which print the results.
- Experiment with the field widths in `@printf` to see what effect it has on your output.

This is the first part of the required output. We must now add statements to P4.19 to count the number of employees, calculate the total gross pay and find the highest-paid employee. How we can add these features is shown in Program P4.20. When run with the sample data, it produces all the required output as specified above.

```
# Program P4.20 - Calculate Pay All Features
using Printf
const MaxRegularHours = 40
const OvertimeFactor = 1.5

function calculatePay()
```

```
inn = open("paydata.txt", "r")
out = open("payroll.txt", "w")
numEmp, wageBill = 0, 0.0
bestPaid, mostPay = "", 0.0
print(out,"Name          Hours   Rate  Regular  Overtime   Gross\n\n")

while (eData = readline(inn)) != ""
    eData = split(eData) # eData[1]=first, eData[2]=last, eData[3]=hours...
    name = eData[1] * " " * eData[2] # make one name
    hours = parse(Float64, eData[3])
    rate = parse(Float64, eData[4])

    if hours <= MaxRegularHours
        regPay = hours * rate
        ovtPay = 0.0
    else
        regPay = MaxRegularHours * rate
        ovtPay = (hours - MaxRegularHours) * rate * OvertimeFactor
    end
    grossPay = regPay + ovtPay
    @printf(out, "%-13s %4.1f %6.2f", name, hours, rate)
    @printf(out, "%9.2f %9.2f %7.2f\n", regPay, ovtPay, grossPay)

    numEmp += 1
    wageBill += grossPay
    if grossPay > mostPay
        mostPay = grossPay
        bestPaid = name
    end
end # while

@printf(out, "\nNumber of employees: %d\n", numEmp)
@printf(out, "Total wage bill: \$%0.2f\n", wageBill)
@printf(out,"%s earned the most pay of \$%0.2f\n", bestPaid, mostPay)

close(inn)
close(out)
end # calculatePay

calculatePay()
```

4.12 break/continue in while

In Section 4.4 we met the break/continue statements and discussed how to use them in a for loop. We now show how to use them in a while loop.

Suppose we want to find the sum of the numbers from 1 to 10 *except* 7. We can do it as follows:

```
function whileAllBut7()
    sum = 0
    n = 0
    while n < 10
        n += 1
        if n == 7 continue end
        sum += n
    end
    println("Sum is $sum")
end # whileAllBut7

whileAllBut7()
```

When used in a while loop, continue causes the *current iteration* of the loop to cease; control goes to the top of the loop to prepare for the next iteration, if any (test the loop condition).

When n is 7, the statement that adds n to the sum is skipped. When run, the program prints

```
Sum is 48
```

Next, suppose we replace `continue` with `break` in the `if` statement:

```
if n == 7 break end
```

When run, the program prints this:

```
Sum is 21
```

When n is 7, `break` causes control to break out of the `while` loop entirely; execution continues with the `println` statement after the loop. 7 is not added to the sum, so 21 (sum from 1 to 6) is printed.

Let's do an example which involves *random numbers*. Imagine you throw a normal 6-sided die repeatedly, and note the numbers which show. What you get are *random numbers uniformly distributed in the range 1 to 6*. For our purpose, all you need to know is you get random numbers from 1 to 6.

We will write a program which *simulates* the throwing of a die. We use the standard Julia function `rand`; `rand()` returns a random decimal fraction from 0 (inclusive) to 1 (exclusive). We write a function `random(m,n)` which returns a random *integer* from m to n, inclusive.

```
function random(m, n)
    m + trunc(Int64, (n-m+1)*rand())
end
```

We want to throw a die and count how many throws we make to get the first 6. We show how to do so in the function `throw6` in Program P4.21.

```
# Program P4.21 - Throw Die Until You Get 6
function random(m, n)
    m + trunc(Int64, (n-m+1)*rand())
end

function throw6()
    numThrow = 0
    while true
        numThrow += 1
        throw = random(1, 6)
        if throw == 6 break end
    end
    println("Number of throws to get 6 = $numThrow")
end

throw6()
```

This `while` loop is a *do forever* loop since the `while` condition is always `true`. Hopefully, this means we will break out of the loop when some condition arises. In this case, we break out if a 6 is thrown.

Here's some sample output from a few runs of the program:

```
Number of throws to get 6 = 3
Number of throws to get 6 = 9
Number of throws to get 6 = 13
Number of throws to get 6 = 5
```

EXERCISES 4

1. Write a program to print 100 mailing labels for

    ```
    The Computer Store
    57 First Avenue
    San Fernando
    ```

2. Write a program to print a conversion table from miles to kilometers. The table ranges from 5 to 100 miles in steps of 5. (1 mile = 1.61 km).

3. Write a program which requests a user to enter an amount of money. The program prints the interest payable per year for rates of interest from 5% to 12% in steps of 0.5%.

4. Write a program to request a value for n; the user is then asked to enter n numbers, one at a time. The program calculates and prints the sum of the numbers. The following is a sample run:

    ```
    How many numbers? 3
    Enter a number? 12
    Enter a number? 25
    Enter a number? 18

    The sum of the 3 numbers is 55
    ```

5. Write a program to print the following 99 times:

    ```
    When you have nothing to say, it is a time to be silent
    ```

6. Write a program to print 3 copies of your favourite song.

7. Write a program to print a table of squares from 1 to 10. Each line of the table consists of a number and the square of that number.

8. Write a program to request a value for n and print a table of squares from 1 to n.

9. Write a program to request values for first and last, and print a table of squares from first to last.

10. The manager of a hotel wants to calculate the cost of carpeting the rooms in the hotel. All the rooms are rectangular in shape. He has a file, rooms.in, which contains data for the rooms.

    The first line contains the number of rooms, n. Each of the next n lines contains a room number, the length and breadth of the room (in meters), and the cost per square meter of the carpet for that room. For example, the data line:

    ```
    325  3.0  4.5  40.00
    ```

    means that room 325 is 3.0 meters by 4.5 meters, and the cost of the carpet for that room is $40.00 per square meter.

    Write a program to read the data and do the following, sending output to the file rooms.out:

    - Print a suitable heading and under it, for each room, print the room number, the area of the room and the cost of the carpet for the room.
    - Print the number of rooms processed.
    - Print the total cost of carpeting all the rooms.
    - Print the number of the room which will cost the most to carpet (ignore ties).

11. A fixed percentage of water is taken from a well each day. Request values for W and P where

   - W is the amount (in liters) of water in the well at the start of the first day
   - P is the percentage of the water in the well taken out each day

   Write a program to print the number of the day, the amount taken for that day and the amount remaining at the end of the day (both amounts rounded). The output should be terminated when 30 days have been printed or the amount remaining is less than 100 liters, whichever comes first. For example, if W is 1000 and P is 10, the output should start as follows:

```
Day    Amount    Amount
       Taken     Remaining
 1      100        900
 2       90        810
 3       81        729
```

12. Solve problem 13, above, but this time print the table for exactly 30 days. If necessary, continue printing the table even if the amount of water falls below 100 liters.

13. Write a program to read data for several items from a file. For each item, the price and a discount percent is given. For each item, print the original price, the discount amount and the amount the customer must pay. At the end, print the number of items and the total amount the customer must pay.

14. Write a program which reads several lengths in inches and, for each, converts it to yards, feet and inches. (1 yard = 3 feet, 1 foot = 12 inches). For example, if a length is **100**, the program should print **2 yd 2 ft 4 in**.

15. Each line of data in a file consists of two lengths. Each length is given as two numbers representing feet and inches. For each pair of lengths, print their sum. For example, if the lengths are **5 ft. 4 in.** and **8 ft. 11 in.**, your program should print **14 ft. 3 in.** The line of data for this example would be given as

```
5 4 8 11
```

16. You are given a file containing an unknown amount of numbers. Each number is one of the numbers 1 to 9. A number can appear zero or more times and can appear anywhere in the file. Some sample data are:

```
5 3 7 7 7 4 3 3 2 2 2 6 7 4 7 7
2 2 9 6 6 6 6 6 8 5 5 3 7 9 9 9
```

   Write a program to read the data *once* and print the number which appears the most in consecutive positions and the number of times it appears. Ignore the possibility of a tie. For the above data, output should be 6 5.

17. The price of an item is p dollars. Due to inflation, the price increases by r% each year. For example, the price might be $79.50 and inflation might be 7.5%. Write a program which reads values for p and r, and, starting with year 1, prints a table consisting of year and year-end price. The table ends when the year-end price is at least twice the original price.

18. Write a program to calculate electricity charges for several customers. The data for each customer consists of a name, the previous meter reading and the current meter reading. The difference in the two readings gives the number of units of electricity used. The customer pays a fixed charge of $25 plus 20 cents for each unit used. The data is stored in a file.

Assume that the fixed charge and the rate per unit are the same for all customers and are given on the first line. This is followed by the data for the customers. Each set of data consists of two lines: a name on the first line and the meter readings on the second line. Print the information for the customers under a suitable heading. Also,

- Count how many customers were processed
- Print the total due to the electricity company
- Find the customer whose bill was the highest

19. A file contains data for several persons. The data for each person consists of their gross salary, deductions allowed and rate of tax (e.g. 25, meaning 25%). Tax is calculated by applying the rate of tax to (gross salary minus deductions). Net pay is calculated by gross salary minus tax.

Under an appropriate heading, print the gross salary, tax deducted, net pay and the percentage of the gross salary that was paid in tax.

For each person, the data consists of two lines: a name on the first line and gross salary, deductions allowed and rate of tax on the second line. The 'name' xxxx ends the data. Also,

- Count how many persons were processed
- Print totals for gross salary, tax deducted and net pay
- Find the person who earned the highest net pay

20. A contest was held for the promotion of SuperMarbles. Each contestant was required to guess the number of marbles in a jar. Write a program to determine the Grand Prize winner (ignoring the possibility of a tie) based on the following:

The first line of data contains a single integer (answer, say) representing the actual number of marbles in the jar. Each subsequent line contains a contestant's ID number (an integer) and an integer representing that contestant's guess.

The Grand Prize winner is that contestant who guesses closest to answer *without exceeding it*. There's no winner if all guesses are too big. Assume all data are valid. Print the number of contestants and the ID number of the winner, if any.

CHAPTER 5

Functions

In this chapter, we will explain:

- Why functions are important in programming
- How to write functions
- What happens when a function is called
- Where functions are placed in a program
- Some important concepts relating to functions using several examples
- How to write *recursive* functions—functions that call themselves

5.1 Introduction

So far, all our programs have consisted of a single function and a statement to call that function. For example, we wrote a function called `calculatePay` and called it with `calculatePay()`.

In addition, we have used predefined Julia functions such as `parse`, `readline`, `round`, `print` and `open`. When we call one of *our* functions, it starts executing with the first statement and ends when it reaches the last statement or a `return` statement.

As we have seen, it is possible to write reasonably useful programs this way. However, there are many limitations to this approach. The problem to be solved may be too complex to be solved with one function. We may need to break it up into subproblems and try to solve each of these individually. It would be impractical to solve all the subproblems in one function. It might be better to write a separate function to solve each subproblem.

We may want to reuse the solution to common problems. It would be difficult to reuse a solution if it is part of the solution to a bigger problem. For example, if we have three numbers and we need to know what type of triangle, if any, can be formed from them, we could write a function `typeOfTriangle(a, b, c)` which, given the three numbers, returns a value indicating the type.

A well-written function performs some well-defined task; for example, skip a specified number of lines in the output or arrange some numbers in ascending order. So far, the functions we wrote performed a task but did not return a value. Essentially, we wrote our code in a function which performed the designated task but was not required to return any answer.

However, quite often, a function performs a task *and* returns a value; for example, calculate the salary of a person and return the answer

Or, given 3 numbers, return the type of triangle they can form, if any. The value returned is normally used at the point from which the function was called.

© The Author(s), under exclusive license to Springer Nature Switzerland AG 2021
N. Kalicharan, *Julia - Bit by Bit*, Undergraduate Topics in Computer Science,
https://doi.org/10.1007/978-3-030-73936-2_5

Previously, we used `readline` to fetch a line of input, `parse` to convert a string to a number, and `round` to round a number to a specified number of decimal places. We are now ready to learn more about how to write our own functions (*user-defined* functions) and we will see several examples in the rest of this book.

5.2 Function Basics

In Chapter 2, we wrote a function which requested a whole number and printed its square.

Now we take a slightly different approach. We want to write a function which, *given* a number (n, say) *returns* the square of the number. We say that n is an *argument* to the function `square`, or, the function `square` takes an argument n. We write `square` as follows:

```
# Given n, return n squared

function square(n)
     return n*n
end
```

(In this book, we use the term *parameter* when referring to the *definition* of the function and the term *argument* when the function is *called*. Others use the terms interchangeably. So `square` takes one parameter n and we supply the argument 6 in the call `square(6)`.)

First, we have the *function header*. In those we've written previously, the header took this form:

```
function fname()
# nothing inside the brackets meaning "no arguments" needed when called
```

The brackets are required but were *empty* (nothing inside). This simply meant that when we called the function, we didn't have to supply any *argument(s)*. As you saw, we called the function like this:

```
fname()
```

Here, the *body* of `square` contains one statement:

```
return n*n
```

When called with `square(8)`, say, it *returns* the value of 8*8=64. We illustrate with the following:

```
julia> function square(n)
             return n*n
       end
square (generic function with 1 method) # Julia acknowledges the definition of
square

julia> square(8)
64

julia> println("Square of 17 is ", square(17))
Square of 17 is 289
```

When we make the call `square(8)`, control is transferred to the function `square` and the parameter n takes on the value supplied, 8. The body is executed, returning 8*8=64 to the place at which the call `square(8)` was made.

We could also use `square` like this:

```
julia> m = 6;

julia> mm = square(m);

julia> println(mm)
36
julia> mm1 = 2square(m ÷ 2) + 5    # argument to square can be an expression
23
```

As a matter of interest, note that in this example, we can get the same effect with this:

```
function square(n)
    n*n
end
```

The word `return` is not needed. That's because the *value* of a function is the value of the last statement executed. Consider this:

```
julia> function test(n)
           if n > 0 m = true else m = false end
       end
test (generic function with 1 method)
```

The function `test` does not *return* a value explicitly. But note the following:

```
julia> test(1)
true

julia> test(-1)
false
```

`test(1)` has the value `true` since the last statement executed for that call is m = true.

`test(-1)` has the value `false` since the last statement executed for that call is m = false.

(As a reminder, the *value* of an assignment statement is the *value assigned* to the variable on the left hand side.)

The function `square` is more general than you might think. Note this:

```
julia> square(1.2)
1.44
```

The value of the *argument* can be any valid number, with or without a decimal point. Not many languages give you this flexibility so simply. If we assign the result to a variable, the *type* of the variable becomes the type of the result:

```
julia> sqn = square(5)
25

julia> fsqn = square(5.0)
25.0

julia> typeof(sqn)
Int64

julia> typeof(fsqn)
Float64
```

And what about this?

```
julia> square("hi")
"hihi"
```

Interesting. This works, but only because `*` is also the string concatenation operator and `"hi"*"hi"` = `"hihi"`.

Nice to know: Polymorphism - the word means "many forms". The function `square` illustrates what is called *polymorphism* in computer programming. Here, `square` takes one argument, n, whose type is unspecified. Only when the function is called (at *run-time*) do we know the *type* of n. The *type* of n is *bound* to the *type* of the argument supplied for *that* call. (This is referred to as *dynamic binding*.) The *type* of the result varies depending on whether n is Int, Float or String.

Now consider these:

```
function square(n::Int64)
    return n*n
end

function square(n::Float64)
    return n*n
end
```

Here, both functions have the same name but take different arguments. This is sometimes referred to as *overloading* (the name `square`) or *static binding*, and is also a type of polymorphism.

The call `square(7)` will invoke the first function and the call `square(1.5)` will invoke the second. However, the call `square("hi")` will now produce an error to the effect that there is no function matching `square(::String)`. In other words, we have not defined any function `square` which takes a `String` argument.

Sometimes, letting Julia perform dynamic binding, one of its strengths, can be advantageous.

Of course, there are times when we may want to specify precisely what *type* of argument `square` can take. For instance, if we want arguments to be integer only, we could define `square` like this:

```
function square(n::Int64)
    return n*n
end
```

With this definition, we get the following:

```
julia> square(5)
25

julia> square(5.0)
ERROR: MethodError: no method matching square(::Float64)
```

Now, an attempt to call `square` with a `Float` argument results in an error. Julia gives us the flexibility to specify precisely the kind of function we want.

It is worth emphasizing that the functions from earlier chapters got their data by using `readline/parse` to read and store the data in variables. On the other hand, a function like `square` gets its data, via its parameter `n`, when it is called. The data is supplied as an argument to the function.

To put what we've discussed so far in context, we write a complete program P5.1 which requests the user to enter a number. The program then prints its square by calling `square`.

 # Program P5.1 - Illustrate Use of Function

```
function square(n)
    n*n
end # square

function testSquare()
    print("Enter a number: ")
    num = parse(Float64, readline())
    println("\nSquare of $num is $(square(num))")
end # testSquare

testSquare()
```

Here's a sample run:

```
Enter a number: 1.2
Square of 1.2 is 1.44
```

We delegate the overall logic of the program to the function testSquare. Here, the logic is fairly simple: fetch a number and print its square by calling square(). However, this framework will serve us well as we write more complicated programs.

When a function returns a value (like square does), it makes sense for this value to be used in a situation where a value is required. Above, we printed the value. We could also assign the value to a variable, as we did before:

```
sqn = square(num)
```

or use it as part of an expression, as in

```
ans = 2square(n) + 1
```

What does *not* make sense is to use it in a statement by itself, like this:

```
square(n)   # a useless statement
```

Here, the value is not being used in any way, so the statement makes no sense at all. It is the same as if we had written a number on a line by itself, like this

```
36    # a useless statement
```

Think carefully when you call a function which returns a value. Be very clear in your mind for what purpose you intend to use the value.

5.2.1 How an Argument Is Passed to a Function

One of the key issues to understand about functions is *how* argument values are passed to a function. In programming, we commonly use the terms "pass by value" and "pass by reference".

If an argument is passed "by value", the *value* of the argument is made available to the function, where it becomes known by the name of the corresponding parameter. The function can do what it pleases with the value supplied but it has no access to the *original* source of the value and, hence, cannot change it . Consider this:

```
function test(n)
    println("In test, before increment, n is $n")
    n += 7
    println("In test, after increment, n is $n")
end

function main()
    n = 5
    println("In main, n is $n")
    test(n)
    println("On return to main, n is $n")
end

main()
```

We have deliberately used the same name n for the variable in main and the parameter of test to show that, even though they have the *same* name, they refer to *different* entities. When run, this is printed:

```
In main, n is 5
In test, before increment, n is 5
In test, after increment, n is 12
On return to main, n is 5
```

When n is printed in main, its value is the same (5) before and after the call test(n). This shows that test has no access to "n in main". When the call test(n) is made, the *value* of n is copied to a temporary location and *this* location is passed to test where it becomes known as n.

Another example might help. Consider the call test(n+3) in main. The argument is evaluated (8); this value is stored in a temporary location and made available to test where it becomes known as n, nothing to do with "n in main". In test, n refers to this temporary location, so 8 and 15 are printed. When test is finished, this n is discarded.

In this example, we say n is passed *by value*.

When an argument is passed *by reference*, the *location* of the argument (as opposed to its *value* only) is made available to the called function; any change the function makes to the argument would be known in the calling function. Most commonly, *arrays* are passed *by reference*. We will see examples when we discuss arrays in Chapter 7.

5.3 Function - Examples

In this section, we discuss several examples which illustrate various aspects and principles of writing and using functions in Julia.

5.3.1 How to Swap Two Variables

We now pursue an example to further explain how arguments are passed in Julia. We want to write a function which, given two variables a and b, swaps their values.

This might be our first attempt:

```
function swap(a, b)  # this won't work
    t = a
    a = b
    b = t
    println(("$a $b")
end
```

Now suppose we execute the following:

```
a = 3; b = 8;
swap(a, b)
println("$a $b")
```

When we do this is printed:

```
8 3      # printed in swap
3 8      # printed after swap(a,b) returns
```

Inside swap, the values are exchanged but the change is not known when swap returns. (The simple explanation is that *copies* of a and b are sent to swap; it can't change the original a and b.) One could be forgiven for thinking there's an honour code among functions: whatever happens in a function stays in the function. And while this is true to some extent, we can still get what we want. How?

It's actually much easier than we might think. All we need is this:

```
function swap(a, b)
    b, a
end
```

Now, when we execute this:

```
a = 3; b = 8;
```

```
a, b = swap(a, b)
println("$a $b")
```

we get this:

```
8 3
```

The values of a and b have been swapped.

The function is easy to write because Julia gives us great flexibility in what we can return from a function. In this case, we return the pair of values b, a. (The value returned by a function is the last statement executed; in this case, the *only* statement executed is b, a. We could also have used return b, a.) When we assign this to a, b, we are effectively swapping the values of a and b.

We used this example to illustrate certain features about functions. If all we really need to do is swap the values of a and b, this would suffice:

```
a, b = b, a
```

5.3.2 Yesterday, Today and Tomorrow

In this example, we prompt the user for a number from 1 to 7 and print the corresponding day of the week. Program P5.2 shows how.

```
# Program P5.2 - Print Day of Week

function getDay(d)
# Given d, return the corresponding day of the week
    if d == 1 "Sunday"
    elseif d == 2 "Monday"
    elseif d == 3 "Tuesday"
    elseif d == 4 "Wednesday"
    elseif d == 5 "Thursday"
    elseif d == 6 "Friday"
    elseif d == 7 "Saturday"
    else "No such day"
    end
end # getDay

function testGetDay()
    print("Enter a number (1-7): ")
    n = parse(Int64, readline())
    println(getDay(n))
end # testGetDay

testGetDay()
```

Here are some sample runs:

```
Enter a number (1-7): 5
Thursday
```

```
Enter a number (1-7): 9
No such day
```

Note: In getDay, we did not use the word return (and say, for instance, return "Sunday"). In the call getDay(5), d is 5, so the *value* of getDay is "Thursday" and this is returned.

Let us pursue this example some more. Now, given the number (1 to 7), we want to print today, yesterday and tomorrow, as in the following:

```
Enter a number (1-7): 5
Today: Thursday
Yesterday: Wednesday
Tomorrow: Friday
```

```
Enter a number (1-7): 1
Today: Sunday
Yesterday: Saturday
Tomorrow: Monday
```

```
Enter a number (1-7): 7
Today: Saturday
Yesterday: Friday
Tomorrow: Sunday
```

Monday to Friday (2 to 6) is straightforward. Adding or subtracting 1 gives us a valid day. But the day after 7 is 1 and the day before 1 is 7. Weekends are problematic, it seems!

For *tomorrow*, this is the logic we want to implement:

```
if day == 7 set day to 1 else add 1 to day
```

We *could* implement it like this:

```
if (day == 7) day = 1 else day += 1 end
```

However, we can get the same result more neatly with this:

```
day = (day % 7) + 1  # when day=7, d%7 is 0.
```

For *yesterday*, this is the logic we want to implement:

```
if day == 1 set day to 7 else subtract 1 from day
```

We can implement it with the ternary operator ? : like this:

```
day == 1 ? 7 : day-1  # if day is 1, return 7 else day-1
```

We can rewrite testGetDay as follows to produce the results shown above:

```
function testGetDay()
    print("Enter a number (1-7): ")
    n = parse(Int64, readline())
    if 1 <= n <= 7
        println("Today: ", getDay(n))
        println("Yesterday: ", getDay(n == 1 ? 7 : n-1))
        println("Tomorrow: ", getDay(n%7+1))
    else
        println("No such day")
    end
end # testGetDay
```

Observe, we take advantage of the fact that the argument to getDay can be any expression that yields a numeric value.

5.3.3 GCD, Greatest Common Divisor

The *greatest common divisor* GCD (also called the *highest common factor*, HCF) of two integers is the highest number that's a factor of both. For example, GCD(42, 24) is 6 and GCD(9, 14) is 1.

We could find GCD(m, n) using Euclid's algorithm, as follows:

```
while n is not 0
    set r to m % n
    set m to n
    set n to r
endwhile
GCD is m
```

It would be nice if, whenever we want to find the GCD of two numbers (m and n, say), we could make a function call gcd(m, n) to get the answer. For instance, the call gcd(42, 24) would return the answer 6. To be able to do this, we write the function as follows:

```
# Returns the gcd of m and n
function gcd(m, n)
    while n != 0
        r = m % n
        m = n
        n = r
    end
    return m
end # gcd
```

When the following is executed:

```
println("GCD(42, 24) is $(gcd(42, 24))")
```

it prints this:

```
GCD(42, 24) is 6
```

When the call gcd(42, 24) is made, the following occurs:

- Each of the arguments is copied to a temporary memory location. These locations are passed to the function gcd where 42 is labelled with m, the first argument, and 24 is labelled with n, the second argument. We can picture this as follows:

m | 42 | n | 24 |

- The while loop is executed, working out the GCD. On exit from the loop, the GCD is stored in m, which will contain 6 at this time. This is the value returned by the function to the place from where it was called.
- Just before the function returns, the locations containing the arguments are thrown away; control then returns to the place from where the call was made.

We write Program P5.3 to test gcd more extensively:

```
# Program P5.3 - Test GCD

# Returns the gcd of m and n
function gcd(m, n)
    while n != 0
        r = m % n
        m = n
        n = r
    end
    return m
end # gcd

function testGCD()
    print("Enter two positive numbers: ")
    a, b = [parse(Int, x) for x in split(readline())]
    while a > 0 && b > 0
        println("The GCD is $(gcd(a, b))\n")
        print("Enter two positive numbers: ")
        a, b = [parse(Int, x) for x in split(readline())]
    end
end # testGCD
testGCD()
```

The following is a sample run:

```
Enter two positive numbers: 42 24
The GCD is 6

Enter two positive numbers: 32 512
The GCD is 32

Enter two positive numbers: 100 31
The GCD is 1

Enter two positive numbers: 84 36
The GCD is 12

Enter two positive numbers: 0 0
```

If necessary, we can enforce the *type* of arguments with which gcd can be called with this:

```
function gcd(m::Int64, n::Int64)
```

5.3.4 Using GCD to Find LCM

A common task in arithmetic is to find the *lowest common multiple* (LCM) of two numbers. For example, the LCM of 8 and 6 is 24 since 24 is the smallest number which can divide both 8 and 6 exactly.

If we know the GCD of the two numbers, we can find the LCM by multiplying the numbers and dividing by their GCD.

Given that the GCD of 8 and 6 is 2, we can find their LCM by working out $(8 \times 6) \div 2$ which is 24. In general,

```
LCM(m, n) = (m x n) ÷ GCD(m, n)
```

Knowing this, we can write a one-line function lcm which, given two arguments m and n, returns the LCM of m and n.

```
# Returns the lcm of m and n; enforce types
function lcm(m::Int64, n::Int64)
    m*n÷gcd(m, n)
end # lcm
```

We leave it as an exercise for you to write a program to test lcm. Remember to include gcd in your program. You may place gcd before or after lcm.

Tip: Julia provides the standard functions gcd(m,n), which returns the *greatest common divisor* of m and n, and lcm(m,n), which returns the lowest common multiple of m and n.

5.3.5 Factorial and Big Integers

An important concept in mathematics is that of *factorial*. We use $n!$ (pronounced "n factorial") to denote the product of the integers from 1 to n. It is defined for n >= 0, with 0! = 1. For example, we have 4! = 4.3.2.1 = 24. Julia provides the function factorial which, given n, returns $n!$

The statement

```
println("4! = $(factorial(4))")
```

prints this:

```
4! = 24
```

One of the characteristics of `factorial` is that its value increases very quickly, as we can see here:

n	n!
1	1
2	2
3	6
4	24
5	120
6	720
7	5,040
8	40,320
9	362,880
10	3,628,800
11	39,916,800
12	479,001,600
13	6,227,020,800
14	87,178,291,200
15	1,307,674,368,000
16	20,922,789,888,000
17	355,687,428,096,000
18	6,402,373,705,728,000
19	121,645,100,408,832,000
20	2,432,902,008,176,640,000
21	51,090,942,171,709,440,000

The maximum values which can be stored in various integer types are as follows:

Int8	127
Int16	32,767
Int32	2,147,483,647
Int64	9,223,372,036,854,775,807

A mere `8!` is too big to store in `Int16`, `16!` is too big to store in `Int32` and `21!` is too big to store in `Int64`.

When we print big integers, it would be nice if we could print them with commas separating every three digits from the right, like this: `35,012,748,905`. Since we can't do this easily in standard Julia, we could write a bare-bones function to help us. Here it is:

```
function formatInt(n::Int64)
    nd = 0
    nstr = ""
    while n > 0
        d = n % 10   # get the last digit
        n = n ÷ 10   # discard the last digit
        nd +=1       # count this digit
        if nd % 3 == 1 && nd != 1  # if nd = 4,7,10,13, etc
            nstr = "," * nstr      # we would need a comma
        end
        nstr = string(d) * nstr
    end # while
    return nstr
end # formatInt
```

We could test it with the following:

```
function testFormatInt()
    print("Enter a number : ")
    n = parse(Int64, readline())
    print(formatInt(n))
end # testFormatInt

testFormatInt()
```

The following are some sample runs:

```
Enter a number : 123
123
```

```
Enter a number : 1234
1,234
```

```
Enter a number : 123456
123,456
```

```
Enter a number : 1234567
1,234,567
```

```
Enter a number : 12345678987654
12,345,678,987,654
```

```
Enter a number : 123456789009010234219
12,345,678,900,901,023,421
```

This would work provided the number entered can fit in an `Int64` variable (up to 19 digits). If we enter a 20-digit number (like `123456789009010234219`, the last number entered above with `9` added on the right), we would get this message:

```
ERROR: LoadError: OverflowError: overflow parsing "123456789009010234219"
```

We can easily extend the range of numbers we can work with by replacing `Int64` with `Int128`:

```
julia> print("Int128: ",  typemin(Int128), " to ", typemax(Int128))
Int128: -170141183460469231731687303715884105728 to
170141183460469231731687303715884105727
```

```
julia> formatInt(typemax(Int128))
"170,141,183,460,469,231,731,687,303,715,884,105,727"
```

We can now handle numbers up to 39 digits long! And `factorial(21)` has "only" 20 digits:

```
julia> factorial(Int128(21))  # work out 21! as an Int128
51090942171709440000
```

```
julia> formatInt(factorial(Int128(21)))
"51,090,942,171,709,440,000"
```

And if we need more than 39 digits, Julia provides `BigInt`, enabling us to work with arbitrary precision. The following is instructive:

```
julia> ni30 = factorial(Int128(30))    # 30! is small enough to fit in Int128
265252859812191058636308480000000
```

```
julia> formatInt(ni30)
"265,252,859,812,191,058,636,308,480,000,000"
```

```
julia> typeof(ni30)
Int128
```

But look what happens when we try this:

```
ni40 = factorial(Int128(40))
ERROR: OverflowError: 40 is too large...; consider using `factorial(big(40))` instead
```

And, indeed, we get the following when we use `big(40)`:

```
julia> ni40 = factorial(big(40))
815915283247897734345611269596115894272000000000

julia> formatInt(ni40)
"815,915,283,247,897,734,345,611,269,596,115,894,272,000,000,000"

julia> typeof(ni40)
BigInt
```

We *could* have used the type name `BigInt` instead of `big` (Julia gives us a choice):

```
julia> ni40 = factorial(BigInt(40))
815915283247897734345611269596115894272000000000
```

And our last example with big integers:

```
julia> ni50 = factorial(BigInt(50))
30414093201713378043612608166064768844377641568960512000000000000    # 65 digits
long

julia> formatInt(ni50)
"30,414,093,201,713,378,043,612,608,166,064,768,844,377,641,568,960,512,000,
000,000,000"

julia> typeof(ni50)
BigInt
```

No matter what size of integers we need to use, Julia has the answer.

5.3.6 Combinations

Suppose there are 7 people on a committee. How many subcommittees of 3 people can be formed? The answer is denoted by $^7C_3$ and calculated as follows:

$$\frac{7!}{4!\,3!}$$

This gives us a value of 35. We say there are 35 combinations of 7 objects taken 3 at a time.

In general, ^nC_r denotes the number of combinations of n objects taken r at a time and is calculated by the formula:

$$\frac{n!}{(n-r)!\,r!}$$

Using `factorial`, we can write a function, `combinations`, which, given `n` and `r`, returns the number of combinations of `n` objects taken `r` at a time. Here it is:

```
function combinations(n, r)
    factorial(n) ÷ (factorial (n-r) * factorial (r))
end #combinations
```

The body consists of one statement with 3 calls to `factorial`.

We note that this is perhaps the easiest, but not the most efficient, way to evaluate ^nC_r. For instance, if we were calculating $^7C_3$ by hand, we would use this:

$$\frac{7.6.5}{3.2.1}$$

rather than this that the function uses:

7.6.5.4.3.2.1

4.3.2.1.3.2.1

We show the efficient version of combinations in program P5.4 which reads values for n and r, and prints the number of combinations we can get from n objects taken r at a time.

```
# Program P5.4 - Test Combinations
function combinations(n::Int64, r::Int64)
    if n < r return 0 end
    if n == r return 1 end
    num = 1
    for v = n-r+1:n num *= v end
    num ÷ factorial(r)
end #combinations

function testCombinations()
    print("\nEnter values for n and r: ")
    while (nr = readline()) != ""
        n, r = [parse(Int64, x) for x in split(nr)]
        nCr = combinations(n, r)
        if nCr == 1
            if n == 1
                println("There is 1 combination of 1 object taken 1 at a time")
            else
                println("There is 1 combination of $n objects taken $r at a
                time")
            end
        else
            if n == 1
                println("There are $nCr combinations of 1 object taken $r at a
                time")
            else
                println("There are $nCr combinations of $n objects taken $r at a
                time")
            end
        end
        print("\nEnter values for n and r: ")
    end
end # testCombinations

testCombinations()
```

The program reads values for n and r and prints the number of combinations. This is done until Enter/Return only is pressed. The following is a sample run:

```
Enter values for n and r: 7 3
There are 35 combinations of 7 objects taken 3 at a time

Enter values for n and r: 1 4
There are 0 combinations of 1 object taken 4 at a time

Enter values for n and r: 6 6
There is 1 combination of 6 objects taken 6 at a time

Enter values for n and r: 3 5
There are 0 combinations of 3 objects taken 5 at a time

Enter values for n and r:
```

Observe the use of if...else to get the program to "speak" correct English; it says "1 combination" instead of "1 combinations" and "1 object" instead of "1 objects".

5.3.7 Calculate Pay

In Program P4.19 we wrote some code which used hours (hours worked) and rate (rate of pay) to calculate grossPay. Here it is:

```
if hours <= MaxRegularHours
    regPay = hours * rate
    ovtPay = 0.0
else
    regPay = MaxRegularHours * rate
    ovtPay = (hours - MaxRegularHours) * rate * OvertimeFactor
end
grossPay = regPay + ovtPay
```

We can write a function (we call it getGrossPay) which, given hours and rate, returns grossPay.

```
function getGrossPay(hours::Float64, rate::Float64)
    MaxRegularHours = 40
    OvertimeFactor = 1.5

    if hours <= MaxRegularHours
        regPay = hours * rate
        ovtPay = 0.0
    else
        regPay = MaxRegularHours * rate
        ovtPay = (hours - MaxRegularHours) * rate * OvertimeFactor
    end
    regPay+ovtPay
end
```

The function returns the value of the last statement executed. We could have achieved the same result with return regPay+ovtPay. We test getGrossPay as follows:

```
julia> @printf("\$%0.2f\n", getGrossPay(40,10))
$400.00

julia> @printf("\$%0.2f\n", getGrossPay(50,10))
$550.00

julia> @printf("\$%0.2f\n", getGrossPay(30,25))
$750.00
```

If you choose to, you could pass MaxRegularHours and OvertimeFactor as arguments to the function or declare them globally with const.

5.3.8 Sum of Exact Divisors

Let us write a function to return the sum of the exact divisors of a given integer. We assume the divisors include 1 but not the given number. For example, the exact divisors of 50 are 1, 2, 5, 10 and 25. Their sum is 43. The function is shown below.

```
function sumDivisors(n::Int64)
# returns the sum of the exact divisors of n
    sumDiv = 1            # 1 is a divisor
    for d = 2 : n ÷ 2  # try numbers from 2 to n÷2
        if n % d == 0 sumDiv += d end
    end
    sumDiv
end # sumDivisors

julia> println(sumDivisors(50))
43
```

- sumDiv is used to hold the sum of the exact divisors; it is set to 1 since 1 is always an exact divisor.
- Other possible divisors are 2, 3, 4 and so on up to n÷2. The for loop checks each of these in turn.
- If n%d, the remainder when n is divided by d, is 0, d is an exact divisor of n. In that case, we add d to sumDiv.
- The last statement returns the value of sumDiv to the place from which sumDivisors is called.

In the next example, we will see how sumDivisors may be used.

5.3.9 Perfect, Abundant or Deficient

Positive integers can be classified based on the sum of their exact divisors. If n is an integer and s is the sum of its exact divisors (including 1 but not including n) then:

- if $s < n$, n is *deficient*; e.g. 15 (divisors 1, 3, 5; sum 9)
- if $s = n$, n is *perfect*; e.g. 28 (divisors 1, 2, 4, 7, 14; sum 28)
- if $s > n$, n is *abundant*; e.g. 12 (divisors 1, 2, 3, 4, 6; sum 16)

To simplify our task, we write a function classifyNumber which, given an integer num, returns its classification (Deficient, Perfect or Abundant). It is shown as part of Program P5.5 which reads several numbers and, for each, prints whether it is deficient, perfect or abundant.

```
# Program P5.5 - Classify Numbers
# For each number read, determine if it's deficient, perfect or abundant

function sumDivisors(n::Int64)
    # returns the sum of the exact divisors of n
    sumDiv = 1          # 1 is a divisor
    for d = 2 : n ÷ 2  # try numbers from 2 to n÷2
        if n % d == 0 sumDiv += d end
    end
    sumDiv
end # sumDivisors

function classifyNumber(num)
    sum = sumDivisors(num)

    if sum < num
        "Deficient"
    elseif sum == num
        "Perfect"
    else
        "Abundant"
    end
end # classifyNumber

function main()
    print("Enter a number: ")
    while (snum = readline()) != ""
        num = parse(Int64, snum)
        println("$(classifyNumber(num))")
        print("Enter a number: ")
    end # while
end # main

main()
```

In `classifyNumber`, we call `sumDivisors` once and stores the result in `sum`. We use `sum` when we need the "sum of divisors" rather than re-calculate it each time.

The following is a sample run:

```
Enter a number: 15
Deficient

Enter a number: 12
Abundant

Enter a number: 28
Perfect

Enter a number: 0
```

Exercise: Write a program to find all the perfect numbers less than 10,000.

5.3.10 Letter Position in Alphabet

Let us write a function which, given a character, returns 0 if it is not a letter of the English alphabet; otherwise, it returns the position—an integer value—of the letter in the alphabet. The function should work if the character is either an uppercase or a lowercase letter. For example, given `'T'` or `'t'`, the function should return 20.

The function takes a `Char` argument and returns an `Int` value. Using the standard functions `isuppercase` and `islowercase`, we write the function `position` as follows:

```
function position(ch)
# If ch is a letter, return its position in the alphabet; else return 0
    if isuppercase(ch) return ch-'A'+1 end
    if islowercase(ch) return ch-'a'+1 end
    return 0
end # position
```

We use `isuppercase` and `islowercase` to establish what kind of character we have. If it is neither, control goes to the last statement and 0 is returned.

If we have an uppercase letter, we find the *distance* between the letter and A by subtracting the code for A from the code for the letter. For example, the distance between A and A is 0 and the distance between A and F is 5. Adding 1 gives the position of the letter in the alphabet. Here, adding 1 gives us 1 for A and 6 for F.

If we have a lowercase letter, we find the distance between the letter and a by subtracting the code for a from the code for the letter. For example, the distance between a and b is 1 and the distance between a and z is 25. Adding 1 gives the position of the letter in the alphabet. Here, adding 1 gives us 2 for b and 26 for z.

To illustrate how the function may be used, we write Program P5.6 which reads a line of input; for each character on the line, it prints 0 if it is not a letter and its position in the alphabet if it is a letter.

```
# Program P5.6 - Test Letter Position
using Printf

function position(ch::Char)
# If ch is a letter, return its position in the alphabet; else return 0
    if isuppercase(ch) return ch-'A'+1 end
    if islowercase(ch) return ch-'a'+1 end
    return 0
```

```
end # position
function testLetterPosition()
    print("Type some letters and non-letters and press 'Enter'\n")
    line = readline()
    for i = 1 : length(line)
        @printf("%c %4d\n", line[i], position(line[i]))
    end
end # testLetterPosition

testLetterPosition()
```

Here is a sample run of P5.6:

```
Type some letters and non-letters and press 'Enter'
FaT($h7Y&n
F    6
a    1
T   20
(    0
$    0
h    8
7    0
Y   25
&    0
n   14
```

For each letter, its position in the alphabet is printed; for each non-letter, 0 is printed. We will use this function as the basis of a program to find the frequency with which each letter occurs in a given passage (Section 7.6).

5.4 Introduction to Recursion

A *recursive definition* is one which is defined in terms of itself. Perhaps the most common example is the *factorial* function. The factorial of a non-negative integer, n, (written as $n!$) is defined as:

```
0! = 1
n! = n(n - 1)!, n > 0
```

Here, $n!$ is defined in terms of $(n - 1)!$ What is $(n - 1)!$? To find out, we must apply the definition of factorial! In this case, we have this:

```
(n - 1)! = 1, if (n - 1) = 0
(n - 1)! = (n - 1)(n - 2)! if (n - 1) > 0
```

What is 3!?

- Since $3 > 0$, it is 3.2!
- Since $2 > 0$, 2! is 2.1! and 3! is 3.2.1!
- Since $1 > 0$, 1! is 1.0! and 3! is 3.2.1.0!
- Since 0! is 1, we have 3! is $3.2.1.1 = 6$

Informally, we say that $n!$ is the product of all integers from 1 to n.

Let us rewrite the definition using programming notation; we call it fact:

```
fact(0) = 1
fact(n) = n * fact(n - 1), n > 0
```

The recursive definition of a function consists of two parts:

- The *base* case, which gives the value of the function for a specific argument. This is also called the *anchor*, *end* case or *terminating* case and allows the recursion to terminate.
- The recursive (or general) case where the function is defined in terms of itself.

We have seen many examples of functions which call other functions. What we have not seen is a function which calls itself—a *recursive function*. We start off with fact:

```
function fact(int n)
    if n < 0 return 0 end
    if n == 0 return 1 end
    n * fact(n - 1)
end
```

In the last statement, we have a call to fact, the function we are writing. The function calls itself.

Consider this statement:

```
n = fact(3)
```

It is executed as follows:

- 3 is copied to a temporary location and this location is passed to fact where it becomes the value of n.
- Execution reaches the last statement and fact attempts to return 3 * fact(2). However, fact(2) must be calculated before the return value is known. Think of this as just a call to some function fact with argument 2.
- As usual, 2 is copied to a temporary location and this location is passed to fact where it becomes the value of n. If fact were a different function, there would be no problem. But since it's the *same* function, what happens to the first value of n? It has to be saved somewhere and reinstated when *this* call to fact finishes.
- The value is saved on something called the *run-time stack*. Each time a function calls itself, its arguments (and local variables, if any) are stored on the stack before the new arguments take effect. Also, for each call, new local variables are created. Thus *each call has i*ts own *copy* of arguments and local variables.
- When n is 2, execution reaches the last statement and fact attempts to return 2 * fact(1). However, fact(1) must be calculated before the return value is known. Think of this as just a call to some other function fact with argument 1.
- This call reaches the last statement and fact attempts to return 1 * fact(0). However, fact(0) must be calculated before the return value is known. Think of this as just a call to some function fact with argument 0.
- At this time, the run-time stack contains the arguments 3, 2 and 1. The call fact(0) reaches the second statement and returns a value of 1.
- The calculation 1 * fact(0) can now be completed, returning 1 as the value of fact(1).
- The calculation 2 * fact(1) can now be completed, returning 2 as the value of fact(2).
- The calculation 3 * fact(2) can now be completed, returning 6 as the value of fact(3).

We should emphasize that this recursive version of fact is merely for illustrative purposes. It is not an efficient way to calculate a factorial—think of all the function calls, the stacking and unstacking of arguments, just to multiply the numbers from 1 to n. This is a more efficient function:

```
function fact(n)
    if n < 0 return 0 end
    f = 1
    for k = 2:n
        f *= k
    end
    f
end
```

5.4.1 GCD, Greatest Common Divisor

In Section 5.3.3, we wrote an *iterative* function to find the GCD of two positive integers, m and n. We now write a *recursive* function to do the same thing. We first give a recursive definition:

```
gcd(m, n) is
    (1) m, if n is 0
    (2) gcd(n, m % n), if n > 0
```

If $m = 70$ and $n = 42$, we have this:

```
gcd(70,42) = gcd(42,70%42) = gcd(42,28) = gcd(28,42%28)
           = gcd(28,14) = gcd(14,28 % 14) = gcd(14,0) = 14
```

We can write gcd like this:

```
function gcd(m, n)
    if n == 0 return m end
    gcd(n, m % n)
end
```

Effectively, the iterative function does explicitly what the recursive one does implicitly.

5.4.2 Fibonacci Numbers

Another example of a recursively defined function is that of the Fibonacci numbers. We define the first two Fibonacci numbers as 1 and 1. Each new number is obtained by adding the previous two. So the first few numbers of the Fibonacci sequence are these:

```
1, 1, 2, 3, 5, 8, 13, 21
```

Recursively, we define the nth Fibonacci number, F(n), like this:

```
F(0) = F(1) = 1
F(n) = F(n-1) + F(n-2), n > 1
```

A function to return the nth Fibonacci number is this:

```
function fib(n)
    if n == 0 || n == 1 return 1 end
    fib(n-1) + fib(n-2)
end
```

Again, we emphasize that while this function is neat, concise and easy to understand, it is not efficient. For example, consider the calculation of F(5):

```
F(5) = F(4) + F(3)
= F(3) + F(2) + F(3)
= F(2) + F(1) + F(2) + F(3)
= F(1) + F(0) + F(1) + F(2) + F(3)
= 1 + 1 + 1 + F(1) + F(0) + F(3)
```

```
= 1 + 1 + 1 + 1 + 1 + F(2) + F(1)
= 1 + 1 + 1 + 1 + 1 + F(1) + F(0) + F(1)
= 1 + 1 + 1 + 1 + 1 + 1 + 1 + 1
= 8
```

Notice the number of function calls and additions which have to be made whereas we can calculate F(5) straightforwardly using only 4 additions:

```
F(2) = F(1) + F(0) = 1 + 1 = 2
F(3) = F(2) + F(1) = 2 + 1 = 3
F(4) = F(3) + F(2) = 3 + 2 = 5
F(5) = F(4) + F(3) = 5 + 3 = 8
```

We urge you to write an efficient, iterative function to return the *n*th Fibonacci number.

5.4.3 Decimal to Binary

Suppose n is 13; this is 1101 in binary. Recall that n % 2 gives us the *last* bit of the binary equivalent of n. If, somehow, we have a way to print all but the last bit, we can then follow this with n % 2. But "printing all but the last bit" is the same as printing the binary equivalent of n÷2.

For example, 1101 is 110 followed by 1; 110 is the binary equivalent of 6, which is 13÷2 and 1 is 13 % 2. So, we can print the binary equivalent of n as follows:

```
print binary of n ÷ 2
print n % 2
```

We use the *same* method to print the binary equivalent of 6. This is the binary equivalent of 6÷2 = 3, which is 11, followed by 6 % 2, which is 0; this gives 110.

We use the *same* method to print the binary equivalent of 3. This is the binary equivalent of 3÷2 = 1, which is 1, followed by 3 % 2, which is 1; this gives 11.

We use the *same* method to print the binary equivalent of 1. This is the binary equivalent of 1÷2 = 0 followed by 1 % 2, which is 1; if we "do nothing" for 0, this will give us 1.

We stop when we get to the stage where we need to find the binary equivalent of 0. This leads us to the following function:

```
function decToBin(n)
    if n > 0
        decToBin(n ÷ 2)
        print("$(n % 2)")
    end
end # decToBin
```

The call decToBin(13) will print 1101. Here is a trace of its execution:

```
decToBin(13)    →    decToBin(6)
                     print(13 % 2)

                →    decToBin(3)
                     print(6 % 2)
                     print(13 % 2)

                →    decToBin(1)
                     print(3 % 2)
                     print(6 % 2)
                     print(13 % 2)

                →    decToBin(0) = do nothing
                     print(1 % 2) = 1
```

```
print(3 % 2) = 1
print(6 % 2) = 0
print(13 % 2) = 1
```

We re-state an important property of recursive functions. Keep in mind the statement will be modified if an argument is an array or structure. We will discuss this in Chapters 8 and 9.

When a function calls itself, the current arguments and local variables, if any, are pushed onto a stack. The function executes with the new arguments and new local variables. When execution is completed, arguments and local variables are popped from the stack and execution resumes (with *these* popped values) with the statement following the recursive call.

Consider the following function fragment:

```
function test(m, n)
    ch = 'x'
    .
    .
    test(m+1, n-1)
    print("$m $n")
    .
    .
end # test
```

Suppose we call test(4, 9). The function executes with $m = 4$, $n = 9$ and the local variable, ch. When the (recursive) call to test is made,

- The values of m, n and ch are saved (pushed onto a stack).
- test begins execution, again, with $m = 5$, $n = 8$ and a new copy of ch.
- Whenever *this* call to test finishes, (perhaps even after calling itself several times), the stack is popped and the program resumes execution with print (the statement after the recursive call) and the popped values of m, n and ch. In this example, 4 9 would be printed.

5.4.4 Towers of Hanoi

The *Towers of Hanoi* puzzle is a classic problem that can be solved using recursion. Legend has it that, when the world was created, some high priests in the Temple of Brahma were given three golden pins. On one pin, 64 golden disks were placed. The disks were all of different sizes with the largest at the bottom, the smallest on the top, and no disk was placed on top of a smaller one.

They were required to move the 64 disks from the given pin to another one according to the following rules:

- Move one disk at a time. Only a disk at the top of a pin can be moved, and it must be moved to the top of another pin.
- No disk must be placed on top of a smaller one.

When all 64 disks have been transferred, the world will come to an end.

This is an example of a problem which can be solved easily by recursion but for which a non-recursive solution is quite difficult. Let us denote the pins by A, B and C with the disks originally placed on A and the destination pin being B. Pin C is used for temporary placement of disks.

Suppose there is one disk. This can be move directly from A to B.

Next, suppose there are five disks on A, as shown:

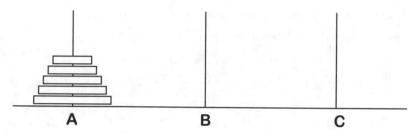

Assume we know how to transfer the top four from *A* to *C* using *B*. When this is done, we have this:

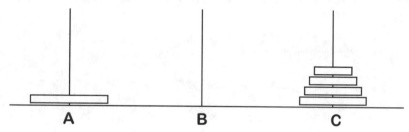

We can now move the fifth disk from *A* to *B*, giving this:

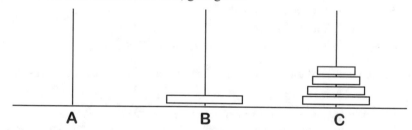

It remains only to transfer the four disks from *C* to *B* using *A*, which we assume we know how to do. When done, we will have this:

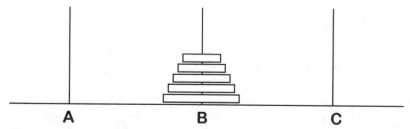

The job is finished.

We have reduced the problem of transferring 5 disks to a problem of transferring 4 disks from one pin to another. This, in turn, can be reduced to a problem of moving 3 disks from one pin to another; *this* can be reduced to 2 and then to 1, which we know how to do. The recursive solution for *n* disks can be expressed like this:

- Transfer *n* - 1 disks from *A* to *C* using *B*.
- Move *n*th disk from *A* to *B*.
- Transfer *n* - 1 disks from *C* to *B* using *A*.

Interestingly, we can use this same solution for transferring the *n* - 1 disks.

The function `hanoi` transfers `n` disks from `startPin` to `endPin` using `workPin`:

```
function hanoi(n, startPin, endPin, workPin)
    if n > 0
        hanoi(n-1, startPin, workPin, endPin)
        println("Move disk from $startPin to $endPin")
        hanoi(n-1, workPin, endPin, startPin)
    end
end # hanoi
```

Suppose we make this call:

```
hanoi(3, 'A', 'B', 'C')  # transfer 3 disks from A to B using C
```

The following will be printed:

```
Move disk from A to B
Move disk from A to C
Move disk from B to C
Move disk from A to B
Move disk from C to A
Move disk from C to B
Move disk from A to B
```

How many moves are required to transfer *n* disks?

- When *n* is 1, 1 move is required; $(1 = 2^1 - 1)$
- When *n* is 2, 3 moves are required; $(3 = 2^2 - 1)$
- When *n* is 3, 7 moves (see above) are required; $(7 = 2^3 - 1)$

For *n* disks, the number of moves is $2^n - 1$. When *n* is 64, the number of moves is

$$2^{64} - 1 = 18,446,744,073,709,551,615$$

Assuming the priests can move 1 disc per second, never make a mistake and never take a rest, it will take them about 585 billion years to complete the task. Rest assured the world is not about to end any time soon!

5.4.5 The Power Function

Given a number, *x*, and an integer, $n \geq 0$, how do we calculate *x* raised to the power *n*, that is, x^n? We can use the definition that x^n is *x* multiplied by itself `n-1` times. Thus, 3^4 is $3 \times 3 \times 3 \times 3$. Here is a function which uses this method:

```
function power(x, n)
    pow = 1
    for h = 2:n
        pow = pow * x
    end
    pow
end # power
```

Note that if *n* is `0` or `1`, `power` returns `1`, the correct answer.

As written, this function performs *n* multiplications. However, we can write a faster function if we adopt a different approach. Suppose we want to calculate x^{16}. We can do it as follows:

- If we know $x8 = x^8$, we can multiply `x8` by `x8` to get x^{16}, using just one more multiplication.

- If we know x4 = x^4, we can multiply x4 by x4 to get x8, using just one more multiplication.

- If we know x2 = x^2, we can multiply x2 by x2 to get x4, using just one more multiplication.

We know x; therefore we can find x2 using one multiplication; knowing x2, we can find x4 using one more multiplication; knowing x4, we can find x8 using one more multiplication; and knowing x8, we can find x^{16} using one more multiplication. We can find x^{16} using just four multiplications.

What if n were 15? First, we would work out $x^{15\div 2}$, that is, x^7 (call this x7). We would then multiply x7 by x7 to give x^{14}. Recognizing that n is odd, we would then multiply this value by x to give the required answer. To summarize,

```
xⁿ = xⁿ÷².xⁿ÷²,    if n is even and
     x.xⁿ÷².xⁿ÷²,  if n is odd
```

We use this as the basis for a recursive power function which calculates x^n more efficiently than the function above.

```
function power(x, n)
    if n == 0 return 1 end
    y = power(x, n ÷ 2)  # careful not to use / => infinite loop
    y = y * y
    if n % 2 == 0 return y end
    x * y
end # power
```

As an exercise, trace the execution of the function with n = 5 and n = 6.

5.4.6 Find Path Through Maze

Advice: This is a non-trivial example which highlights the power of recursion for solving a complex problem. If you do not understand all of it at a first reading, don't worry. You can return to it later.

Consider the following diagram which represents a maze:

```
##########
# #   #   #
# # # ## #
# #     #
# ##### #
# # #S##
#     ## #
##########
```

Problem: Starting at S, and moving along the open spaces, try to find a way out of the maze. The following shows how to do it with x marking the path:

```
#########
#  #xxx#   #
#  #x#x## #
#xxx#xxxx#
#x######x#
#x#  #S##xx
#xxxxx## #
#########
```

Our goal is to write a program which, given a maze and a starting point, determines whether or not a path exists to get out of the maze. If one exists, mark the path with x.

Given any position in the maze, there are four possible directions in which one can move: North (N), East (E), South (S) and West (W). You will not be able to move in a particular direction if you meet a wall. However, if there is an open space, you can move into it.

In writing the program, we will try the directions in the order N, E, S and W. We will use the following strategy:

```
try N
if there is a wall, try E
else if there is a space, move to it and mark it with x
```

Whenever we go to an open space, we repeat this strategy. So, for instance, when we go East, if there is a space, we mark it and try the four directions *from this new position*.

Eventually, we will get out of the maze or we will reach a dead-end position, having tried all possibilities. For example, suppose we get to the position marked C:

```
#########
#C#     #   #
#B#  #  ## #
#A   #      #
#x######  #
#x#  #x##
#xxxxx## #
#########
```

There are walls in all directions except South, from which we came. In this situation, we go back to the previous position and try the next possibility from there. This is called *backtracking*. In this example, we go back to the position south of C (call this B).

When we were at B, we would have gotten to C by trying North. Since this failed, when we go back to B, we will try the 'next' possibility, that is, East. This fails since there is a wall. So we try South; this fails since we have already been there. Finally, we try West which fails since there is a wall.

So, from B, we *backtrack* to the position from which we moved to B (call this A).

When we backtrack to A, the 'next' possibility is East. There is a space so we move into it, mark it with x and try the first direction (North) from there.

When we backtrack from a failed position, we must 'unmark' that position, that is, we must erase the x. This is necessary since a failed position will not be part of the solution path.

How do we backtrack? The recursive mechanism will take care of that for us. The following algorithm shows how:

```
function findPath(P) # find a path from position P
    if P is outside the maze, return 0
```

```
    if P is at a wall, return 0
    if P was considered already, return 0
    # if we get here, P is a space we can move into
    mark P with x
    if P is on the border of the maze, we are out of the maze; return true
    # try to extend the path to the North; if successful, return true
    if (findPath(N)) return true
    # if North fails, try East, then South, then West
    # however, if North succeeds, there is no need to try other directions
    if (findPath(E)) return true
    if (findPath(S)) return true
    if (findPath(W)) return true
    # if all directions fail, we must unmark P and backtrack
    mark P with space
    return false # we have failed to find a path from P
end # findPath
```

Write the program

First we must determine how the maze data will be supplied. In the example, above, the maze consists of 8 rows and 10 columns. If we represent each 'wall' by 1 and each 'space' by 0, the maze is represented by the following:

```
1 1 1 1 1 1 1 1 1 1
1 0 1 0 0 0 1 0 0 1
1 0 1 0 1 0 1 1 0 1
1 0 0 0 1 0 0 0 0 1
1 0 1 1 1 1 1 1 0 1
1 0 1 0 1 0 1 1 0 0
1 0 0 0 0 0 1 1 0 1
1 1 1 1 1 1 1 1 1 1
```

The start position, S, is at row 6, column 6. The first line of data will specify the number of rows and columns of the maze, and the coordinates of S. Thus, the first line of data will be this:

```
8 10 6 6
```

This will be followed by the maze data, above.

When we need to mark a position with an x, we will use the value 2.

Our program will read data from the file maze.in and send output to maze.out. The complete program is shown as Program P5.7. When this program is run with the above data, it produces the following output:

```
##########
#  #xxx#   #
#  #x#x## #
#xxx#xxxx#
#x######x#
#x#  #S##xx
#xxxxx## #
##########
```

Program P5.7 - Maze

```
function findPath(M, r, c)
# Find a path through the maze M starting at row r, column c
    if r < 1 || r > size(M,1) || c < 1 || c > size(M,2) return false end
```

```
    if M[r,c] == 1 return false end # into a wall
    if M[r,c] == 2 return false end # already considered

    # else M[r,c] = 0
    M[r,c] = 2 # mark the path
    if r == 1 || r == size(M,1) || c == 1 || c == size(M,2) return true end
    # path found - space located on the border of the maze

    if findPath(M, r-1, c) return true end
    if findPath(M, r, c+1) return true end
    if findPath(M, r+1, c) return true end
    if findPath(M, r, c-1) return true end
    M[r,c] = 0    # no path found; unmark
    return false
end # findPath

function printMaze(out, M, sr, sc)
    for r = 1:size(M,1)
        for c = 1:size(M,2)
            if r == sr && c == sc
                print(out,'S')
            elseif M[r,c] == 0
                print(out,' ')
            elseif M[r,c] == 1
                print(out,'#')
            else
                print(out,'x')
            end
        end
        println(out)
    end
end # printMaze

function getData(inn, M)
# size(M,1) - number of rows of M; size(M,2) - number of columns
    for r = 1:size(M,1)
        M[r,1:size(M,2)] = [parse(Int, x) for x  in split(readline(inn))]
    end
end # getData

function main()
    inn = open("maze.in", "r")
    out = open("maze.out", "w")

    m, n, sr, sc = [parse(Int, x) for x  in split(readline(inn))]
    M = Array{Int, 2}(undef, m, n)
    getData(inn, M)
    printMaze(out, M, sr, sc)
    if findPath(M, sr, sc)
        println(out, "\nSolution found\n")
        printMaze(out, M, sr, sc)
    else
        println(out, "\nNo solution")
    end
    close(inn)
    close(out)
end # main

main()
```

EXERCISES 5

1. Explain why functions are important in writing a program.
2. Explain carefully what happens when the following function is called with `test(5)`

```
function test(n)
    <body>
end
```

3. Given the function header

```
function fun(n)
```

   explain carefully what happens when the following statement is executed:

```
println("The answer is $(fun(9))")
```

4. Given the function header

```
function test(m, n, x)
```

   say whether each of the following calls to `test` is valid or invalid. If invalid, state why.

```
test(1, 2, 3)
test(-1, 0.0, 3.5)
test(7, 2)
test(14, '7', 3.14)
```

5. Write a function `sqr1` which, given an integer n, returns n^2+1.
6. Write a function `isEven` which, given an integer n, returns `true` if n is even and `false` if n is odd.
7. Write a function `isOdd` which, given an integer n, returns `true` if n is odd and `false` if even.
8. Write a function `isPerfectSquare` which, given an integer n, returns `true` if n is a perfect square (e.g. 25, 81) and `false` if it is not. Use only elementary arithmetic operations. *Hint*: Try numbers starting at 1. Compare a number times itself with n.
9. Write a function `isVowel` which, given a character c, returns `true` if c is a vowel and `false` if it is not.
10. Write a function which, given an integer n, returns the sum

```
1 + 2 +...+ n
```

11. Write a function which, given an integer n, returns the sum

$$1^2 + 2^2 +...+ n^2$$

12. Write a function which, given three integer values representing the sides of a triangle, returns `true` if the triangle is right-angled and `false` if it is not.
13. Write a function `power` which, given a value x and an integer n, returns x^n.
14. Given values for `month` and `year`, write a function to return the number of days in the month.
15. Using the algorithm of problem 13, Exercises 3 , write a function which, given a year between 1900 and 2099, returns a value indicating the day on which Easter Sunday falls in that year.

Write another function which returns an *integer* value: If d is the day of the month, return d if the month is March and -d if the month is April. For example, if the year is 1999, return -4 since Easter Sunday fell on April 4 in 1999. Assume the year is valid.

Write a program which reads two years, y1 and y2. Print the day on which Easter Sunday falls for each year between y1 and y2.

16. Write a function isPrime which, given an integer n, returns true if n is a prime number and false if it is not. A prime number is an integer > 1 which is divisible only by 1 and itself.

Using isPrime, write a program to prompt for an even number n greater than 4 and print all pairs of prime numbers which add up to n. Print an appropriate message if n is not valid. For example, if n is 22, your program should print this:

```
 3    19
 5    17
11    11
```

17. You are required to generate a sequence of integers from a given positive integer *n*, as follows. If *n* is even, divide it by 2. If *n* is odd, multiply it by 3 and add 1. Repeat this process with the new value of *n*, stopping when *n* = 1. For example, if *n* is 13, the following sequence will be generated:

```
13  40  20  10  5  16  8  4  2  1
```

Write a function which, given *n*, returns the length of the sequence generated, including *n* and 1. For *n* = 13, your function should return 10.

Write a program to read two integers *m* and *n* (*m* < *n*), and print the maximum sequence length for the numbers between *m* and *n*, inclusive. Also print the number which gives the maximum length. For example, if *m* = 1 and *n* = 10, your program should print this:

```
9 generates the longest sequence of length 20
```

18. We can code the 52 playing cards using the numbers 1 to 52. We can assign 1 to the Ace of Spades, 2 to the Two of Spades and so on, up to 13 to the King of Spades. We can then assign 14 to the Ace of Hearts, 15 to the Two of Hearts and so on, up to 26 to the King of Hearts. Similarly, we can assign the numbers 27-39 to Diamonds and 40-52 to Clubs.

   (a) Write a function which, given integers rank and suit, returns the code for that card. Assume rank is a number from 1 to 13 with 1 meaning Ace and 13 meaning King; suit is 1, 2, 3 or 4 representing Spades, Hearts, Diamonds and Clubs, respectively.

   (b) Write another function which, given the *number code* of a card (a number from 1 to 52), returns the *name* of the card. Given 21, it returns "Eight of Hearts".

   (c) Write another function which, given the *name* of a card (e.g. Eight of Hearts), returns its *number code* (e.g. 21).

   (d) Write a function to deal a random hand of 7 cards from a pack of 52 cards. Deal another hand of 7 cards from the remaining cards.

19. Write an efficient, iterative function which, given n, returns the *n*th Fibonacci number.

20. What output is produced by the call W(0) of the following function?

```
function W(n)
    print("$n ")
    if n < 10 W(n+3) end
    print("$n ")
end
```

21. What output is produced by the call S('C') of the following function?

```
function S(ch)
    if ch < 'H'
        S(ch+1)
        print("$ch ")
    end
end
```

22. What output is produced by the call T('C') of the following function?

```
function T(ch)
    if ch < 'H'
        print("$ch ")
        T(ch+1)
    end
end
```

23. What is printed by the call fun(18, 3) of the following recursive function?

```
function T(ch)
    if ch < 'H'
        print("$ch ")
        T(ch+1)
    end
end
```

24. What is returned by the call test(7, 2) of the following recursive function?

```
function test(n, r)
    if r == 0 return 1 end
    if r == 1 return n end
    if r == n return 1 end
    test(n-1, r-1) + test(n-1, r)
end
```

25. Write a recursive function which takes an integer argument and prints the integer with one space after each digit. For example, given 7583, it prints 7 5 8 3 .

26. Consider points (m, n) in the usual Cartesian coordinate system where m and n are positive *integers*. In a *north-east* path from point A to point B, one can move only *up* and only *right* (no *down* or *left* movements are allowed). Write a function which, given the coordinates of any two points A and B, returns the *number* of north-east paths from A to B.

CHAPTER 6

Characters & Strings

In this chapter, we will explain the following:

- Some important features of character sets
- How to work with character constants and values
- How to declare character variables in Julia
- How you can use characters in arithmetic expressions
- How to read, manipulate and print characters
- How to convert characters from one case to the other
- How to test for end-of-line using \n
- How to test for end-of-file using eof
- How to compare characters
- How to read characters from a file
- How to convert a number from character to integer
- How to compare strings
- How to index into a string
- How to create a string from pieces of another
- How to fetch a word embedded among other data
- How to write palindrome and Geography quiz programs
- Array of Characters versus Strings
- Some functions for the advanced user

6.1 Character Sets

Most of us are familiar with a computer or typewriter keyboard (called the *standard English keyboard*). On it, we can type the letters of the alphabet (uppercase and lowercase), the digits and other *special characters* like +, =, <, >, & and %—these are the so-called *printable* characters.

Each character is assigned a unique integer value, called its *code*. This code may be different from one computer system to another depending on the *character set* being used. For example, the code for A might be 65 on one computer but 33 on another.

Inside the computer, this integer code is stored as a sequence of bits; for example, the 7-bit code for 65 is 1000001 and the 6-bit code for 33 is 100001.

Nowadays, most computers use the ASCII (American Standard Code for Information Interchange) character set for representing characters. This is a 7-bit character standard which

© The Author(s), under exclusive license to Springer Nature Switzerland AG 2021
N. Kalicharan, *Julia - Bit by Bit*, Undergraduate Topics in Computer Science,
https://doi.org/10.1007/978-3-030-73936-2_6

includes the letters, digits and special characters found on a standard keyboard. It also includes *control* characters such as backspace, tab, line feed, form feed and carriage return.

The ASCII codes run from 0 to 127 (the range of numbers which can be stored using 7 bits). Interesting features to note are:

- The digits 0 to 9 occupy codes 48 to 57.
- The uppercase letters A to Z occupy codes 65 to 90.
- The lowercase letters a to z occupy codes 97 to 122.

Note, however, that even though the ASCII set is *defined* using a 7-bit code, it is stored on most computers in 8-bit bytes—a 0 is added at the front of the 7-bit code. For example, the 7-bit ASCII code for A is 1000001; on a computer, it is stored as 01000001, occupying one byte.

In this book, as far as is possible, we will write our programs making no assumptions about the underlying character set. Where it is unavoidable, we assume the ASCII character set is used. For instance, we may need to assume that the uppercase letters are assigned consecutive codes; similarly for lowercase letters. This may not necessarily be true for another character set. Even so, we will not rely on the specific values of the codes, only that they are consecutive.

6.2 Character Constants and Values

A character constant is a single character enclosed in single quotes such as 'A', '+' and '5'. Some characters cannot be represented like this because we cannot type them (like tab or backspace). Others play a special role in Julia (e.g. ', \). For these, we use an *escape sequence* enclosed in single quotes. Some examples are shown here:

char	description	code
'\n'	new line	10
'\f'	form feed	12
'\r'	carriage return	13
'\t'	tab	9
'\''	single quote	39
'\b'	backspace	8
'\\'	backslash	92

The *value* of a character constant is the character represented, without the single quotes, and, for the characters playing a special role, without the backslash. So, for instance, the character value of 'T' is T and the character value of '\\' is \.

A character constant has an *integer value* associated with it—the numeric code of the character. Thus, the integer value of 'T' is 84 since the ASCII code for T is 84. The integer value of '\\' is 92 since the ASCII code for \ is 92. And the integer value of '\n' is 10 since the ASCII code for the newline character is 10.

If ch contains a character, Int(ch) returns its numeric code, as shown here:

```
julia> ch = 'T';
julia> Int(ch)
84
```

6.3 The Type Char

In Julia, a character is represented by the *type* Char. If we assign a character constant to a variable, the *type* of that variable becomes Char. Study the following:

```
julia> typeof('B')
Char

julia> typeof('+')
Char

julia> ch = 'B'
'B': ASCII/Unicode U+0042 (category Lu: Letter, uppercase)

julia> typeof(ch)
Char

julia> Int(ch)
66                # U+0042 = 66, Hexadecimal(42) = Decimal(66)
```

If we need to, we can declare a variable to be of type Char, within a function, like this:

```
function test()
    ch::Char = 'R'
    println(ch)
end

test()
```

When run, this will print **R**

Int(c) returns the integer value of the Char argument c. And Char(n) returns the character whose code is n. Examples:

```
julia> Int('0')
48

julia> Int('A')
65

julia> Int('a')
97

julia> Char(48)
'0': ASCII/Unicode U+0030 (category Nd: Number, decimal digit)

julia> Char(65)
'A': ASCII/Unicode U+0041 (category Lu: Letter, uppercase)

julia> Char(97)
'a': ASCII/Unicode U+0061 (category Ll: Letter, lowercase)
```

The following shows the codes for some special characters:

```
julia> Int('\t')    # tab
9

julia> Int('\n')    # line feed LF
10

julia> Int('\r')    # carriage return CR
13

julia> Int('$')     # dollar sign
36

julia> Int('\\')    # backslash
92
```

If ch is a Char variable, we could print its *character value* and its *integer code* with this:

```
julia> ch = 'T';

julia> println("Character: $ch, Integer: $(Int(ch))")
Character: T, Integer: 84
```

We could also print the *character* value using the specification %c in @printf, and the *integer* value using Int(ch) and specification %d. For example, the statement

```
@printf("Character: %c, Integer: %d\n", 'B', Int('B'))
```

will print this:

```
Character: B, Integer: 66
```

We can perform some limited arithmetic with characters. Note the following:

```
julia> 'a'+3    # returns the character 3 away from 'a'
'd'

julia> ch = Char(97)
'a'             # code for a is 97

julia> ch + 3        # adding an Int to a Char give a Char
'd'                  # code for d is 100 (97+3)

julia> Int(ch + 3)
100             # code for 'd'

julia> c = 'a' * 3   # cannot multiply Char by Int
ERROR: MethodError: no method matching *(::Char, ::Int64)
```

But this is valid since Int('a') is an integer:

```
julia> c = Int('a')*3    # 97*3
291
```

Here are some other examples:

```
julia> typeof('A'+1)   # 'A'+1 is 'B'
Char

julia> 'T'-'A'         # 'T'-'A' = 84 - 65 = 19
19

julia> typeof('T'-'A')
Int64

julia> 'T'-'a'         # 84 - 97 = -13
-13
```

6.4. Some Char Functions

Julia provides many functions for working with characters. For example, how do we test if the character in ch is a digit? We must test if

```
ch >= '0' && ch <= '9'
```

If this is true, we know that ch is between '0' and '9', inclusive. In Julia, we can express this test as above or like this:

```
'0' <= ch <= '9'
```

We can also use the standard function isdigit(ch) which returns true if ch is a digit and false, otherwise. Other commonly used functions are:

```
isuppercase(ch)
```

Tests whether ch is an uppercase letter. For ASCII, these are the letters A to Z. We could also test with this: `'A' <= ch <= 'Z'`.

`islowercase(ch)`

Tests whether ch is a lowercase letter. For ASCII, these are the letters a to z. We could also test with this: `'a' <= ch <= 'z'`.

`isletter(ch)`

Tests whether ch is a letter (uppercase or lowercase). We could also test with this: `isuppercase(ch) || islowercase(ch)`.

`isascii(ch)`

Tests whether ch belongs to the ASCII character set. For example, `isascii('$')` is `true` but `isascii('β')` is `false`.

`isascii(str)`

Tests whether all characters in str are ASCII characters. For example, `isascii("A=5%")` is `true` but `isascii("aβc")` is `false`.

`isspace(ch)`

Tests whether ch is a whitespace character. These include `'\t'`, `'\n'`, `'\v'`, `'\f'`, `'\r'`, and `' '`.

`ispunct(ch)`

Tests whether ch is a punctuation character. These include the usual `'.'`, `'!'`, `':'`, `';'`, etc. as well as `'/'`, `'*'`, `'-'`, `'+'` and others like `'@'`, `'#'`, and `'&'`.

6.4.1 Uppercase To/From Lowercase

Suppose ch contains an uppercase letter and we want to convert it to its equivalent lowercase letter. For example, ch contains `'H'` and we want to change it to `'h'`.

First we observe that the ASCII codes for `'A'` to `'Z'` range from 65 to 90 and the codes for `'a'` to `'z'` range from 97 to 122. We further observe that the difference between the codes for the two cases of the same letter is always 32; for example,

```
'r' - 'R' = 114 - 82 = 32
```

Hence we can convert an uppercase letter ch to lowercase by adding 32 to it. This can be done with

```
ch = ch + 32  or  ch += 32
```

If ch contains `'H'` (code 72), either statement will add 32 to 72 giving 104; the "character whose code is 104" is assigned to ch, that is, `'h'`. We have changed the value of ch from `'H'` to `'h'`.

Conversely, to convert a lowercase letter ch to uppercase, we subtract 32 from ch; `ch -= 32`.

By the way, we do not really need to know the codes for the letters. All we need is the difference between the uppercase and lowercase codes. We can let Julia tell us what the difference is by using `'a' - 'A'`, like this:

```
ch += 'a' - 'A'   # convert ch from uppercase to lowercase
```

This works no matter what the actual codes for the letters are. It assumes, of course, that ch contains an uppercase letter and the difference between the uppercase and lowercase codes is the same for all letters.

As an example, we write a function `lowerToUpper` which takes a string argument and returns a string in which all lowercase letters are converted to uppercase, leaving the others unchanged. We test it in Program P6.1, which reads a line of input from the file `input.txt` and does the conversion.

Recall that strings are immutable; we cannot change a character "in place". We must create a new string (upLine) with lowercase letters changed to uppercase. We use the "string concatenation" operator * which joins two strings, or a string and a character.

```
# Program P6.1 - Lower To Upper
# Read input line; convert all lowercase letters to uppercase
function lowerToUpper(line::String)
    dist = 'a' - 'A'
    upLine = ""    # strings are immutable; must create new string
    for ch in line
        if islowercase(ch)
            upLine *= ch - dist # you can concatenate a string and a character
        else
            upLine *= ch   # you can concatenate a string and a character
        end
    end # for
    upLine
end # lowerToUpper

function main()
    inn = open("input.txt", "r")
    upLine = lowerToUpper(readline(inn))
    println(upLine)
    close(inn)
end # main

main()
```

If `input.txt` contains this:

```
World Of Mathematics: x^2 = y^2 + z^2
```

Program P6.1 prints this:

```
WORLD OF MATHEMATICS: X^2 = Y^2 + Z^2
```

Exercise: Modify the program to convert all uppercase letters to lowercase.

uppercase, lowercase

We have gone into some detail here to give you some insight into the nature of characters and how they can be manipulated. However, Julia contains almost all the functions you'll need for working with characters. Here are two of the more common ones (ch is Char and str is String):

uppercase(ch) or uppercase(str)

Converts ch or str to uppercase; only lowercase letters affected. Examples:

```
julia> uppercase('t')
'T'

julia> uppercase("abc %&# fgh PT789")
"ABC %&# FGH PT789"
```

lowercase(ch) or lowercase(str)

Converts ch or str to lowercase; only uppercase letters affected. Examples:

```
julia> lowercase('T')
't'

julia> lowercase("ABC %&# FGH pt789")
"abc %&# fgh pt789"
```

With uppercase, the for loop in the function lowerToUpper of Program P6.1 could have been expressed as follows:

```
upLine = uppercase(readline(inn))
```

6.5 Read and Print Characters

Many programs revolve around the idea of reading and writing one character at a time and developing the skill of writing such programs is an important aspect of programming. We can use read(stdin, Char) to read a *single* character from the standard input (stdin, the keyboard) into a Char variable (ch, say) with this:

```
ch = read(stdin, Char)
```

The *next* character in the data is stored in ch. It is important to note that when reading a character, the *very next character* (whatever it is, even if it's a space) is stored in the variable.

The function read takes two arguments—the first is a *file pointer* (stdin for the keyboard) and the second is a type; we will use Char (for the next *character*) or UInt8 (for the integer value of the next *byte*).

For ASCII characters, the option Char returns the next character and UInt8 returns the *integer code* of the next character. For example, if the next input character is 'A', read(stdin, Char) returns 'A' and read(stdin, UInt8) returns 65 (the code for 'A').

Most times we would be reading from a file. If the file is "input.txt", we can open it for reading with this (using inn as the file pointer):

```
inn = open("input.txt", "r")
```

And to read the first character from the file, and store it in ch, we use this:

```
ch = read(inn, Char)
```

To summarize these ideas, we write Program P6.2 to open a file, read the first character and print it with its numeric code.

```
# Program P6.2 - Read and Print First Character
# Read the first character from a file, print it, and its code
function readPrintChar()
    inn = open("input.txt", "r")
    ch = read(inn, Char)
    println("The first character is $ch")
    println("Its code is $(Int(ch))")
    close(inn)
end

readPrintChar()
```

Suppose the first line of input.txt contains this:

```
Hello
```

When run, the program prints this:

```
The first character is H
Its code is 72
```

In Program P6.2, we read just the first character. If we want to read and print the first 3 characters, we could do so with Program P6.3.

```
# Program P6.3 - Read and Print First 3 Characters
# Read first 3 characters from a file; print each, and its code
function readPrint3Char()
    inn = open("input.txt", "r")
    for h = 1 : 3
        ch = read(inn, Char)
        println("Character $h is $ch; Code = $(Int(ch))")
    end
    close(inn)
end

readPrint3Char()}
```

Suppose the first line of `input.txt` contains this:

```
Fun times ahead!
```

When run, the program prints this:

```
Character 1 is F; Code = 70
Character 2 is u; Code = 117
Character 3 is n; Code = 110
```

Next, suppose the first part of the data line contains an arbitrary number of blanks (or, more generally, whitespace characters like tabs and newlines) including none. How do we find and print the first non-space character?

Terminology: We will use the term *space* or *space character* to refer to any whitespace character like a blank, tab or newline.

Since we do not know how many spaces to read, we cannot say something like "read 7 spaces , then the next character". More likely, we need to say something like "as long as the character read is a space, keep reading". We have the notion of doing something (reading a character) as long as some *condition* is true; the condition here is whether the character is a space. This can be expressed more concisely as follows:

```
read a character
while the character read is a space
    read the next character
endwhile
print non-space character
```

There's only one flaw with this logic. What if all the characters are space characters? The `while` loop will never exit! To fix this, we will have to check for end-of-file. We stop when we reach the end-of-file or encounter a non-space character. We show how to do this in Program P6.4. (Recall `eof(inn)` returns `true` if we've reached the end-of-file and `false`, otherwise.)

```
# Program P6.4 Fetch First Non-space Character
# Print the first non-space character, if any, in the data
function firstNonSpaceChar()
    inn = open("input.txt", "r")
    ch = ' '   # necessary for ch to be known outside while
    while !eof(inn)
        ch = read(inn, Char)
```

```
            if !isspace(ch) break end  # exit while if non-space found
        end
        if eof(inn)
            println("No non-space found")
        else
            println("The first non-space is $ch")
        end
        close(inn)
    end

    firstNonSpaceChar()
```

Suppose the first two lines of input.txt contains this (the first contains spaces, tabs and a newline):

```
        Fun times ahead!
```

When run, the program prints this:

```
The first non-space is F
```

The program will locate the first non-whitespace character no matter how many whitespace characters precede it. Verify that the code works if F is the first character of the first line.

If input.txt is empty or contains only spaces, the program will print this:

```
No non-space found
```

This program also highlights an important aspect of Julia's *scope of variables* rule. If ch = ' ' was omitted, ch would be known only inside the while loop (since it's first used there); on exit from while, its value would not be available for the if...else statement to print the answer.

6.6 Count Space Characters

Program P6.4 prints the first non-space character. Suppose we want to *count* how many spaces there were before the first non-space. We could use a variable numSpace to hold the count. Program P6.5 is the modified program for counting the leading spaces.

```
# Program P6.5 Count Spaces to First Non-space
# Count the number of space characters before first non-space character
function spacesBeforeNonSpaceChar()
    inn = open("input.txt", "r")
    numSpace = 0
    ch = ' '  # necessary for ch to be known outside while
    while !eof(inn)
        ch = read(inn, Char)
        if isspace(ch)
            numSpace += 1
        else
            break     # exit while if non-space found
        end
    end # while
    if eof(inn)
        println("No non-space found")
    else
        println("Number of leading spaces is $numSpace")
        println("The first non-space is $ch")
    end
    close(inn)
end # spacesBeforeNonSpaceChar
```

```
spacesBeforeNonSpaceChar()}
```

Suppose `input.txt` contains this (7 leading spaces):

```
       Fun times ahead!
```

When run, the program prints this:

```
Number of leading spaces is 7
The first non-space is F
```

Comments on Program P6.5:

- `numSpace` is initialized to `0` *before* the `while` loop.
- `numSpace` is incremented by `1` *inside* the loop provided `ch` contains a space character. If `ch` is *not* whitespace, we exit the `while` loop.
- When we exit the `while` loop, the value in `numSpace` will be the number of spaces read. This value is then printed.
- Observe that if the first character in the data were non-space, `isspace(ch)` would be `false`; control goes to `else`, forcing a `break` from the `while` loop. Since it's not end-of-file, control goes to `else`, with `numSpace = 0`. The program will print, correctly:

```
Number of leading spaces is 0
```

- As before, if the file contains only whitespace characters, the program will print this:

```
No non-space found
```

6.7 Compare Characters

Characters can be compared using the relational operators `==`, `!=`, `<`, `<=`, `>` and `>=`. The comparison is done using the numeric code of each character. So, for instance, we have `'0' < 'A' < 'a'`.

Let us write a program to read a line of data from a file and print the 'largest' character, that is, the character with the highest code. For instance, if the line consisted of English words, the letter which comes latest in the alphabet would be printed. (Recall, though, that lowercase letters have higher codes than uppercase letters so that, for instance, `'k'` is greater than `'T'`.)

'Finding the largest character' involves the following steps:

- Choose a variable to hold the largest value; we choose `bigChar`.
- Initialize `bigChar` to a very small value. The value chosen should be such that no matter what character is read, its value would be greater than this initial value. For characters, we normally use `'\0'`—the null character, the 'character' with a code of `0`.
- As each character (`ch`, say) is read, it is compared with `bigChar`; if `ch` is greater than `bigChar`, then we have a 'larger' character and `bigChar` is set to this new character.
- When all the characters have been read and checked, `bigChar` will contain the largest one.

These ideas are expressed in Program P6.6.

Testing for end-of-line: If we are reading character by character, how do we test for end-of-line? It depends on the operating system we are using. On Windows, a line ends with CRLF (\r\n, carriage return-line feed); on Linux and MacOSX, it ends with LF (\n). In our programs, where we need to, we will test for end-of-line by testing for \n.

```
# Program P6.6 Find Largest Char
# Read a line of input and find the character with the highest code
function findLargestChar()
    inn = open("input.txt", "r")
    bigChar = '\0'
    while !eof(inn)    # in case the file is empty
        ch = read(inn, Char)  # get next character
        if ch == '\n' break end # reached end-of-line
        if ch > bigChar bigChar = ch end
    end
    if bigChar == '\0'
        println("Empty file")
    else
        println("The largest character is $bigChar")
    end
    close(inn)
end

findLargestChar()
```

Suppose the file `input.txt` contains this:

```
Where The Mind Is Without Fear
```

When run, the program prints this:

```
The largest character is u
```

u is printed since its code is the highest of all the characters in the data.

On the other hand, if this is the data:

```
Where The Mind ~ Is Without Fear
```

the program will print this (the ASCII code for ~ is 126):

```
The largest character is ~
```

maximum, minimum, argmax, argmin

We explained how to find the 'largest' character to get an appreciation of the details that are involved. However, as you would expect by now, Julia provides standard functions for finding the largest (and smallest) characters in a string. Further, it can tell you the index at which it was found, using `argmax` and `argmin`.

```
julia> str = "Where the mind is Without fear";

julia> maximum(str)
'u': ASCII/Unicode U+0075 (category Ll: Letter, lowercase)

julia> argmax(str)
24

julia> minimum(str)
' ': ASCII/Unicode U+0020 (category Zs: Separator, space)

julia> argmin(str)
6
```

6.8 Echo Input, Number Lines

We now write a program to read data from a file `input.txt` and write back the same data (*echo* the data) to another file (`output.txt`) with the lines numbered starting from 1.

The program would read the data from the file and write it to the screen, like this:

```
1. First line of data
2. Second line of data
     etc.
```

The program is fairly straightforward and is shown as Program P6.7.

```
# Program P6.7 Echo Input Number Lines
# Read data from input.txt and write to output.txt with lines numbered

function echoInputNumberLines()
    inn = open("input.txt", "r")
    out = open("output.txt","w")
    n = 0
    while !eof(inn)
        n += 1
        line = readline(inn)
        write(out,"$n. $line\n")
    end
    close(inn)
    close(out)
end # echoInputNumberLines

echoInputNumberLines()
```

Suppose `input.txt` contains the following:

```
I think that I shall never see
A computer made up quite like me
A me who likes to run and play
And always likes to have my way
```

When the program is run, it sends the following to `output.txt`:

```
1. I think that I shall never see
2. A computer made up quite like me
3. A me who likes to run and play
4. And always likes to have my way
```

6.9 Convert Digit Characters to Integer

We now consider the problem of converting a single-character digit into a number (`'8'` to 8) and then convert a *sequence* of digit-characters to a number (`'3' '8' '5'` to 385). Consider this:

```
d = '5' - '0'
```

The *integer* 5 is assigned to d since the code for `'5'` is 53 and the code for `'0'` is 48.

Observe that the code for a digit in character form is *not* the same as the value of the digit; for instance, the code for the character `'5'` is 53 but the *value* of the digit 5 is 5. Sometimes we know that a `Char` variable contains a digit and we want to get the (integer) value of the digit.

The above statement shows how we can do this—we simply subtract the code for `'0'` from the code for the digit. It does not matter what the actual codes for the digits are; it matters only that the codes for 0 to 9 are consecutive, which is the case for the ASCII character set.

In general, if `ch` contains a digit character (`'0'` to `'9'`), we can obtain the integer value of the digit with this:

```
d = ch - '0'
```

We have used `readline()` to read a line of input (as a string) and, if it contained a number only, used `parse` to convert it from string to number. However, if the input contains anything but a number, Julia reports an error.

As a reminder, the following assumes the input line contains an integer only. It fetches the number as a string, converts it to an integer, and stores it in `num`:

```
num = parse(Int64, readline())
```

Now, suppose we have an input line with a number somewhere in the line, like this:

```
Number of items: 385, all in good condition
```

How do we find the number and convert the individual digits into the *integer* 385?

First, we consider how we can convert a sequence of digits into an integer. When we type the number 385, we are actually typing three individual characters – `'3'` then `'8'` then `'5'`. Inside the computer, the integer 385 is completely different from the three characters `'3'` `'8'` `'5'`. That's why we need `parse`: it converts this sequence of three characters into the integer 385.

To illustrate, the 8-bit ASCII codes for the characters `'3'`, `'8'` and `'5'` are `00110011`, `00111000` and `00110101`, respectively. When typed to the screen or a file, the digits 385 are represented by this:

```
00110011 00111000 00110101
```

Assuming an integer is stored using 16 bits, the integer 385 is represented by its binary equivalent

```
00000001 10000001
```

Observe the character representation is quite different from the integer representation.

To repeat, the function `parse` will convert `00110011 00111000 00110101` to `00000001 10000001`. We now show how this is done, working with the decimal digits.

The basic step requires us to convert a digit character into its equivalent integer value. We showed how to do this above. Once we can convert individual digits, we can construct the value of the number as we read it from left to right, using the following algorithm:

```
set num to 0
get a character, ch
while ch is a digit character
    convert ch to the digit value, d = ch - '0'
    set num to num*10 + d
    get a character, ch
endwhile
num now contains the integer value
```

The sequence of *characters* 385 is converted as follows:

```
num = 0
get '3'; convert to 3
num = num*10 + 3 = 0*10 + 3; num is now 3
get '8'; convert to 8
num = num*10 + 8 = 3*10 + 8; num is now 38
get '5'; convert to 5
num = num*10 + 5 = 38*10 + 5; num is now 385
```

There are no more digits and the final value of `num` is 385.

We are now ready to write a program which scans a line of data, character by character, until it finds an integer. It constructs and prints the integer.

The program will have to read characters until it finds a digit, the first of the integer. Having found the first digit, it must construct the integer by reading characters as long as it keeps getting a digit. For example, suppose the data was this:

```
Number of items: 385, all in good condition
```

The program will read characters until it finds the first digit, 3. It will construct the integer using the 3 and then reading 8 and 5. When it reads the comma, it knows the integer has ended.

This idea can be expressed in the following pseudocode algorithm:

```
get a character, ch
while ch is not a digit
    get a character, ch
endwhile
# at this point, ch contains a digit
num = 0
while ch is a digit
    use ch to build the integer (num = num*10 + ch - '0')
    get a character, ch
endwhile
print num
```

In Program P6.8, we write a function getNumber which fetches the next number from the file designated by inn. Since the function is going to be standalone, it's probably a good idea to remind the user, in the function header, that inn is an input stream. The function searches for an integer until it finds one, or it reaches the end of the file.

```
# Program P6.8 - Fetch a Number
# Read the input file char by char until it finds a number or end-of-file
function getNumber(inn::IOStream)
    ch = ' '          # necessary for ch to be known to the whole function
    while !eof(inn)
        ch = read(inn, Char)  # get another character
        if isdigit(ch) break end # exit while if digit found
    end
    if eof(inn) return nothing end # end-of-file reached, no digit found

    # ch contains the first digit of the number
    num = 0
    while !eof(inn) && isdigit(ch) # as long as we get a digit
        num = num * 10 + ch - '0' # update num
        ch = read(inn, Char)
    end
    return num
end # getNumber

function main()
    inn = open("input.txt", "r")
    if (num=getNumber(inn)) == nothing
        println("No number found")
    else
        println("Number is $num")
    end
end # main

main()
```

Suppose input.txt contains the following:

```
Number of items: 385, all in good condition
```

When the program is run, it prints this:

```
Number is 385
```

Exercise: Modify the function to (a) read a positive or negative integer (b) read a number with or without a decimal point.

We will use this function in Program P6.9 after we get familiar with some `String` basics.

6.10 String Basics

Each ASCII character occupies one byte of storage. So the string `"Computer"` will be stored in 8 bytes (one byte per character):

```
# length is a standard function which returns the number of characters in a
given string
julia> length("Computer")
8
```

We put characters together to from a *string*.

A *string literal* (*constant*) is a finite sequence of characters enclosed in double quotes. Examples:

```
"Once upon a time"
"645-2001"
"Are you OK?"
"c:\\data\\castle.in"
```

The empty string (a string with no characters) is denoted by two consecutive double quotes, `""`.

The *value* of a string literal is the sequence of characters without the beginning and ending quotes: the value of `"Glad to see you"` is `Glad to see you`.

```
julia> str = "Glad to see you"
"Glad to see you"      # a string, the result of the assignment

julia> println(str)
Glad to see you        # the value of str is printed
```

If you want the double quote to be part of a string, you must write it using the escape sequence `\"`, as in

```
"\"Don't move!\", he commanded."
```

The value of this string is

```
"Don't move!", he commanded.
```

Each `\"` is replaced by `"` and the beginning and ending quotes are dropped.

```
julia> dmc = "\"Don't move!\", he commanded."
"\"Don't move!\", he commanded."

julia> print(dmc)
"Don't move!", he commanded      # Each \" replaced by "
```

Previously, we used the following statement to fetch a line of input typed by the user and assign it to `name`:

```
name = readline()
```

Whatever the user types is considered a string. So, essentially, we are assigning a string to `name`. We can assign a string directly to a variable, like this:

```
str = "Once upon a time"
```

Regardless of what it was before, str is now a String variable (uppercase S). We have this:

```
julia> typeof(str)
String
```

Suppose we assign the string "Alice Liddell" to the variable AiW (for *Alice in Wonderland*). We have this:

```
julia> AiW = "Alice Liddell";

julia> typeof(AiW)
String
```

Print a String, %s

The statement:

```
println("Hello, $AiW")
```

prints this:

```
Hello, Alice Liddell
```

We can get the same result with this:

```
@printf("Hello, %s\n", AiW)
```

(*Note*: in order to use @printf, your program must be preceded by the directive using Printf.)

When executed, the string is printed with the specification %s replaced by the *value* of AiW. We say %s matches the String variable AiW.

But %s can do more than that. It can match any numeric variable as well.

Suppose num has the value 32.754. The statement:

```
@printf("Hello, %s\n", num)
```

will print this:

```
Hello, 32.754
```

In other words, %s forces the number 32.754 to be converted to the string "32.754" whose value is then printed.

We could also get the same effect by using %0.3f to print num to 3 decimal places:

```
@printf("Hello, %0.3f\n", num)
```

The above is summarized in the following Julia interaction:

```
julia> AiW = "Alice Liddell";

julia> println("Hello, $AiW")
Hello, Alice Liddell

julia> @printf("Hello, %s\n", AiW)
Hello, Alice Liddell

julia> num = 32.754;

julia> @printf("Hello, %s\n", num)
Hello, 32.754

julia> @printf("Hello, %0.3f\n", num)
Hello, 32.754
```

6.11 Compare Strings

We can compare strings (as we do numbers) using the *relational operators* == (equal to), != (not equal to), < (less than), <= (less than or equal to), > (greater than), >= (greater than or equal to).

To determine if one string is less than (or greater than) another, the ordering in the ASCII character set is used.

When we compare two strings, they are compared character by character. If there is no mismatch, the strings are the same. If there's a mismatch, the ordering of the mismatched characters determines which string is less than the other. To illustrate:

```
julia> "heather" == "weather" # First letters don't match
false

julia> "heather" == "heathen" # First 6 match but r is different from n
false

julia> "man" < "Woman"        # m > W so this is false
false

julia> "woman" > "man"        # w > m so this is true
true

julia> "Excite" == "excite"   # E is different from e
false

julia> "Excite" == "Excite"
true

julia> "Excite" ≡ "Excite"    # you can use ≡ (\equiv Tab) instead of ==
true

julia> "Excite" != "excite"   # E is different from e
true

julia> "excite" > "Excite"    # e is greater than E
true

julia> "man" < "mango"        # First 3 match; nothing left in first string
true
```

Note the last example. If one string, s1, is a proper substring of the other, s2, s1 is considered to be *less than* s2.

The congruence symbol ≡ (\equiv Tab) belongs to the *extended* ASCII character set, and can be used instead of == to check for equality of strings.

cmp - compare two strings

In addition to the relational operators, Julia provides the standard function cmp for string comparison. Assume s1 and s2 are Strings and consider this:

```
cmp(s1, s2)
```

cmp returns -1 if s1 < s2, 0 if s1 = s2 and 1 if s1 > s2.

Here are some examples:

```
julia> cmp("alpha", "beta")  # a < b
-1

julia> cmp("hi", "hello")    # i > e
1
```

```
julia> cmp("Hi", "hello")     # H < h
-1

julia> cmp("hi", "Hi")        # h > H
1

julia> cmp("Hi", "Hi")
0

julia> cmp("man", "mango")    # man < mango
-1

julia>  cmp("mango", "man")   # mango > man
1

julia>  cmp("ethos", "ethos")
0
```

6.12 Index Into a String

If str is a string, we can access individual characters by *indexing* into it using a *subscript*. For instance, str[1] is the first character, str[2] is the second, and so on, up to str[n] if n is the length of the string (number of characters in it).

```
julia> bc = "Blue Christmas"
"Blue Christmas"

julia> println(bc[1])
B

julia> println(bc[begin]) # begin is a synonym for 1
B

julia> print(bc[6])
C

julia> length(bc)          # 14 characters in "Blue Christmas"
14

julia> println(bc[14])     # print the last one
s
julia> print(bc[end])      # end is a synonym for last index position
s

julia> print(bc[length(bc)]) # same as bc[14]
s
```

Sometimes it's helpful to remember that, in Julia, strings are *immutable*—they cannot be changed. In this example, the value of bc is Blue Christmas. We can, of course, assign a different *string* to bc (in which case, the old value is lost) but we cannot, for instance, change bc[1] from B to G.

Suppose we try this: bc[1] = 'G'.

We will get a message to the effect that we are trying to do something illegal. In other words, we can access and use individual characters in myriad ways—we just cannot change them. However, if we want, we can create a *new* string from individual pieces of a given string. To illustrate:

```
julia> bm = bc[1]*bc[4]*bc[8]*bc[12]  # * joins individual pieces
"Berm"
```

Here, we introduce * (star/asterisk) in a new role, that of *string concatenation* operator. It takes individual pieces of a string (called *substrings*) and joins them together.

In the example, it takes the first, fourth, eighth and twelfth characters, creates the new string "Berm", and assigns it to bm. We can now work with bm as a string in its own right, nothing to do with bc, from which it was created.

Here are some other ways we can access portions of a string. We use what is called *range indexing*. [lo : hi] refers to the portion of a string from index lo to index hi, both indices inclusive.

```
julia> bc = "Blue Christmas"
"Blue Christmas"

julia> bc[1:4]          # characters at subscripts 1 to 4
"Blue"

julia> bc[6:11]         # characters 6 to 11
"Christ"

julia> bc[12:end]       # end  denotes the last character index
"mas"

julia> bc[end-2:end]    # last 3 characters; we can use end as we would a variable
"mas"

julia> bc[begin:end]    # the whole string
"Blue Christmas"
```

And [lo : step : hi] lets us extract characters starting at index lo, up to index hi, that are step apart. In other words, we can extract characters that are a fixed distance apart in the string.

To extract every other character, we can write this:

```
julia> bc[1:2:14]     # characters in positions 1, 3, 5, 7, 9, 11, 13
"Bu hita"
```

To extract characters from positions 4, 7, 10, 13 (4 to 13 in steps of 3), we can write this:

```
julia> bc[4:3:end]     # start at 4; advance in steps of 3.
"ehsa"
```

or this:

```
julia> bc[begin+3:3:end]
"ehsa"
```

To extract every fourth character, starting at index 3, we can write this:

```
julia> bc[begin+2:4:end]   # characters 3, 7, 11
"uht"
```

To iterate through the characters of a string, we can use the for statement:

```
for c in str  # perform the loop with c assuming each value in str
```

Here's an example:

```
julia> for c in "abcd" print("$(c+4) ") end
e f g h
```

To give us more options, Julia provides a SubString function. The general format is :

```
SubString(str, m, n)
```

where str is a String and m, n are integers. It returns the substring str[m:n]. If m or n is outside the valid range of indices, a BoundsError is reported. The following shows some typical ways to use SubString.

```
julia> str = "Where the mind is without fear"
"Where the mind is without fear"

julia> SubString(str, 1, 5)     # characters 1 to 5
"Where"

julia> SubString(str, 11, 15)    # characters 11 to 15
"mind"

julia> lastindex(str)    # there are 30 (ASCII) characters in str
30

julia> SubString(str, lastindex(str)-3, lastindex(str)) # last 4 chars
"fear"                   # the characters from str[27:30]

julia> SubString(str, 30, 31)    # valid indices run from 1 to 30
ERROR: BoundsError: attempt to access String at index [30:31]
```

The following shows the difference between a *character* of a string and a *substring* consisting of one character:

```
julia> bc = "Blue Christmas"
"Blue Christmas"

julia> c = bc[6]
'C': ASCII/Unicode U+0043 (category Lu: Letter, uppercase)

julia> typeof(c)
Char

julia> s = bc[6:6]
"C"

julia> typeof(s)
String
```

bc[6] refers to the sixth character (of type Char) of bc.

bc[6:6] refers to a (sub) String consisting of a single character.

In general, these are very different from each other—c is a Char, and can be used only in places where a Char can be used; s is a String, and can be used only in places where a String can be used.

6.13 Example - Sum of Distances

In Section 3.4.1 we wrote a program to find the sum of two lengths. Here, we will refer to them as distances so as not to confuse the word *length* (meaning distance) with the Julia function, length, which returns the length of a string, among other things. We had the following sample run:

```
Enter values for m and cm: 3 75
Enter values for m and cm: 5 50

Sum is 9m 25cm
```

Each distance was entered as two integers only—no other characters. But let's suppose we want the program to run like this (we use bigger numbers so we don't confuse a number with an index in the explanation):

```
Enter first distance: 23m 75cm
Enter second distance: 25m 50cm

Sum is 49m 25cm
```

Now we no longer have a *pure* number; we can't read it with `readline/parse`. We must scan the input character by character and decipher the two numbers that were entered. The approach is similar to what we presented above to find the number hidden among other characters. However, to do something different, we will store the data entered in a `String` variable (we use `line`), and scan the string for the numbers.

Like before, the program will prompt for the first distance, like this:

```
print("Enter first distance: ")
line = readline()
```

But, now, whatever the user types will be stored in `line`. Suppose she types this:

```
23m 75cm
```

The program will make the call `getInteger(line, 1)` to find the first number, `23`. Here is `getInteger`:

```
function getInteger(line, n)
# line is a String; return the next integer starting at line[n]

    while n <= length(line) && !isdigit(line[n])
        n += 1
    end
    if n > length(line) return -1, n end

    # at this point, line[n] contains the first digit of the number
    num = 0
    while n <= length(line) && isdigit(line[n]) # as long as we get a digit
        num = num * 10 + line[n] - '0'
        n += 1
    end
    return num, n # the number and the index of the last char scanned
end # getInteger
```

Starting at index n (initially 1), the function searches for the first digit of the next number (first `while` loop). The second `while` loop fetches the other digits, if any. Any non-digit character or the end of `line` signals the end of the number. The function returns the number found and the index of the character immediately following the number. If required, future scanning will start from the next character. If no number is found, the function returns -1. We don't use it here but it can be used for error-checking.

In the example, the number `23` is found at `line[1:2]`; `m` in `line[3]` ends the number. The function returns `23  3`. Future scanning will start from `line[4]`.

On the next call to `getInteger`, scanning starts at `line[4]`. The number `75` is found at `line[5:6]` with `c` at `line[7]` indicating the end of the number. The function returns `75  7`.

The complete program is shown as P6.9. A sample run was shown at the beginning of this section.

```
# Program P6.9 - Sum Two Distances Given in Free Format
# Find the sum of two distances which may be given with labels

function getInteger(line, n)
    # line is a Char array; return the next integer; start scan at line[n]
    while n <= length(line) && !isdigit(line[n])
        n += 1
    end
    if n > length(line) return -1, n end

    # at this point, line[n] contains the first digit of the number
    num = 0
```

```
        while n <= length(line) && isdigit(line[n]) # as long as we get a digit
            num = num * 10 + line[n] - '0' # update num
            n += 1
        end
        return num, n # the number and the index of the last char scanned
    end # getInteger

function sumDistances()
    print("Enter first distance: ")
    line = readline()
    m1, n = getInteger(line, 1)
    cm1, n = getInteger(line, n+1) # scan from the next char in line

    print("Enter second distance: ")
    line = readline()
    m2, n = getInteger(line, 1)
    cm2, n = getInteger(line, n+1)  # scan from the next char in line

    mSum = m1 + m2      # add the metres
    cmSum = cm1 + cm2   # add the centimetres
    if cmSum >= 100
        mSum = mSum + cmSum ÷ 100
        cmSum = cmSum % 100
    end
    print("\nSum is $(mSum)m $(cmSum)cm\n")
end # sumDistances

sumDistances()
```

We take a closer look at this statement in `getInteger`:

```
return num, n # the number and the index of the last char scanned
```

Julia makes it easy for a function to return more than one value. Here, the function returns the number found (`num`) and the index (`n`) of the last character accessed. Since the function returns two values, they must be assigned to two variables in the calling function, like this:

```
m1, n = getInteger(line, 1)
```

6.14 Concatenation

Previously, we introduced *, the string concatenation operator. It is used to join pieces of strings to make a bigger one. For example:

```
julia> "Blue Christmas" * " by " * "Elvis Presley"
"Blue Christmas by Elvis Presley"
```

We could have done it like this:

```
julia> song = "Blue Christmas";
julia> singer = "Elvis Presley";
julia> println(song * " by " * singer)
Blue Christmas by Elvis Presley
```

Even better, we could write this:

```
julia> ss = "$song by $singer"
"Blue Christmas by Elvis Presley"
```

or this:

```
julia> println("$song by $singer")
Blue Christmas by Elvis Presley
```

6.15 Example - Get Words From Random Data

Consider a file (`input.txt` designated by `inn`) in which words are dispersed randomly. For the purpose of this example, we define a word as a contiguous sequence of letters. A word is delimited by any non-letter character or end-of-line. The following shows some sample data:

```
>>>Goodness ^ Of ^ Grace: Come :;You broken! > Heavy laden..  ..
<<<+Come! You helpless!?.() come You in despair:-(..
```

We first write a function which will pick out the next word in the input. It uses this statement to read the next character and store it in `ch`:

```
ch = read(inn, Char)
```

Here is the function, `getNextWord`:

```
function getNextWord(inn::IOStream)
# A word is defined as a contiguous sequence of letters
    ch = ' '         # necessary for ch to be known to the whole function
    while !eof(inn) && !isletter(ch) # Search for next letter
        ch = read(inn, Char)
    end
    if eof(inn) return nothing end  # None found; end of file reached

    # At this point, ch contains the first letter of the word
    wrd = string(ch)    # convert a single letter to String
    ch = read(inn, Char)
    while isletter(ch) # as long as we get a letter
        wrd *= ch       # add it to the word
        ch = read(inn, Char)
    end
    return wrd
end # getNextWord
```

We can test it by writing code to read and print each word in the file, like this:

```
function testGetWord()
    inn = open("input.txt", "r")
    wrd = getNextString(inn)
    while wrd != nothing
        print(wrd, " ")      # print words on one line
        wrd = getNextString(inn)
    end
    close(inn)
end
```

When we call `testGetWord()` with the above data in `input.txt`, it prints this:

```
Goodness Of Grace Come You broken Heavy laden Come You helpless come You in
despair
```

Now that we are assured the program is fetching the words correctly, we can add the code to find the 'smallest' and the 'largest' (first and last in alphabetical order). The complete program is shown as Program P6.10.

```
# Program P6.10 - Find First and Last Words in Alphabetical Order
# Read a file with arbitrary words; print first and last in alpha order
# A word is a string of letters; any non-letter is a delimiter

function getNextWord(inn::IOStream)
# A word is defined as a contiguous sequence of letters
    ch = ' '         # necessary for ch to be known to the whole function
    while !eof(inn) && !isletter(ch) # Search for next letter
        ch = read(inn, Char)
```

```
    end
    if eof(inn) return nothing end  # None found; end of file reached

    # At this point, ch contains the first letter of the word
    wrd = string(ch)   # convert a single-letter to String
    ch = read(inn, Char)
    while isletter(ch) # as long as we get a letter
        wrd *= ch
        ch = read(inn, Char)
    end
    return wrd
end # getNextWord

function firstLastWord()
    inn = open("input.txt", "r")
    first = "~"      # any ASCII letter will be less than ~
    last = ""        # any ASCII letter will be greater than ""
    word = getNextWord(inn)
    while word != nothing
        println(word)
        if (word < first) first = word end
        if (word > last) last = word end
        word = getNextWord(inn)
    end
    close(inn)
    println("\nFirst word is $first")
    println("Last word is $last")
end # firstLastWord

firstLastWord()
```

When run with the sample data, above, in `input.txt`, the program prints this:

```
Goodness
Of
Grace
Come
You
broken
Heavy
laden
Come
You
helpless
come
You
in
despair

First word is Come
Last word is laden
```

Recall that lowercase letters have higher codes than uppercase letters so, for instance, `laden` comes *after* `You`. If we want to compare the words, ignoring the case of the letters, we can replace these statements:

```
if (word < first) first = word end
if (word > last) last = word end
```

with these:

```
if (lowercase(word) < lowercase(first)) first = word end
if (lowercase(word) > lowercase(last)) last = word end
```

We convert both words to lowercase before comparing. (We could also have converted both to uppercase with the same result.) Note, however, we save the word with its original spelling if it is the smallest or largest so far.

With these changes, and the same data, the program now prints these for the last two lines:

```
First word is broken
Last word is You
```

The words have been compared in true alphabetical order.

6.16 Example - Palindrome

Consider the problem of determining if a given string is a palindrome (the same when spelt forwards or backwards). Examples of palindromes (ignoring case, punctuation and spaces):

```
civic
Race car
Madam, I'm Adam.
A man, a plan, a canal, Panama.
```

If all the letters were of the same case (upper or lower) and the string (`phrase`, say) contained no spaces or punctuation marks, we could write `isPalindrome` as follows:

```
function isPalindrome1(phrase)
    phrase == reverse(phrase)  # reverse(String) is a standard Julia function
end
```

It takes the given phrase (`p`), reverses the letters in it (`rp`), and compares `p` with `rp`. If they are the same, the phrase is a palindrome. The function returns `true` for `civic` but `false` for `Civic`. Easy, but too restrictive.

The next version can do a bit more. It does not assume the letters are all the same case. Before comparing, it converts `p` and `rp` to lowercase.

```
function isPalindrome2(phrase)
    lowercase(phrase) == lowercase(reverse(phrase))
end
```

Now, both `civic` and `Civic` return `true`. And the same holds for `MadamImAdam`.

Again, the function is easy to write but is it efficient? Is it doing more work than is necessary to determine if a given word/phrase is a palindrome? We observe there's a lot of hidden work in that one statement. The phrase has to be reversed, and then the reversed string compared with the original. Let's explore this some more.

Suppose the word, when converted to lowercase, is `thermostat`. This method would reverse `thermostat` to get `tatsomreht`. Comparing the two tells us that `thermostat` is not a palindrome. But we can get the answer more quickly as follows:

```
compare the first and last letters, t and t
they are the same, so
compare the second and second to last letters, h and a
these are different so the word is not a palindrome
```

Using this idea, we tackle the more general problem of determining if a given phrase (including spaces and punctuation) is a palindrome.

The first task would be to reduce the phrase to letters of one type only (lowercase or uppercase); we choose lowercase. All spaces and punctuation will be removed. We do this by creating a new string which includes only the letters from the original phrase, all converted to lowercase. So, for instance, `Madam I'm Adam` would be reduced to `madamimadam`.

The function `lettersOnlyLower` does all of this:

```
function lettersOnlyLower(phrase)
# Return a string with the letters only, all converted to lowercase
    word = ""
    for ch in phrase
        if isletter(ch)
            word *= lowercase(ch) # add this letter to word
        end
    end
    return word
end # lettersOnlyLower
```

All that's left to do is compare first and last, then second and second to last, and so on, until we get a mismatch (and it's not a palindrome) or we check the whole string (and it's a palindrome).

The details are shown in Program P6.11.

```
# Program P6.11 - Test for Palindrome
#Check if a given word/phrase is a palindrome

function lettersOnlyLower(phrase)
# Return a string with the letters only, all converted to lowercase
    word = ""
    for ch in phrase
        if isletter(ch)
            word *= lowercase(ch) # add this letter to word
        end
    end
    return word
end # lettersOnlyLower

function isPalindrome(phrase)
    word = lettersOnlyLower(phrase)
    lo = 1
    hi = length(word)
    while lo < hi
        if word[lo] != word[hi] return false end
        lo += 1; hi -= 1
    end
    return true # no mismatch found
end   # isPalindrome

function main()
    print("\nWord or phrase? (To stop, press Enter): ")
    phrs = readline()
    while phrs != ""
        if isPalindrome(phrs)
            println("is a palindrome")
        else
            println("is not a palindrome")
        end
        print("\nWord or phrase? (To stop, press Enter): ")
        phrs = readline()
    end
end # main()

main()
```

The following shows a sample run:

```
Word or phrase? (To stop, press Enter): Madam I'm Adam
is a palindrome
```

```
Word or phrase? (To stop, press Enter): Flo, gin is a sin. I golf.
is a palindrome

Word or phrase? (To stop, press Enter): Never odd or even.
is a palindrome

Word or phrase? (To stop, press Enter): This and That
is not a palindrome

Word or phrase? (To stop, press Enter): Pull up if I pull up.
is a palindrome

Word or phrase? (To stop, press Enter):
```

6.17 A Flexible `getString` Function

So far, we have used `readline` to fetch a line of input, and `split` to break up the line into individual substrings. (We can then use `parse`, if necessary, to convert individual substrings to numbers.)

But what if we wanted to read a string delimited by double quotes or some other character? Suppose we had data in the following format:

```
"Margaret Dwarika" "Managing Director"
```

Each item of data is a string delimited by double quotes.

We will write a function, `getString`, which will read a string enclosed within *delimiter* characters. For example, we could specify a string as `$John Smith$` or `"John Smith"`. This is a very flexible way of specifying a string.

Each string can be specified with its own delimiters which could be different for the next string. It is particularly useful for specifying strings which may include special characters such as the double quotes without having to use an escape sequence like `\"`.

For instance, to specify the following string in Julia:

```
"Don't move!" he commanded.
```

we must write this:

```
"\"Don't move!\" he commanded."
```

With `getString`, we would be able to supply it like this:

```
$"Don't move!" he commanded.$
```

or

```
%"Don't move!" he commanded.%
```

or using any other character as a delimiter, provided it is not one of the characters in the string. We could even use something like this:

```
7"Don't move!" he commanded."7
```

However, we normally use special characters like `"`, `$`, `%` or `#` as delimiters.

We will write `getString` with one parameter: a file designated by `inn`. The function will read and return the next string from `inn`.

The function assumes that the first non-whitespace character met (`delim`, say) is the delimiter. Characters are read and stored until `delim` is met again, indicating the end of the string. The delimiter characters are not stored since they are not part of the string.

Given the data above, we would be able to read it like this:

```
name = getString(inn) # would store Margaret Dwarika in name
jobtitle = getString(inn) # would store Managing Director in jobtitle
```

We would get the same result even if the data was supplied like this:

```
*Margaret Dwarika*      +Managing Director+
```

Here is getString:

```
function getString(inn::IOStream)
# Return the next string within delimiters.
# Delimiter is the first non-whitespace character encountered
    str = ""; ch = ' '
    while !eof(inn) && isspace(ch)
        ch = read(inn, Char)  # get another character
    end
    if eof(inn) return str end
    delim = ch

    while !eof(inn) && ((ch=read(inn, Char)) != delim)
        str *= ch
    end
    return str
end # getString
```

Comments on getString

- The predefined function isspace returns true if its argument is a space, tab or newline and false, otherwise.
- If getString encounters end-of-file before finding a non-whitespace character (the delimiter), the empty string is returned. Otherwise, it builds the string by reading one character at a time; the string is terminated by the next occurrence of the delimiter or end-of-file, whichever comes first.
- We can read a string from the standard input (the keyboard) by calling getString with stdin as the argument.

6.18 Example - Geography Quiz Program

Let us write a program which quizzes a user on countries and their capitals. The program will illustrate some useful programming concepts like reading from the keyboard *and* a file and being very flexible in terms of user input. The following is a sample run of the program, indicating how we want the finished program to work. The user is given two tries at a question. If she gets it wrong both times, the program tells her the correct answer.

```
What is the capital of Trinidad? Tobago
Wrong. Try again.

What is the capital of Trinidad? Port of Spain
Correct!

What is the capital of Jamaica? Kingston
Correct!

What is the capital of Grenada? Georgetown
Wrong. Try again.

What is the capital of Grenada? Castries
Wrong. Answer is St. George's
```

We will store the names of the countries and their capitals in a file (quizdata.txt, say). For each country, we will store its name and its capital. The following shows some sample data:

```
"Trinidad" "Port of Spain"
"Jamaica" "Kingston"
"Grenada" "St. George's"
```

In the program, we will convert the capital to a string consisting of the letters only in the capital, all converted to uppercase. For instance, we will convert Port of Spain to PORTOFSPAIN.

This will enable users to type their answers with a lot of flexibility. For instance, Port of Spain, port of spain and portof Spain will all be converted to the same answer, PORTOFSPAIN.

We can use any character to delimit a string, provided it is not a character in the string. And we can use different delimiters for different strings. It is perfectly okay to supply the above data as follows:

```
"Trinidad" $Port of Spain$
%Jamaica% "Kingston"
$Grenada$ %St. George's%
```

We can do this because of the flexibility of getString. We will use getString to read strings from the file and readline to get the user's answers typed at the keyboard.

Suppose a country's data are read into the variables country and capital. The letters only from capital are converted to uppercase and stored in CAPITAL. (Remember, in Julia, capital is a different variable from CAPITAL). When the user types an answer (answer, say), it must be compared with capital. Suppose we use a straightforward comparison like this to check if answer is the same as capital:

```
if answer == capital ...
```

Answers like "Portof Spain", "port of spain", " Port ofSpain" and "st georges" would all be considered wrong. If we want these answers to be correct (and we probably should) we must convert all user answers to a common format before comparing.

We take the view that as long as all the letters are there, in the correct order, regardless of case, the answer is correct. When the user types an answer, we ignore spaces and punctuation and convert *the letters only* to uppercase. This is then compared with CAPITAL. For example, the answers above would be converted to "PORTOFSPAIN" and "STGEORGES" and would elicit a "Correct!" response.

Earlier, we wrote a function lettersOnlyLower which kept the letters only from a string and converted them to lowercase. Here, we want a similar function but we convert to uppercase instead. We name the function lettersOnlyUpper. The code is identical to lettersOnlyLower except that lowercase is replaced by uppercase. Our test for correctness now becomes this:

```
ANSWER = lettersOnlyUpper(answer)
if ANSWER == CAPITAL
    println("Correct!")
```

All the details are captured in Program P6.12.

Program P6.12 - Geography Quiz

```
function getString(inn::IOStream)
# Return the next string within delimiters. Delimiter is first non-whitespace
    str = ""; ch = ' '
    while !eof(inn) && isspace(ch)
        ch = read(inn, Char)  # get another character
    end
    if eof(inn) return str end
    delim = ch
```

```
        while !eof(inn) && ((ch=read(inn, Char)) != delim)
            str *= ch
        end
        return str
    end # getString

    function lettersOnlyUpper(phrase)
    # Return a string with the letters only, all converted to uppercase
    word = ""
    for ch in phrase
        if isletter(ch)
            word *= uppercase(ch) # add this letter to word
            end
        end
        return word
    end # lettersOnlyUpper

    function askOneQuestion(country, capital)
        CAPITAL = lettersOnlyUpper(capital)
        print("\nWhat is the capital of $country? ")
        answer = readline()
        ANSWER = lettersOnlyUpper(answer)
        if ANSWER == CAPITAL
            println("Correct!")
        else
            println("Wrong. Try again")
            print("\nWhat is the capital of $country? ")
            answer = readline()
            ANSWER = lettersOnlyUpper(answer)
            if ANSWER == CAPITAL
                println("Correct!")
            else
                println("Wrong. Answer is $capital")
            end
        end
    end # askOneQuestion

    function main(dataFile)
        if !isfile(dataFile)           # does file exist?
            println("Data file not found")
            exit(1)
        end
        inn = open(dataFile, "r")
        while (country = getString(inn)) != ""
            capital = getString(inn)
            askOneQuestion(country, capital)
        end
        close(inn)
    end # main

    main("quizdata.txt")
```

6.19 Other String Functions

We discuss five functions that can be useful when working with strings: findfirst, findlast, findnext, findprev and occursin.

6.19.1 findfirst

findfirst(c::Char, str::String)

Find the first occurrence of c in str. If found return its index, else return nothing.

```julia
julia> findfirst('a', "La Isla Bonita")
2

julia> findfirst('B', "La Isla Bonita")
9

julia> findfirst('b', "La Isla Bonita")

julia>
```

The last case is a little disconcerting because there's no feedback and you wonder what was the answer. All you see is the cryptic julia> prompt. It would be nice if Julia returned *something* (0 or -1, perhaps?) to indicate the character wasn't found.

To be fair, though, Julia does return the keyword nothing but doesn't indicate this in the REPL. However, one can test for it like this:

```julia
julia> findfirst('b', "La Isla Bonita") == nothing
true
```

We can also search a substring of str like this:

```julia
julia> lib = "La Isla Bonita";

julia> findfirst('a', lib[3:end])  # search from index 3 to the end
5
```

The answer 5 is obtained; we start counting from 1 at index 3, the beginning of the substring.

If we want to find the next a starting from B, we can write this:

```julia
julia> findfirst('a', lib[findfirst('B', lib):end])
6
```

findfirst('B', lib) returns 9 since B is at lib[9]. We then look in lib[9:end], that is, Bonita for a; it is found at position 6.

findfirst(p::String, str::String)

Find the first occurrence of the pattern p in the string str. If found, return its *index range*, else return nothing.

The first argument is a String, even a 1-character string, as we see in this example:

```julia
julia> lib = "La Isla Bonita";

julia> findfirst("a", lib)
2:2
```

Here, findfirst finds the String "a" at lib[2:2]. Note that a *substring* is specified with two indices, a *from* index and a *to* index; so "a" was found from index 2 to index 2. Other examples:

```julia
julia> findfirst("sla", lib)    # "sla" found from lib[5] to lib[7]
5:7

julia> findfirst("it", lib)     # "it" found from lib[12] to lib[13]
12:13

julia> findfirst("nip", lib)    # returns nothing, meaning "not found"
julia>
```

6.19.2 findlast

findlast(c::Char, str::String)

Find the last occurrence of c in str. If found, return its index, else return nothing.

```
julia> findlast('a', "La Isla Bonita")
14
julia> findlast('s', "La Isla Bonita")
5
julia> findlast('b', "La Isla Bonita") # 'b' not found
julia>
julia> findlast('b', "La Isla Bonita") == nothing
true
```

findlast(p::String, str::String)

Find the last occurrence of the pattern p in the string str. If found, return its *index range*, else return nothing.

```
julia> findlast("a", "La Isla Bonita")
14:14
julia> findlast("it", "La Isla Bonita")
12:13
julia> findlast("bra", "Abracadabra")
9:11
julia> findlast("ajj", "Ajji majji la tarajji")
18:20
julia> findlast("bro", "Abracadabra") # returns nothing
julia>
```

6.19.3 findnext

findnext(c::Char, str::String, n::Int)

Find the next occurrence of c in str, starting from str[n]. If found, return its index in str, else return nothing. The index returned is the *absolute index* in str, not relative to where you started the search.

```
julia> spell = "Abracadabra"
"Abracadabra"
 123456789    (the position in the string)
julia> findnext('b', spell, 1)  # start search at 1; 'b' found at 2
2
julia> findnext('b', spell, 2)  # start search at 2; 'b' found at 2
2
julia> findnext('b', spell, 7)  # start search at 7; 'b' found at 9
9
julia> findnext('c', spell, 5)  # start search at 5; 'c' found at 5
5
julia> findnext('c', spell, 6)  # start search at 6; 'c' not found; return
nothing
julia>
```

findnext can find the next occurrence of a character starting at some given index. But what if we want to find *all* occurrences of a given character. We can do this as follows:

```
function findall(ch::Char, str::String)
# print the indices of all occurrences of ch in str
    k = 1
    while (n = findnext(ch, str, k)) != nothing
        println(n)
        k = n + 1     # move to the index after the one just found
    end
    println("End of list")
end # findall
```

When called with this:

```
findall('p', "hippopotamus")
```

the function prints this:

```
3
4
6
End of list
```

findnext(p::String, str::String, n::Int)

Find the next occurrence of the pattern p in a string str, starting from str[n]. If found, return its *index range* in str, else return nothing. The index range returned is the *absolute index range* in str, not relative to where you started the search.

```
julia> spell = "Abracadabra"
"Abracadabra"
 123456789    (the position in the string)

julia> findnext("bra", spell, 1)  # start search at 1; "bra" found at 2:4
2:4

julia> findnext("bra", spell, 5)  # start search at 5; "bra" found at 9:11
9:11

julia> findnext("cada", spell, 3) # start search at 3; "cada" found at 5:8
5:8

julia> findnext("cad", spell, 6)  # start search at 6; "cad" not found; return
nothing

julia>
```

Terminology: An index range (like 2:4) is called a UnitRange in Julia. The following refers:

```
julia> n = 2:4;

julia> typeof(n)
UnitRange{Int64}

julia> n[1]
2

julia> n[2]
3

julia> n[3]
4
```

We now write a function to find *all* occurrences of a pattern p in a string str.

```
function findall(p::String, str::String)
# print the indices of all occurrences of ch in str
    k = 1
    while (n = findnext(p, str, k)) != nothing
```

```
        println(n)
        k = n[1] + length(p)  # move to the index after the one just found
    end
    println("End of list")
end # findall
```

When called with this:

```
findall("bra", "Abracadabra")
```

the function prints this:

```
2:4
9:11
End of list
```

6.19.4 findprev

findprev(c::Char, str::String, n::Int)

Find the previous occurrence of c in str, starting from str[n]. If found, return its index in str, else return nothing. The index returned is the *absolute index* in str, not relative to where you started the search.

```
julia> spell = "Abracadabra"
"Abracadabra"
 123456789    (the position in the string)

julia> findprev('b', spell, 5)
2

julia> findprev('b', spell, 7)
2

julia> findprev('b', spell, length(spell)) # start at the end
9

julia> findprev('d', spell, 5) # not found; nothing returned

julia>
```

findprev(p::String, str::String, n::Int)

Find the previous occurrence of the pattern p in a string str, starting from str[n]. If found, return its *index range* in str, else return nothing. The index range returned is the *absolute index range* in str, not relative to where you started the search.

```
julia> spell = "Abracadabra"
"Abracadabra"
 123456789    (the position in the string)

julia> findprev("bra", spell, 10)  # start at 10; "bra" found at 2:4
2:4

julia> findprev("cad", spell, 7)  # start at 7; "cad" found at 5:7
5:7

julia> findprev("ada", spell, 8)  # start at 8; "ada" found at 6:8
6:8

julia> findprev("ada", spell, 7)  # start at 7; "ada" not found; nothing
returned

julia> julia>
```

6.19.5 occursin

occursin(c::Char, str::String)

Returns `true` if `c` occurs in `str` and `false`, otherwise.

```
julia> magic = "Ajji majji la tarajji"
"Ajji majji la tarajji"

julia> occursin('m', magic)
true

julia> occursin('b', magic)
false
```

occursin(p::String, str::String)

Returns `true` if `p` is a substring of `str` and `false`, otherwise.

```
julia> occursin("tara", magic)
true

julia> occursin("zara", magic)
false
```

6.20 Array of Characters

A string is a sequence of characters enclosed in double quotes. Previously, we've used strings in various ways. We've printed them, we've entered them as input and we've extracted portions of a string to make another one. Here are some more examples of what we can do:

```
julia> st = "Save The Last Dance For Me"
julia> length(st)   # number of characters
26
julia> sizeof(st)   # same as length since each char occupies 1 byte
26
julia> st[1] * st[end] * st[(end+1)÷2]
"Set"
```

One thing we cannot do is change individual characters in a string—strings are *immutable*.

We now discuss some other characteristics of strings. Since we're assuming that all the characters in our string are ASCII, its length (number of characters in it) is the same as its size (number of bytes needed to store it).

Given a string `st`, we can access individual characters by supplying a subscript: `st[1]` is the first, `st[end]` is the last and `st[(end+1)÷2]` is the one in the middle. In general, `st[n]` refers to the character in the nth position.

Even though strings are immutable, Julia provides functions which allow us to perform operations on a string that we can't do directly.

The first is `collect`. Among other roles, `collect` takes a string and converts it to an *array of characters*. For example, the following creates an array `sta` with 4 elements, each being one letter of the word `Save`.

```
julia> sta = collect("Save")
4-element Array{Char,1}:
 'S': ASCII/Unicode U+0053 (category Lu: Letter, uppercase)
 'a': ASCII/Unicode U+0061 (category Ll: Letter, lowercase)
 'v': ASCII/Unicode U+0076 (category Ll: Letter, lowercase)
 'e': ASCII/Unicode U+0065 (category Ll: Letter, lowercase)
```

As we see, sta is a Char array; sta[1] is 'S', sta[2] is 'a', sta[3] is 'v' and sta[4] is 'e'.

The big difference between sta and st is we can *change* the value of any element of sta by *assigning* a new value to it. For example,

```julia
julia> sta[1] = 'C';
julia> println(sta)
['C', 'a', 'v', 'e']

julia> sta[3] = 'r';
julia> println(sta)
['C', 'a', 'r', 'e']
```

With the array, not only can we change individual characters, we can also insert/delete a character at/from any given index. Here, we insert a letter at index 2 using **insert!**:

```julia
julia> sta = collect("Save");
julia> insert!(sta, 2, 'h');   # insert 'h' at index 2 in sta
julia> println(sta)
['S', 'h', 'a', 'v', 'e']
```

Next, using **deleteat!**, we delete the letter we inserted (or any other):

```julia
julia> deleteat!(sta, 2);   # delete character at index 2 in sta
julia> println(sta)
['S', 'a', 'v', 'e']
```

What if we want to insert a character *after* the last one? If we *know* the last index of sta is 4, we can insert the new character at index 5. If we don't know the size, we can use lastindex, like this:

```julia
julia> insert!(sta, lastindex(sta)+1, 'd');
# we must use +1; if we insert 'd' at index 4, 'e' will move to 5
julia> println(sta)
['S', 'a', 'v', 'e', 'd']
```

To delete the last character, we can use this:

```julia
julia> deleteat!(sta, lastindex(sta));
julia> println(sta)
['S', 'a', 'v', 'e']
```

Suppose after working with sta, we end up with this:

```julia
julia> println(sta)
['S', 'h', 'a', 'r', 'e', 'd']
```

We can now convert it back into a String with **join**:

```julia
julia> st = join(sta)
"Shared"
julia> typeof(st)
String
```

To emphasize, a *string* is a sequence of characters and an *array* is a sequence of values, but we can manipulate an array of characters more flexibly than we can a string. However, we can easily convert a string to an array and vice versa, so we can choose the format that best suits our purpose in any given situation.

Tip: collect converts a String to a Char array; join converts a Char array to a String.

6.21 For the Curious Reader

Advice: This section may be omitted at a first reading. It is included as a challenge to the adventurous and curious student.

In the world of ASCII characters, life is straightforward. Each character occupies exactly one byte. We have this:

```
julia> length("The King and I")
14
julia> sizeof("The King and I")
14
```

The *length* of a string (number of *characters* in it) and its *size* (amount of storage needed to store it, in bytes) are the same.

But it's not so straightforward with characters in other languages (Greek, Indian, Chinese, Japanese, Korean, to name a few). In the Greek alphabet, for instance, each character is two bytes long; *one* character, *two* bytes. To illustrate:

```
julia> length("αβθ")
3

julia> sizeof("αβθ")
6
```

Moral: Except for ASCII, the *length* of a string is not necessarily the same as its *size*.

To further complicate matters, some characters occupy three bytes. The symbols ∀ (for all) and ∃ (there exists) occupy three bytes each.

```
julia> length("∀ ∃")        # three characters; count the space
3

julia> sizeof("∀ ∃")        # one byte for the space; 3 each for ∀, ∃
7
```

Understanding the difference between *length* and *size* is key to what follows.

String indices in Julia refer to *code units* (think *bytes*), the fixed-width building blocks that are used to encode arbitrary characters. This means that not every index into a `String` is necessarily a valid index for a character. If you index into a string at an invalid byte index, you will get a `StringIndexError`.

Consider the following:

```
julia> grk = "β+θ"
"β+θ"
julia> length(grk)
3
julia> sizeof(grk)
5
```

Since β and θ occupy two bytes each, the *valid* indices into `grk` are 1 (β), 3 (+) and 4 (θ). If we try to access `grk[2]` or `grk[5]`, we will get an error:

```
julia> print(grk[2])
ERROR: StringIndexError("β+θ", 2)
```

However, there's no problem with these:

```
julia> print(grk[1])
β
```

```
julia> print(grk[3])
+
julia> print(grk[4])
θ
```

You might be tempted to ask, do I have to remember the length of each character I may want to use? And if I have a string containing English letters, Greek letters and mathematical symbols, how do I tell which indices are valid and which are not? Well, you're in luck since Julia provides a number of functions for working with arbitrary strings.

The most common are: `firstindex`, `lastindex`, `nextind`, `prevind`, `eachindex`. (The inconsistency in naming these functions—some with `index` and some with `ind`—is mildly annoying, to say the least. Couldn't find the rationale for it.) We use the following in our examples:

```
julia> str = "β+θ=∀"    # valid indices are 1, 3, 4, 6, 7
"β+θ=∀"
julia> length(str)
5
julia> sizeof(str)
9
```

firstindex(str)

Return the index of the first byte of the first character. In most cases, this is 1. (For those of us who need it, Julia provides us with the flexibility to define arrays that start with an *arbitrary* index. For these situations, `firstindex` would be more useful; however, this topic is beyond the scope of this book.)

lastindex(str)

Return the index of the *first* byte of the last character. Here it returns 7 since ∀ is the last character and occupies `str[7:9]`.

nextind(str, n)

Return the index of the *first* byte of the *next* valid character following byte n. Here, we have this:

```
julia> nextind(str, 1)
3
julia> nextind(str, 2)    # valid call even though 2 is not a valid index
3
julia> nextind(str, 3)
4

julia> nextind(str, 4)
6
julia> nextind(str, 6)
7
julia> nextind(str, 7)
10
# there is no 'next' character but it would start at 10 if there was one;
# since there is none, attempting to access str[10] would give a BoundsError
```

prevind(str, n)

If n is the index of a *valid* character, return the index of the *first* byte of the *preceding* character. If n is *not* a valid index, return the index of the *first* byte of the character to which byte n belongs. Recall our sample string:

```
julia> str = "β+θ=∀"  # valid indices are 1, 3, 4, 6, 7
```

We have this:

```
julia> prevind(str, 6)
4
```

6 is a valid index; the preceding valid index is 4.

```
julia> prevind(str, 5)
4
```

5 is *not* a valid index; it is the second byte of θ, which occupies str[4] and str[5]. The valid index to which str[5] belongs is 4.

As another example, we have this:

```
julia> prevind(str, 9)    # ∀ occupies str[7] to str[9]
7
```

Observe this:

```
julia> prevind(str, 1)
0
```

The index previous to 1 is 0 but keep in mind there is no character at index 0. Trying to access str[0] will give a BoundsError.

eachindex(str)

We can use eachindex(str) to iterate over the valid indices of str. We can print them:

```
julia> for i in eachindex(str) println(i) end
1
3
4
6
7
```

To be more useful, we can use collect to return these indices in an array:

```
julia> strind = collect(eachindex(str));

julia> print(strind)
[1, 3, 4, 6, 7]
```

strind[i] refers to the starting byte number of the ith character.

With strind, we can access the elements of str in a seamless manner without having to worry about, or needing to know, the size of each character. We don't even need to know how many characters are in str (but we can with length(str)) since strind[end] will give us the index of the last character.

We show two ways to print the characters of the string str="β+θ=∀". The most direct is this:

```
julia> for c in str println(c) end
β
+
θ
=
∀
```

The next is indirect, using strind, but may give you more flexibility in some situations:

```
julia> for i in strind println(str[i]) end
β
+
θ
=
∀
```

Note that str[end] and str[strind[end]] give us the last character of str:

```
julia> str[end]
'∀'

julia> str[strind[end]]
'∀'
```

thisind(str, i)

Given an index i into a string str, find the *start index* of the character to which str[i] belongs.

Consider, again, this:

```
julia> str = "β+θ=∀"  # valid indices are 1, 3, 4, 6, 7
```

What is the value of thisind(str, 2)? We first ask *to which character does* str[2] *belong*? β occupies str[1] and str[2], so str[2] belongs to β; its *start index* is 1 so 1 is the answer.

What is thisind(str, 9)? We first ask *to which character does* str[9] *belong*? ∀ occupies str[7] to str[9], so str[9] belongs to ∀; its *start index* is 7 so 7 is the answer.

By the same token, we have these:

```
julia> thisind(str, 3)
3
julia> thisind(str, 4)
4
julia> thisind(str, 5)
4
julia> thisind(str, 6)
6
```

```
julia> thisind(str, 7)
7
julia> thisind(str, 8)
7
```

Caution: Extraction of a substring using *range indexing* also expects valid byte indices or an error is thrown.

We illustrate with our earlier example:

```
julia> str = "β+θ=∀"  # valid indices are 1, 3, 4, 6, 7
```

Suppose we attempt to extract this substring: str[lo:hi]

lo and hi *must* take on values from the set 1, 3, 4, 6, 7; any other value will throw an error.

Examples:

```
julia> str[1:4]
"β+θ"

julia> str[4:6]
"θ="

julia> str[4:7]
"θ=∀"

julia> str[4:8]     # error since 8 is an invalid index
ERROR: StringIndexError("β+θ=∀", 8)

julia> str[7:9]   # error - 9 is an invalid index; even though 7:9 contains ∀
ERROR: StringIndexError("β+θ=∀", 9)

julia> str[7:7]   # this is how to access the substring "∀"
"∀"
```

Using the functions just discussed, you can write your programs making no assumptions about any underlying character set. They will work for all.

EXERCISES 6

1. Give the range of ASCII codes for the (a) digits (b) uppercase letters (c) lowercase letters.

2. How is the single quote represented as a character constant?

3. What is the character value of a character constant?

4. What is the numeric value of a character constant?

5. How is the expression `5 + 'T'` evaluated? What is its value?

6. What character is stored in `ch` by `ch = 4 + 'n'`?

7. If `ch = '8'`, what value is assigned to `d` by `d = ch - '0'`?

8. If `ch` contains an uppercase letter, explain how to change `ch` to its lowercase equivalent.

9. If `ch` contains a lowercase letter, explain how to change `ch` to its uppercase equivalent.

10. Write a program to read a line of data and print the first digit on the line.

11. Write a program to read a line of data and print the first letter on the line.

12. Write a program to read a line of data and print the number of digits and letters on the line.

13. Write a program to read a passage from a file and print how many times each vowel appears.

14. Write a function which, given a string of arbitrary characters, returns the number of consonants in the string.

15. Modify Program P6.8 so it will find negative integers as well. (Caution: A minus sign by itself is not an integer.)

16. Write a program which reads a file containing a Julia program and outputs the program to another file with all the # comments removed.

    Write a program to read the data, character by character, and store the next number (with or without a decimal point) in a `Float64` variable (`fv`, say). For example, given the following data, your program should store `43.75` in `fv`.

    ```
    Mary works for $43.75 per hour
    ```

17. Someone has typed a letter in a file `letter.txt`, but does not always start the word after a period with a capital letter. Write a program to copy the file to another file `format.txt` so that all words after a period now begin with a capital letter. Also ensure there is exactly one space after each period. For example, the text

    ```
    Things are fine.    we can see you now.        let us know when is a good
    time.  bye for now.
    ```

    must be re-written as

    ```
    Things are fine. We can see you now. Let us know when is a good time. Bye
    for now.
    ```

CHAPTER 7

Arrays

In this chapter, we will explain the following:

- The difference between simple variable and array variable
- How to declare and store values in an array
- How to process elements of an array using a `for` loop
- How to the calculate average and differences from average of a set of numbers
- How to read the entire contents of a file as a `String`
- How to write a *Letter Frequency* program
- How to test if a file exists
- How an array is passed as an argument to a function
- How to find the sum, average of numbers stored in an array
- How to use an array to keep several counts
- How to pass an array as an argument to a function
- How to find the largest and smallest values in an array
- How to write a program to process the results of an election

7.1 Introduction

In the last chapter, we worked with strings and got a brief introduction to the notion of *arrays*. We saw that a string is a `Char` array. When we write the following, it defines `tag` (short for Rabindranth Tagore who wrote it in *Gitanjali*) as a `String` variable with the value shown:

```
tag = "Where knowledge is free"
```

To all intents and purposes, `tag` is an array of `Char` with the one proviso that it is *immutable*—we cannot change individual characters (see Section 6.12).

We can refer to an individual element of `tag` using a *subscript* inside the array brackets, [and]. So `tag[1]` is W and `tag[7]` is k. Here are some other examples:

```
julia> tag = "Where knowledge is free"
"Where knowledge is free"

julia> length(tag)
23

julia> tag[11:15]
"ledge"

julia> tag[4:5] * tag[13]
"red"

julia> tag[end-3:end-2] * tag[17] * tag[13:15]
"fridge"
```

N. Kalicharan, *Julia - Bit by Bit*, Undergraduate Topics in Computer Science, https://doi.org/10.1007/978-3-030-73936-2_7

```
julia> tag[2] * tag[17] * tag[13]*tag[13] * tag[5] * tag[8]
"hidden"
```

In this chapter, we delve deeper into the many ways we can use arrays to solve various problems.

7.2 Simple vs Array Variable

The variables we have been using so far (such as ch, n, sum, name) are normally called *simple* variables. At any given time, a simple variable can be used to store one item of data, for instance, one number or one character. Of course, the value stored in the variable can be changed, if we wish. However, there are many situations in which we wish to store a group of related items and to be able to refer to them by a common name. The *array variable* allows us to do this.

For example, suppose we wish to store a list of scores made by 42 students in a test. We can do this by inventing 42 different Int variables and storing one score in one variable. But it would be quite tedious, cumbersome, unwieldy and time-consuming to write code to manipulate these 42 variables. (Think of how you would assign values to these 42 variables.) And what if we needed to deal with 200 scores?

A better way is to use an *array* to store the 42 scores. We can think of this array as having 42 *locations*—we use one location to store one *element*, in this case, one score. To refer to a particular score, we use a *subscript*. For example, if Score is the name of the array, then Score[5] refers to the score in location 5—here 5 is used as a subscript. It is written inside square brackets, [and]. (In this book, we use the *convention* of using a capital letter to begin an array name.)

Normally, an array is used to store a list of values of the *same type*; for instance, we speak of an array of integers, an array of characters, an array of strings or an array of floating-point numbers. However, if you need it, Julia lets you store elements of *different* types in the same array.

Using an array allows us to work with a list of values in a simple, systematic way, regardless of its size. We can process all or some items using a simple loop. We can also do things like search for an item in the list or sort the list in ascending or descending order.

7.3 Array Declaration

The simplest way to declare an array variable is to assign a list of values enclosed in [and] to it:

```
julia> A = [17, 15, 19, 12]
4-element Array{Int64,1}:
 17
 15
 19
 12
```

This declares A as an integer (Int64) array with the four values shown: A[1] is 17, A[2] is 15, A[3] is 19 and A[4] is 12. The 1 after Int64 indicates 1-dimensional. In Julia, a *column* vector is considered one-dimensional.

Compare the following where we use spaces, rather than commas, to separate the numbers:

```
julia> B = [17 15 19 12]
1×4 Array{Int64,2}:
 17  15  19  12
```

This declares B as an integer (Int64) array with the four values shown: B[1] is 17, B[2] is 15, B[3] is 19 and B[4] is 12. The 2 after Int64 indicates 2-dimensional. In Julia, a *row* vector is considered two-dimensional. The phrase 1×4 Array also indicates two dimensions.

Is there a difference between A and B? No, and yes.

Both A and B can be treated as one-dimensional *flat* arrays with a single subscript. So we can talk about A[i] or B[i] where i can be 1, 2, 3 or 4. And that's what we'd do most of the time.

However, technically speaking, A is a 4×1 array and B is a 1×4 array. We illustrate with this:

```
julia> A[3]
19

julia> B[3]
19

julia> A[3,1]
19

julia> B[1,3]
19

julia> A[1,3]
ERROR: BoundsError: attempt to access 4-element Array{Int64,1} at index [1, 3]

julia> B[3,1]
ERROR: BoundsError: attempt to access 1×4 Array{Int64,2} at index [3, 1]
```

We can also think of A as a *column vector* and B as a *row vector*. The difference is important in matrix multiplication, for instance. So, yes, there is a difference but we won't be dwelling on it in this book.

Here are some other examples of arrays with elements of the same type.

The following declares C as a 4-element Char array with the initial values shown:

```
julia> C = ['f','a','t','e']
4-element Array{Char,1}:
 'f': ASCII/Unicode U+0066 (category Ll: Letter, lowercase)
 'a': ASCII/Unicode U+0061 (category Ll: Letter, lowercase)
 't': ASCII/Unicode U+0074 (category Ll: Letter, lowercase)
 'e': ASCII/Unicode U+0065 (category Ll: Letter, lowercase)
```

The following declares TF as a 4-element Bool array with the initial values shown:

```
julia> TF = [true,false,true,false]
4-element Array{Bool,1}:
 1
 0
 1
 0

julia> TF[3]
true
```

The following declares F as a 4-element Float64 array with the initial values shown:

```
julia> F = [7.2, 3.1, 9.5, 6.7]
4-element Array{Float64,1}:
 7.2
 3.1
 9.5
 6.7
```

And the following declares Y as a 4-element array with values of different types:

```
julia> Y = ["hi", 53, false, 3.14]
4-element Array{Any,1}:
 "hi"
 53
 false
 3.14
```

```
julia> Y[4]
3.14
```

Above, we specified the name of the array; its size would be deduced from what we assign to it. The arrays were all of size 4. This means their *valid* subscripts range from 1 to 4. If we attempt to access A[0] or A[5], say, we will get an *array subscript error*.

A subscript can be written using a constant (like 3), a variable (like i) or an expression (like i+1). The *value* of the subscript determines which element is being referenced.

We end this section with a more practical example. Suppose we want to store the number of days in a month during a leap year. We could use this:

```
Month = [31,29,31,30,31,30,31,31,30,31,30,31]
```

We have this:

- Month[1]=31, the number of days in January;
- Month[2]=29, the number of days in February (in a leap year);
  and so on, up to
- Month[12]=31, the number of days in December.

We can do something similar for the days of the week. This is left as an exercise.

To pursue the example, suppose we want to print the names of the months with less than 31 days. One way would be to store the names of the months in an array. Next, we loop through the array Month; if a month has less than 31 days, its name is printed. Program P7.1 shows how.

```
# Program P7.1 # Months With Less Than 31 Days
using Printf
function monthName(n::Int64)
    # Given n, return the name of the nth month
    Name = ["January","February","March","April","May","June","July",
            "August","September","October","November","December"]
    Name[n]
end # monthName

function monthsLess31()
    Month = [31,29,31,30,31,30,31,31,30,31,30,31]
    for i = 1:12
        if Month[i] < 31
            @printf("%2d - %s\n", i, monthName(i))
        end
    end
end # monthsLessThan31

monthsLess31()
```

When run, the program prints this:

```
 2 - February
 4 - April
 6 - June
 9 - September
11 - November
```

We can use declarations like the ones above if we know the *size* of the array and the *values* we want to store in it. However, most times we know only the maximum size (100, say) and want to initialize the elements to the same value (perhaps 0, the empty string or a space character). Julia makes it easy to do this, in more ways than one.

We can use the `fill` function:

```
X = fill(0,100)   # create/fill Int64 array X[1:100] with 0s; (X is 100x1)
X = fill(0.0,100) # create/fill Float64 array X[1:100] with 0s; (X is 100x1)
```

We can initialize to any value we choose:

```
X = fill(3.14,100)  # create Float64 array X[1:100]; set all elements to 3.14
```

To create an array and initialize it to zero, we can also use the `zeros` function:

```
Z = zeros(100)        # create Float64 array Z[1:100]; set all elements to 0.0
Z = zeros(Int32,100) # create Int32 array Z[1:100]; set all elements to 0
```

We can use `zeros` to create a 2-dimensional array like this:

```
Z = zeros(Int32,3,5) # create Int32 3x5 array Z; set all elements to 0
```

In general, the call `fill(v, n)` creates an array of size n and sets all elements to v. The *type* of v determines the type of the array. If v is `1`, it's an `Int` array; if v is `1.0`, it's a `Float` array; if v is `""`, it's a `String` array.

We can use `fill` to create a 2-dimensional array, like this:

```
julia> A = fill(3.14, 2, 3)
2×3 Array{Float64,2}:
 3.14  3.14  3.14
 3.14  3.14  3.14

julia> B = fill(99, 3, 5)
3×5 Array{Int64,2}:
 99  99  99  99  99
 99  99  99  99  99
 99  99  99  99  99
```

In general, `fill(v, m, n)` creates an m×n array and sets all elements to v. The *type* of v determines the type of the array.

We've shown how to declare an array of a specific size and fill it with specific values. However, there are times when all we know is the maximum amount of items we *may* get but their values are will be supplied at some later time, such as when the program is run.

For example, we may need to store the scores obtained in a test by students in a class. All we know is the maximum size of the class. The actual size of a given class can be less than this maximum. And the scores will be known only at some later time when the test is given.

In these cases, we can use this declaration, assuming there are ≤ 40 students in a class:

```
Score = Array{Int64,1}(undef,40)
```

Tip: `Array{Int64}` is the same as `Array{Int64, 1}`

This declares an array `Score[1:40]` with *undefined* values. That just means we can make no assumptions about the values `Score` contains. For example:

```
julia> Score = Array{Int,1}(undef,4)
4-element Array{Int64,1}:
 219406560
 377160880
 217139856
 312594480
```

As you can see, the array is filled with random, *nonsense* values; we use the term *undefined*.

We can picture `Score` as follows. We leave the locations blank to indicate we haven't stored anything there as yet.

	Score[1]
	Score[2]
. . .	
. . .	
	Score[39]
	Score[40]

To give another example, suppose we need to store the item numbers (integers) and prices (floating-point numbers) of 100 items.

We can use one array (`Item`, say) to hold the item numbers and another array (`Price`, say) to hold the prices. These can be declared like this:

```
Item  = Array{Int64,1}(undef,100)
Price = Array{Float64,1}(undef,100)
```

The elements of `Item` range from `Item[1]` to `Item[100]` and the elements of `Price` range from `Price[1]` to `Price[100]`. When we store values in these arrays (see next), we will ensure that

`Price[1]` holds the price of `Item[1]`;
`Price[2]` holds the price of `Item[2]`;

and, in general,

`Price[i]` holds the price of `Item[i]`.

7.4 Store Values in an Array

Consider the array `Score`. If we wish, we could set selected elements to specific values, like this:

```
Score[3] = 56
Score[7] = 81
```

But what if we wish to set the 40 locations to 40 scores? Would we have to write 40 statements like these?

```
Score[1] = 45
Score[2] = 63
Score[3] = 39
.
Score[40] = 78
```

This is certainly one way of doing the job, but it is very tedious, time-consuming and inflexible. A neater way is to let the subscript be a *variable* rather than a *constant*. For example, `Score[h]` can be used to refer to the score in location h; the specific score depends on the value of h. If the value of h is 37, then `Score[h]` refers to `Score[37]`, the score in location 37.

Note that `Score[h]` can be used to refer to another score simply by changing the value of h, but, at any one time, `Score[h]` refers to one specific score, determined by the current value of h.

Suppose the 40 scores are stored in a file `scores.txt`, one per line. The following code will read and store them in the array `score`:

```
Score = Array{Int64}(undef,40)
inn = open("scores.txt", "r")
for h = 1 : 40
    Score[h] = parse(Int64,readline(inn))
end
```

Suppose the file `scores.txt` begins with the following data:

```
45
63
39
...
```

The `for` loop is executed with the value of h ranging from 1 to 40:

- When h is 1, the first score, 45, is read and stored in `Score[1]`;
- When h is 2, the second score, 63, is read and stored in `Score[2]`;
- When h is 3, the third score, 39, is read and stored in `Score[3]`;

and so on, up to

- When h is 40, the 40th score is read and stored in `Score[40]`.

This method is much more concise than writing 40 assignment statements. We use one statement

```
Score[h] = parse(Int64,readline(inn))
```

to store the scores in 40 different locations. This is achieved by varying the value of the *subscript*, h. This method is also more flexible.

If we had to deal with 200 scores, we need only change 40 to 200 in the declaration of `score` and in the `for` statement (and supply the 200 scores in the data file). The previous method would require us to write 200 assignment statements.

If we want to print the scores as they are read, we could write the `for` loop like this:

```
for h = 1 : 40
    Score[h] = parse(Int64,readline(inn))
    println(Score[h])
end
```

On the other hand, if we want to print the scores *after* they are read and stored in the array, we could write *another* `for` loop:

```
for h = 1 : 40
    println(Score[h])
end
```

We have used the same loop variable h that was used to read the scores. But it is not required that we do so. Any other loop variable would have the same effect. For instance, we could write this:

```
for i = 1 : 40
    println(Score[i])
end
```

What's important is the *value* of the subscript, *not the variable* that is used as the subscript.

It should be noted that even though we have declared `score` to be of size 40, it is not required that we use all the elements. For example, suppose we want to set just the first 20 elements of `score` to 0, we could do this with the following:

```
for i = 1 : 20
    Score[i] = 0
end
```

This sets elements Score[1], Score[2], Score[3], up to Score[20] to 0. Elements Score[21] to Score[40] remain undefined.

We could accomplish the same thing with fill:

```
Score[1:20] = fill(0, 20) #Store 20 0s in the 20 locations on the left hand side
```

Observe that we could specify the *portion* of the array to be filled on the left hand side. To store the number 99 in Score[25:30] (six locations), we could use this:

```
Score[25:30] = fill(99, 6)
```

The number of locations on the left *must match* the amount specified in fill.

We illustrate with a smaller array, Num[1:4].

```
julia> Num = Array{Int64}(undef,4)
4-element Array{Int64,1}:
 217238192
 311796208
 311475648
 312134144

julia> Num[1:2] = fill(0, 2)
2-element Array{Int64,1}:
 0
 0

julia> Num
4-element Array{Int64,1}:
         0
         0
 311475648
 312134144
```

The first two elements are set to 0; the others remain undefined.

Above, we explained the traditional method of reading a set of numbers from a file. We also assumed the numbers were supplied one per line. Now we show you a few of the many options Julia provides for reading the same data.

First, we introduce read which lets us read the entire contents of a file as a String.

```
txtfile = read("scores.txt", String)
```

If we had opened the file with this;

```
inn = open("scores.txt", "r")
```

we could read it with

```
Txtfile = read(inn, String)
```

Either way, Txtfile now contains the contents of the file as a String. There is no line structure in the string. However end-of-line characters are read and stored just as ordinary characters.

Suppose scores.txt contains this (one number per line):

```
9
4
7
2
```

After the read statement, Txtfile contains this:

```
"9\r\n4\r\n7\r\n2\r\n"
```

(Recall that, on Windows, a line is terminated with \r\n; on Linux and MacOS, \n alone is used.)

Recall also that \r, \n and the space character are all considered *whitespace* which Julia treats as *separators* in looking for a number. If we replace all separators by a single space, we end up with this:

```
"9 4 7 2 "
```

Next, suppose `scores.txt` contains this (all on one line):

```
9 4 7 2
```

After the read statement, `Txtfile` contains this:

```
"9 4 7 2\r\n"
```

If we replace all separators by a single space, we end up with this:

```
"9 4 7 2 "
```

This is the same as what we obtained above when the data was entered one per line.

To give one more example, suppose `scores.txt` contains this (two per line):

```
9 4
7 2
```

After the read statement, `Txtfile` contains this:

```
"9 4\r\n7 2\r\n"
```

If we replace all separators by a single space, we end up with this:

```
"9 4 7 2 "
```

In all cases, except for whitespace, the result is the same. What this means is, we can have great flexibility in *how* we supply this data: one per line, all on one line, two per line, or any other combination (like 3 on the first line and 1 on the second).

With the data in the *string* `Txtfile`, we can extract the numbers with `parse`, put them in an array, and call the array `Num`, with this:

```
Num = [parse(Int64, x) for x in split(Txtfile)]
```

Julia can tell us what kind of variable `Num` is:

```
julia> Num
4-element Array{Int64,1}:
 9
 4
 7
 2
```

If we so desired, we could do it all in one statement:

```
Num = [parse(Int64, ns) for ns in split(read("scores.txt", String))]
```

This one statement does all of the following:

- Reads the contents of the file `scores.txt` as one (long) string. (We assume the file contains numbers in free format, any amount, or different amounts, per line.)
- `split` extracts the individual numbers, each as a string `ns`.
- `parse` converts each `ns` from string to `Int64`.
- The numbers are stored in an array `Num` in the order in which they were converted.
- We have `Num[1]=9`, `Num[2]=4`, `Num[3]=7`, `Num[4]=2`.
- The amount of numbers supplied determines the value of `lastindex(Num)`; here it is 4.

7.5 Average and Differences from Average

Consider the problem of finding the average of a set of numbers (integers) and the amount by which each number differs from the average. In order to find the average, we need to know all the numbers. In Section 4.9.2, we saw how to find the average by reading and storing one number at a time. Each new number read replaced the previous one. At the end, we could calculate the average but we've lost all the numbers (except the last one).

Now, if we also want to know how much each number differs from the average, we would need to save the original numbers so that they are available after the average is calculated. We will store them in an array. The program will be based on the following assumptions:

- The numbers will be stored in a file, input.txt.
- Any amount can be supplied.
- They can be supplied in *free format*, any amount per line.

Suppose input.txt contains this:

```
2 7
5 3
```

The following shows the expected output:

```
4 number(s) supplied
Sum is 17
Average is 4.25

Numbers and differences from average
   2  -2.25
   7   2.75
   5   0.75
   3  -1.25
```

Program P7.2 shows one way of solving this problem.

```
# Program P7.2 - Average and Difference from Average
# Find average and difference from average of numbers in a file
using Printf

function averageDiff()
    Num = [parse(Int64, ns) for ns in split(read("input.txt", String))]
    n = lastindex(Num)    # amount of numbers
    if n == 0
        println("No numbers supplied")
        return
    end

    println("$n number(s) supplied")
    total = sum(Num)       # returns sum of elements in array
    println("Sum is $total")
    average = round(total/n,digits=2)
    @printf("Average is %0.2f\n", average)

    println("\nNumbers and differences from average")
    for h = 1 : n
        @printf("%4d %6.2f\n", Num[h], Num[h]-average)
    end
end # averageDiff

averageDiff()
```

As explained above, after the first statement is executed, the array `Num[1:n]` contains the `n` numbers supplied.

The following uses the standard function `sum` to find the sum of the numbers in the array:

```
total = sum(Num)
```

Using `total` and `n`, we calculate the average. We then step through the array, printing the amount by which each number differs from the average. A sample run was shown above.

Tip: Julia provides many statistical functions, among them `mean` (average), `var` (variance) and `std` (standard deviation). To use them, you must precede your code with `using Statistics`, like this:

```
julia> using Statistics

julia> mean([3,5,7])
5.0

julia> var([3,5,7])
4.0

julia> std([3,5,7])
2.0
```

You can also pass an array variable (with numbers) as an argument to these functions.

```
julia> A=[3,5,7,10];
julia> mean(A)
6.25
```

7.6 Letter Frequency

In this example, we want to determine the frequency with which each letter of the alphabet is used in a given passage. For instance, this is the basis used to determine the *value* of each letter in the game of *Scrabble*. Letters which appear in fewer words are worth more than those which occur more frequently.

We now tackle the task of finding how frequently each letter is used in a given passage, stored in the file `passage.txt`.

We will use an integer array `Freq` to hold the frequency count of each letter: `Freq[1]` holds the count for `a`; `Freq[2]` holds the count for `b`; and so on, until `Freq[26]` holds the count for `z`. We call `fill` to set all the counts to `0`.

The file is read one character at a time. For each character `c`, `position` is called. It returns `0` if `c` is not a letter. If `c` is a letter, it returns its position `n` in the alphabet (a number from 1 to 26); `Freq[n]` is incremented by `1`. If needed, see Section 5.3.10 (Letter Position in Alphabet) for more details.

When the entire file is read, we print the results using a `for` loop. We set `ch` to each of the letters from `a` to `z`. For each letter `ch`, its position in the alphabet (`n`, say) is calculated using `ch-'a'+1`; and we print `Freq[n]`. For example, if `ch` is `'e'`, `ch-'a'+1` becomes `'e'-'a'+1`, which is `5`, the position of `e` in the alphabet.

All the details are shown in Program P7.3.

```
# Program P7.3 - Letter Frequency
using Printf
```

```
function position(ch::Char)
    # If ch is a letter, return its position in the alphabet; else return 0
    if isuppercase(ch) return ch-'A'+1 end
    if islowercase(ch) return ch-'a'+1 end
    return 0
end # position

function charFrequency(inn::IOStream)
    LettersInAlphabet = 26
    Freq = fill(0, LettersInAlphabet) # set all letter frequencies to 0
    while !eof(inn)
        n = position(read(inn, Char)) # get position of next character
        if n != 0 Freq[n] += 1 end    # if not 0, it's a letter
    end

    println("Letter Frequency\n")
    for ch = 'a' : 'z'
        @printf("%4c %8d\n", ch, Freq[ch-'a'+1])
    end
    close(inn)
end # charFrequency

inn = open("passage.txt", "r")
charFrequency(inn)
```

We ran the program with the following in `passage.txt`:

```
From Desiderata by Max Ehrmann
GO PLACIDLY amid the noise and the haste,
and remember what peace there may be in silence.
As far as possible, without surrender, be on good terms with all persons.
Speak your truth quietly and clearly; and listen to others,
even to the dull and the ignorant; they too have their story.
```

This was the output produced:

```
Letter Frequency

    a       23
    b        5
    c        4
    d       12
    e       35
    f        2
    g        3
    h       15
    i       13
    j        0
    k        1
    l       12
    m        8
    n       17
    o       17
    p        5
    q        1
    r       19
    s       16
    t       24
    u        6
    v        2
    w        3
    x        1
    y        8
    z        0
```

Does the file exist?

Consider this statement:

```
inn = open("passage.txt", "r")
```

This says to "open the file `passage.txt` for reading". It assumes the file has been created and the appropriate data stored in it. But what if the user forgot to create the file or has put it in the wrong place (the wrong folder, for instance) or misspelled the name? We will get an error message to the effect that the file cannot be found.

We can use `isfile()` to check for this:

```
if !isfile("passage.txt")
    println("File not found")
    exit(1)
end
```

The standard function `exit` is used to terminate execution of a program and return control to the operating system. It is conventional to use `exit(0)` to indicate normal termination; other arguments are used to indicate some sort of error.

The file-not-found error arises because the file was not found in the current working directory. You can find out what this is by typing `pwd()`. You might get something like this:

```
julia> pwd()
"C:\\Julia Programs"
```

Therefore, the message means that the file `C:\Julia Programs\passage.txt` does not exist. We must ensure the filename is spelt correctly *and* it is in the designated folder. Also, remember, we always have the option of specifying the complete *file path* in an `open` statement, like this:

```
inn = open("C:\\Julia Programs\\passage.txt", "r")
# within a string \ is represented by \\
```

So far, we specified the name of our file in the `open` statement. To use a different file, we would have to change the name in the statement, and re-compile the program. We can make our program more flexible if we let the user tell us the name of the file when the program is run.

We show one way to do this in P7.3 by writing a function `main`, as follows:

```
function main()
    print("Name of file? ")
    dataFile = readline()
    if !isfile(dataFile)
        println("File not found")
    else
        inn = open(dataFile, "r")
        charFrequency(inn)
    end
end
```

The following shows a sample run with a misspelled file name:

```
Name of file? pasage.txt
File not found
```

7.7 Array as Argument to a Function

In Section 5.2.1, we explained how arguments are passed to a function, and the difference between "pass by value" and "pass by reference".

As a reminder, when an argument is passed "by value", a temporary location is created with the value of the argument, and this temporary location is passed to the function. The function never has access to the original argument.

Now that we have an idea of what arrays are all about, we can explain "pass by reference" in more detail.

In Julia, *an array name denotes the address of its first element*. When we use an array name as an argument to a function, the address of the first element is passed to the function which, therefore, has access to the array. Any change the *called* function makes to the array will be known to the *calling* function. Consider this:

```julia
julia> function change(B)
          B[2] = 25
       end
change (generic function with 1 method)

julia> A = [9, 3, 7];

julia> change(A);

julia> println(A)
[9, 25, 7]
```

When called, the function change will be passed an array; it sets the second element to 25. The call change(A) passes the address of A to change where it is known as B. Any change to B is a change to A.

As written, there is nothing in the function header to indicate that the parameter B is an array. The function figures out the type of B depending on the argument with which it is called. If it is called with change(A) where A is an array, then B is an array. In fact, B is simply an alias for A.

Also, there is nothing in the function to indicate the *number of elements* in B. However, the function knows! If we attempt B[4]=31, say, we get this message:

```
ERROR: BoundsError: attempt to access 3-element Array{Int64,1} at index [4]
```

Of course, if we need to, we could use length(B) or lastindex(B) to find out how many elements B contains.

7.8 Name of Day Revisited

In Program P5.2, we wrote a function getDay which returned the name of a day, given the number of the day. The function used a host of elseif statements to get the job done. We now rewrite the function to do the same thing, using an array to store the names of the days. Here it is:

```julia
function getDay(n::Int64)
    Day =
    ["Sunday","Monday","Tuesday","Wednesday","Thursday","Friday","Saturday"]
    Day[n]
end
```

Notice how much simpler and neater this is, with just two statements. The first creates an array called Day which we can picture as follows:

Day

Sunday	Day[1]
Monday	Day[2]
Tuesday	Day[3]
Wednesday	Day[4]
Thursday	Day[5]
Friday	Day[6]
Saturday	Day[7]

The second statement, Day[n], gives the value returned by the function. If d contains a value from 1 to 7, then Day[d] contains the name of the day corresponding to d. For instance, if d is 3, Day[d] is Tuesday. Any function which calls getDay must ensure the argument supplied is a number from 1 to 7, inclusive. If not, the function will give an *array subscript* error.

7.9 Find Largest, Smallest in Array

Let us consider the problem of finding the largest of a set of values stored in an array. Suppose the integer array Num contains the following values:

Num

25	72	17	43	84	14	61
1	2	3	4	5	6	7

We can easily see that the largest number is 84 and it is in location 5. But how does a program determine this? One approach is as follows:

- Assume that the first element (the one in position 1) is the largest; we do this by setting big to 1. As we step through the array, we will use big to hold the *array index* of the largest number encountered so far; Num[big] will refer to the actual number.
- Next, starting at index 2, we look at the number in each successive location, up to 7, and compare the number with the one at index big.
- The first time, we compare Num[2] with Num[1]; since Num[2], 72, is larger than Num[1], 25, we update big to 2. This means that the largest number so far is at index 2.
- Next, we compare Num[3], 17, with Num[big] (that is, Num[2]), 72; since Num[3] is smaller than Num[2], we go on to the next number, leaving big at 2.
- Next, we compare Num[4], 43, with Num[big] (that is, Num[2]), 72; since Num[4] is smaller than Num[2], we go on to the next number, leaving big at 2.
- Next, we compare Num[5], 84, with Num[big] (that is, Num[2]), 72; since Num[5] is larger than Num[2], we update big to 5. This means that the largest number so far is at index 5.
- Next, we compare Num[6], 14, with Num[big] (that is, Num[5]), 84; since Num[6] is smaller than Num[5], we go on to the next number, leaving big at 5.
- Next, we compare Num[7], 61, with Num[big] (that is, Num[5]), 84; since Num[7] is smaller than Num[5], we go on to the next number, leaving big at 5.

- Since there is no next number, the process ends with the value of `big` being 5, the index of the largest number. The actual number is denoted by `Num[big]`; since `big` is 5, this is `Num[5]`, which is 84.

We can express the process just described by the following pseudocode:

```
big = 1
for h = 2 to 7
    if Num[h] > Num[big] big = h
endfor
print "Largest is ", Num[big], " in location ", big
```

We now write a function, `getLargest`, to find the largest value in an array. To be general, we specify which portion of the array to search for the value. This is important since, many times, we declare an array to be of some maximum size (100, say) but do not always put 100 values in the array.

When we *declare* the array to be of size 100, we are *catering* for 100 values. But, at any time, the array may have less than this amount. We use another variable (n, say) to tell us how many values are currently stored in the array. For example, if n is 36, it means that values are stored in elements 1 to 36 of the array.

When we need to find the largest, we must specify which elements of the array to search. We will write the function such that it takes three arguments—the array `Num`, and two integers `lo` and `hi`—and returns the *index* of the largest number from `Num[lo]` to `Num[hi]`, inclusive. It is up to the caller to ensure `lo` and `hi` are within the range of subscripts declared for the array.

For instance, the call

- `getLargest(Score, 1, 7)` will return the index of the largest number from `Score[1]` to `Score[7]`, inclusive; and the call
- `getLargest(Mark, 10, 20)` will return the index of the largest number from `Mark[10]` to `Mark[20]`, inclusive.

Here is the function, `getLargest` (we explain shortly why we don't specify a type for `Num`):

```
function getLargest(Num, lo::Int64, hi::Int64)
# Return the location of the biggest item from Num[lo:hi]
    big = lo
    for h = lo+1 : hi
        if Num[h] > Num[big] big = h end
    end
    big
end # getLargest
```

The function assumes the largest number is at index `lo`, the first one, by setting `big` to `lo`. In turn, it compares the numbers in locations `lo+1` up to `hi` with the number in location `big`. If a bigger one is found, `big` is updated to the location of the bigger number.

Find smallest

The function, `getLargest`, could be easily modified to find the *smallest* value in an array. Simply change `big` to `small`, say, and replace > by <, giving this:

```
function getSmallest(Num, lo::Int64, hi::Int64)
# Return the location of the smallest item from Num[lo:hi]
    small = lo
    for h = lo+1 : hi
```

```
            if Num[h] < Num[small] small = h end
      end
      small
end # getSmallest
```

This function returns the location of the smallest element from `Num[lo]` to `Num[hi]`, inclusive. Later, we will show you how to use this function to arrange a set of numbers in ascending order.

We have explained how to find the largest and smallest values in an array, assuming the values were integers. But there is nothing in the functions themselves which specify the type of values the array should contain. This means they will work for any types which can be compared using `<` and `>`. These include `char`, `Int32`, `Int64`, `Float32`, `Float64`, even `String`.

To illustrate:

```
julia> T=["gamma","beta","alpha","psi","zeta","theta","rho"];

julia> getSmallest(T,1,7)  # return the index of the smallest
3

julia> T[getSmallest(T,1,7)]
"alpha"

julia> getLargest(T,1,7)  # return the index of the largest
5

julia> T[getLargest(T,1,7)]
"zeta"
```

We have explained in some detail the *process* of finding the largest (and smallest) value in an array, so you would have an idea of what is involved. However, Julia provides standard functions to perform these tasks. We look at some of these next.

7.9.1 min, max, minimum, maximum

We use `min` and `max` to find the smallest and largest of a *list* of values. The list is enclosed in (round) parentheses.

```
julia> min(3,6,8,2)
2

julia> max(3,6,8,2)
8

julia> min("gamma","beta","alpha","psi","zeta","theta","rho")
"alpha"

julia> max("gamma","beta","alpha","psi","zeta","theta","rho")
"zeta"
```

We use `minimum` and `maximum` to find the smallest and largest of an *array* of values. The array is enclosed in square brackets.

```
julia> minimum([9,7,3,6])
3

julia> maximum([9,7,3,6])
9

julia> minimum(["gamma","beta","alpha","psi","zeta","theta","rho"])
"alpha"

julia> maximum(["gamma","beta","alpha","psi","zeta","theta","rho"])
"zeta"
```

Suppose A and B are defined like this:

```
julia> A = [15,17,19,14,11]
julia> B = ["gamma","beta","alpha","psi","zeta","theta","rho"]
```

We can find the minimum, maximum and their indexes as follows:

```
julia> minimum(A)
11

julia> argmin(A)  # the index of A which holds the minimum
5

julia> maximum(A)
19

julia> argmax(A)  # the index of A which holds the maximum
3

julia> minimum(B)
"alpha"

julia> argmin(B)
3

julia> maximum(B)
"zeta"

julia> argmax(B)
5
```

If we need both the value *and* the index, we can get them using findmin and findmax:

```
julia> findmin(A)
(11, 5)

julia> findmax(A)
(19, 3)

julia> findmin(B)
("alpha", 3)
julia> findmax(B)
("zeta", 5)
```

7.10 A Voting Problem

We now illustrate how to use some of the ideas just discussed to solve the following problem.

In an election, there are seven candidates. Each voter is allowed one vote for the candidate of his/her choice. The vote is recorded as a number from 1 to 7. The number of voters is unknown beforehand. Any vote which is not a number from 1 to 7 is an invalid (spoilt) vote.

A file, votes.txt, contains the names of the candidates. The first name is considered as candidate 1, the second as candidate 2, and so on. The names are followed by a blank line (the program will stop reading names when it hits the blank line), followed by the votes. Write a program to read the data and evaluate the results of the election. Print all output to the file, results.txt.

Your output should specify the total number of votes, the number of valid votes and the number of spoilt votes. This is followed by the votes obtained by each candidate and the winner(s) of the election.

Suppose we are given the following data in the file, `votes.txt`:

```
Victor Taylor
Denise Duncan
Kamal Ramdhan
Michael Ali
Anisa Sawh
Carol Khan
Gary Oliver

3 1 2 5 4 3 5 3 5 3 2 8 1 6 7 7 3 5
6 9 3 4 7 1 2 4 5 5 1 4
```

Our program should send the following output to the file, `results.txt`:

```
Invalid vote: 8
Invalid vote: 9

Number of voters: 30
Number of valid votes: 28
Number of spoilt votes: 2

Candidate        Score

Victor Taylor      4
Denise Duncan      3
Kamal Ramdhan      6
Michael Ali        4
Anisa Sawh         6
Carol Khan         2
Gary Oliver        3

The winner(s):
Kamal Ramdhan
Anisa Sawh
```

We need to store the names of the 7 candidates and the votes obtained by each. We will use a `String` array `Candidate` for the names of the candidates and an integer array `Vote` for the votes.

`Vote[i]` will hold the vote count for `Candidate[i]`.

To make the program flexible, we will define the following, catering for up to 10 candidates (we will see shortly how to cater for an unlimited number of candidates):

```
MaxCandidates = 10
```

The first thing the program must do is read the names. We write a function `getNames` to do this.

```
function getNames(inn, Cand)
# get the names of the candidates; count them
    n = 0
    while (name = readline(inn)) != ""
        if n < MaxCandidates
            n += 1
            Cand[n] = name
        else
            println("\nToo many candidates")
            println("Working with first $n")
        end
    end
    return n
end # getNames
```

The function reads names, one per line, until the blank line (empty string) is encountered. It keeps count. If more names than `MaxCandidates` are supplied, we *could* abort the program (with `exit(1)`, say). However, we choose to continue, ignoring the extra names, if only to illustrate how it could be done.

Next, we read and process the votes. This is handled by the function `processVotes`. We read the votes line by line. The following reads one line of votes and stores them in the array `Num`:

```
line = readline(inn)
Num = [parse(Int, x) for x in split(line)]
```

We then process each vote in `Num`. Processing vote `v` involves checking that it is valid. If it is, we add 1 to the score for candidate `v`. We process the votes with the following:

```
for v in Num
    if v < 1 || v > numCand
        println(out, "Invalid vote: $v")
        spoiltVotes += 1
    else
        Vote[v] +=1
        validVotes += 1
    end
end
```

The key statement here is

```
Vote[v] +=1
```

This is a clever way of using the vote `v` as a subscript to add 1 for the right candidate. For example, if `v` is 3, we have a vote for candidate 3, `Kamal Ramdhan`. We wish to add 1 to the vote count for candidate 3. This count is stored in `Vote[3]`. When `v` is 3, the statement becomes

```
Vote[3] +=1
```

This adds 1 to `Vote[3]`. The beauty is the same statement will add 1 for any of the candidates, depending on the value of `v`. This illustrates some of the power of using arrays. It does not matter whether there are 7 candidates or 700; the one statement will work for all.

Now that we know how to read and process the votes, it remains only to determine the winner(s) and print the results. We delegate this task to the function `printResults`.

Using the sample data, the array `vote` will contain the following values after all the votes have been tallied.

Vote

4	3	6	4	6	2	3
1	2	3	4	5	6	7

To find the winning vote, we use the standard function `maximum`, applied to the array `vote`:

```
winVote = maximum(Vote)   # returns the maximum value in vote
```

Here, `winVote` will be set to 6.

Now that we know the winning vote, we can 'step through' the array `vote`, looking for those candidates with that value. This way, we will find *all* the candidates (one or more) with the highest vote and declare them as winners. In other words, this caters for ties.

The details are given in the function `printResults` shown as part of Program P7.4, our solution to the voting problem posed at the beginning of this section.

```
# Program P7.4 - Vote Counting
MaxCandidates=10
using Printf
```

```
function getNames(inn, Cand)
# get the names of the candidates; count them
    n = 0
    while (name = readline(inn)) != ""
        if n < MaxCandidates
            n += 1
            Cand[n] = name
        else
            println("\nToo many candidates")
            println("Working with first $n")
        end
    end
    return n
end # getNames

function printResults(out, max, Name, Vote, valid, spoilt)
    println(out, "\nNumber of voters: $(valid + spoilt)")
    println(out, "Number of valid votes: $valid")
    println(out, "Number of spoilt votes: $spoilt")
    println(out, "\nCandidate        Score\n")
    for c = 1 : max
        @printf(out, "%-15s %3d\n", Name[c], Vote[c])
    end

    println(out, "\nThe winner(s)")
    winVote = maximum(Vote)  # returns the maximum value in vote
    for c = 1 : max
        if (Vote[c] == winVote) println(out, "$(Name[c])") end
    end
end # printResults

function processVotes(inn, out, numCand, Vote)
    validVotes = spoiltVotes = 0
    while (line = readline(inn)) != "" # get the data, one line at a time
        Num = [parse(Int, x) for x in split(line)] # all the numbers on one line
        for v in Num
            if v < 1 || v > numCand
                println(out, "Invalid vote: $v")
                spoiltVotes += 1
            else
                Vote[v] +=1
                validVotes += 1
            end
        end
    end # while
    validVotes, spoiltVotes # return values
end # processVotes

function main()
    inn = open("votes.txt", "r")
    out = open("results.txt", "w")

    Candidate = fill("", MaxCandidates)
    numCand = getNames(inn, Candidate)
    Vote = fill(0, numCand)

    valid, spoilt = processVotes(inn, out, numCand, Vote)

    printResults(out, numCand, Candidate, Vote, valid, spoilt)

    close(inn)
    close(out)
end # main

main()
```

7.10.1 How to Handle Any Number of Candidates

One of the drawbacks of P7.4 is that we must estimate and specify the maximum number of candidates expected. We do so by setting the value of MaxCandidates to 10. If there are more candidates, we can always reset MaxCandidates to the higher number. However, we can solve this problem more neatly by taking advantage of Julia's ability to add elements to an array.

We start by declaring candidate as a String array of length 0:

```
Candidate = Array{String}(undef,0)
```

We pass this array to getNames where it is known as Cand. Here is the new version of getNames:

```
function getNames(inn, Cand::Array{String})
# get the names of the candidates; count them
    if (aName = readline(inn)) == ""
        println("No names supplied")
        exit(1)
    end
    while aName != ""
        push!(Cand, aName)  # add name to the list
        aName = readline(inn)
    end
    return length(Cand)    # the number of candidates in the election
end # getNames
```

If the first line is empty, we assume no names are supplied and the program halts. Otherwise, we add the name to Cand. For each new name, we add an element to Cand and store the name there, using the standard Julia function push!, like this:

```
push!(Cand, aName)
```

In other words, the array Cand expands to suit the amount of names supplied. With this change, we get a more flexible program which adapts to fit the actual number of candidates in the election.

7.10.2 How to Sort the Results

Another improvement we can make is to sort the results, either by names or by votes received. Julia provides several options for sorting arrays.

First, suppose we want to print the results in alphabetical order. We would need to sort the Candidate array. But if we do, and don't adjust the Vote array accordingly, at the end, the wrong score would be associated with a given candidate.

For instance, these are the names in alphabetical order:

```
Anisa Sawh
Carol Khan
Denise Duncan
Gary Oliver
Kamal Ramdhan
Michael Ali
Victor Taylor
```

But, now, Vote[1], which is 4, is not Anisa's score. When we sort, we want to ensure a score remains with its owner. Fortunately, this is easy to do in Julia.

Consider this statement:

```
sc = sortperm(Candidate)
```

This does not rearrange the names in `Candidate` but, rather, returns a permutation of the array's indices that tells us what is the sorted order. Recall, this is `Candidate`:

```
1 Victor Taylor
2 Denise Duncan
3 Kamal Ramdhan
4 Michael Ali
5 Anisa Sawh
6 Carol Khan
7 Gary Oliver
```

The call to `sortperm` would store the following in `sc`:

```
[5, 6, 2, 7, 3, 4, 1]
```

This order of the indices gives the names in alphabetical order. So `Anisa` (5) is followed by `Carol` (6) is followed by `Denise` (2), and so on, with the last being `Victor` (1).

If we print the names in the order of the indices in `sc`, they will print in alphabetical order.

Even better, if we print the corresponding element in `Vote`, it would be *that* person's score. For example, `Candidate[5]` is `Anisa` and `Vote[5]` is her score. The following will print the results in alphabetical order:

```
println(out, "\nResults in alphabetical order")
sc = sortperm(Candidate)
for i in sc
    @printf(out, "%-15s %3d\n", Cand[i], Vote[i])
end
```

It produced the following output for the sample data:

```
Results in alphabetical order
Anisa Sawh        6
Carol Khan        2
Denise Duncan     3
Gary Oliver       3
Kamal Ramdhan     6
Michael Ali       4
Victor Taylor     4
```

Tip: If we want to sort an array `A`, we could do so as follows:

```
SA = sort(A) # A is sorted and stored in SA; A is unchanged
sort!(A)     # 'destructive' sort; this changes A to sorted order
```

Next, suppose we want to print the results from the highest votes received to the lowest. We must now sort `vote` in descending (reverse) order. We do this with the option `rev=true` in `sortperm`.

The following shows how:

```
println(out, "\nResults in descending order by score")
sv = sortperm(Vote, rev=true)
for i in sv
    @printf(out, "%-15s %3d\n", Candidate[i], Vote[i])
end
```

It produced the following output for the sample data:

```
Results in descending order by score
Kamal Ramdhan     6
Anisa Sawh        6
Victor Taylor     4
Michael Ali       4
```

```
Denise Duncan     3
Gary Oliver       3
Carol Khan        2
```

Note that ties are listed in the order the names appeared in the original array. For instance, Victor and Michael tied; Victor appears before Michael in the original array, so they retain that order in the sorted array. This is a characteristic of what is called *stable* sorting; equal items retain their original, relative order after sorting.

Sort by last name

We end this section by asking the question, how can we print the results in order by last name? That would be trivial if a name was given in the form `last, first`. But, remember, the name is given as `first last`. The problem to solve is this: given a name in the format `first last`, how do we convert it to `last, first`?

When we solve it, we would print the results like this:

```
Results sorted by last name
Ali, Michael      4
Duncan, Denise    3
Khan, Carol       2
Oliver, Gary      3
Ramdhan, Kamal    6
Sawh, Anisa       6
Taylor, Victor    4
```

The following shows how the name `"Carol Khan"` is converted to `"Khan, Carol"`.

```
julia> nm = "Carol Khan";

julia> fst, lst = split(nm)
2-element Array{SubString{String},1}:
 "Carol"
 "Khan"

julia> cnm = lst * ", " * fst
"Khan, Carol"
```

The key is to use `split` to break up the name into its two parts, then recombine them in a different order with a comma in between.

To solve our problem, we apply this technique to each element of the candidate array (called `Cand` in the function). For each name `Cand[i]`, we replace it with the reformatted name. The details are shown in the function `resultsByLastName`:

```
function resultsByLastName(out, n, Cand, Vote)
    # names in "John Smith" format; convert to "Smith, John"
    for i = 1:n
      first, last = split(Cand[i]) # separate first and last names
      Cand[i] = last*", "*first # replace Cand[i] with reformatted name
    end
    println(out, "\nResults sorted by last name")
    sc = sortperm(Cand)
    for i in sc
        @printf(out, "%-15s %3d\n", Cand[i], Vote[i])
    end
end # resultsByLastName
```

When called as follows, it prints the results shown above:

```
resultsByLastName(out, numCand, Candidate, Vote)
```

EXERCISES 7

1. Explain the difference between a simple variable and an array variable.

2. Write array declarations for each of the following: (a) a floating-point array of size 25 (b) an integer array of size 50 (c) a character array of size 32.

3. What is a subscript? Name 3 ways in which we can write a subscript.

4. What values are stored in an array when it is first declared?

5. Name 2 ways in which we can store a value in an array element.

6. You declare an array of size 500. Must you store values in all elements of the array?

7. Write code to read 200 names from a file and store them in an array.

8. An array `Num` is of size `100`. You are given two values `i` and `k`, with `1 ≤ i < k ≤ 100`. Write code to find the average of the numbers from `Num[i]` to `Num[k]`, inclusive.

9. Modify the letter frequency count program to count the number of non-letters as well. Make sure you do not count the end-of-line characters.

10. Write a function which, given an array of integers and an integer *n*, reverses the first *n* elements of the array.

11. Write a program to read names and phone numbers into two arrays. Request a name and print the person's phone number. Use at least one function.

12. The number `27472` is *palindromic* since it reads the same forwards and backwards. Write a function which, given an integer n, returns `true` if n is palindromic and `false` if it is not.

13. Write a function `substring` which, given two strings `s1` and `s2`, returns the starting position of the first occurrence of `s1` in `s2`. If `s1` is not in `s2`, return `-1`. For example, `substring("mom", "thermometer")` returns `5` but `substring("dad", "thermometer")` returns `-1`.

14. Write a function `remove` which, given a string `str` and a character `c`, removes all occurrences of `c` from `str`. For example, if `str` contains `"brother"`, `remove(str, 'r')` should return `"bothe"`.

15. Write a program to read English words and their equivalent Spanish words into two arrays. Request the user to type several English words. For each, print the equivalent Spanish word. Modify the program so that the user types Spanish words instead.

16. Write a program to find out, for a class of students, the number of families with 1, 2, 3, ... up to 8 or more children. The data consists of the number of children in each pupil's family.

17. A survey of 10 pop artists is made. Each person votes for an artist by specifying the number of the artist (a value from 1 to 10). Write a program to read the names of the artists, followed by the votes, and find out which artist is the most popular.

18. The children's game of 'count-out' is played as follows. *n* children (numbered 1 to *n*) are arranged in a circle. A sentence consisting of *m* words is used to eliminate one child at a time until one child is left. Starting at child 1, the children are counted from 1 to *m* and the *m*th child is eliminated. Starting with the child after the one just eliminated, the children are again counted from 1 to *m* and the *m*th child eliminated. This is repeated until one child is left. Counting is done circularly and eliminated children are not counted. Write a program to read values for *n* (assumed <= 100) and *m* (> 0) and print the number of the last remaining child.

19. The prime numbers from 1 to 2500 can be obtained as follows. From a list of the numbers 1 to 2500, cross out all multiples of 2 (but not 2 itself). Then, find the next number (n, say) that is not crossed out and cross out all multiples of n (but not n). Repeat this last step provided that n has not exceeded 50 (the square root of 2500). The numbers remaining in the list (except 1) are prime. Write a program which uses this method to print all primes from 1 to 2500. Store your output in a file called `primes.out`. This method is called the Sieve of Eratosthenes, named after the Greek mathematician, geographer and philosopher.

20. There are 500 light bulbs (numbered 1 to 500) arranged in a row. Initially, they are all OFF. Starting with bulb 2, all even numbered bulbs are turned ON. Next, starting with bulb 3, and visiting every third bulb, it is turned ON if it is OFF, and it is turned OFF if it is ON. This procedure is repeated for every fourth bulb, then every fifth bulb, and so on up to the 500th bulb. Write a program to determine which bulbs are OFF at the end of the above exercise.

What is special about the bulbs that are OFF? Can you explain why this is so?

CHAPTER 8

Searching, Sorting and Merging

In this chapter, we will explain the following:

- How to search a list using sequential search
- How to sort a list using selection sort
- How to sort a list using insertion sort
- How to sort a list of strings
- How to sort parallel arrays
- How to search a sorted list using binary search
- How to merge two sorted lists

8.1 Sequential Search

In many cases, an array is used for storing a list of information. Having stored the information, it may be required to find a given item in the list. For example, an array may be used to store a list of the names of 50 people. It may then be required to find the position in the list at which a given name (Indira, say) is stored.

We need to develop a technique for searching the elements of an array for a given one. Since it is possible that the given item is not in the array, our technique must also be able to determine this. The *technique* for searching for an item is the same regardless of the *type* of elements in the array. However, the *implementation* of the technique may be different for different types of elements.

We will use an integer array to illustrate the technique called *sequential search*. Consider the array Num of 7 integers:

Num

35	17	48	25	61	12	42
1	2	3	4	5	6	7

We wish to determine if the number 61 is stored. In search terminology, 61 is called the *search key* or, simply, the *key*. The search proceeds as follows:

- Compare 61 with the 1st number, Num[1], which is 35; they do not match so we move on to the next number.
- Compare 61 with the 2nd number, Num[2], which is 17; they do not match so we move on to the next number.
- Compare 61 with the 3rd number, Num[3], which is 48; they do not match so we move on to the next number.

© The Author(s), under exclusive license to Springer Nature Switzerland AG 2021
N. Kalicharan, *Julia - Bit by Bit*, Undergraduate Topics in Computer Science,
https://doi.org/10.1007/978-3-030-73936-2_8

- Compare 61 with the 4th number, Num[4], which is 25; they do not match so we move on to the next number.
- Compare 61 with the 5th number, Num[5], which is 61; they match, so the search stops and we conclude that the key is in location 5.

But what if we were looking for 32? In this case, we will compare 32 with all the numbers in the array and none will match. We conclude that 32 is not in the array.

Assuming the array contains n numbers, we can express the above logic as follows:

```
for h = 1:n
    if key == Num[h]
        key found at location h
        search is over
    endif
endfor
key not found # all numbers checked
```

We express this technique in a function search which, given an array Num, an integer key, and two integers lo and hi, searches for key from Num[lo] to Num[hi]. If found, the function returns the position in the array. If not found, it returns -1. For example, consider the statement:

```
n = search(Num, 61, 1, 7)
```

This will search Num[1] to Num[7] for 61. It will find it in position 5 and return 5, which is stored in n. The call

```
search(Num, 32, 1, 7)
```

returns -1 since 32 is not stored in the array. Here is the function, search:

```
function search(Num, key, lo, hi)
# Search for key in Num[lo:hi]; if found, return its location else -1
    for h = lo:hi
        if key == Num[h] return h end
    end
    -1
end # search
```

The for loop 'steps through' the array until it finds the key or all values are checked, and it's not there.

To give an example of how search may be used, consider the voting problem of the last chapter. After the votes have been tallied, our arrays Candidate and Vote look like this:

1	Victor Taylor	4
2	Denise Duncan	3
3	Kamal Ramdhan	6
4	Michael Ali	4
5	Anisa Sawh	6
6	Carol Khan	2
7	Gary Oliver	3

Suppose we want to know how many votes Carol Khan received. We would have to search for her name in the Candidate array. When we find it (in position 6), we can retrieve her votes from Vote[6]. In general, if a name is in position n, the number of votes received will be Vote[n].

Above, we wrote the function search and explained how it works using an integer array as our example. However, the observant reader will notice that nothing in the function makes any assumption about what *type* of values it will be asked to search. This means we can use the *same* function to search `Candidate`, the array of strings which contains the names of the candidates. Consider this:

```
n = search(Candidate, "Carol Khan", 1, 7)
```

This will return `6`; printing `Vote[n]` will print the number of votes `Carol Khan` received.

Tip: If all we need to know is whether an item `k` is present in an array `Num`, we can write this:

```
if k in Num
```

8.2 Selection Sort

In Section 7.10, we used some predefined Julia functions to sort the data in various ways. Now we take a look "under the hood" to see what is involved in sorting a list of items.

Sorting is the process by which a set of values are arranged in ascending or descending order. There are many reasons to sort. Sometimes we sort in order to produce more readable output (for example, to produce an alphabetical listing). A teacher may need to sort her students in order by name or by average score. If we have a large set of values and we want to identify duplicates, we can do so by sorting; the repeated values will come together in the sorted list. There are many ways to sort. We start with a method known as *selection sort*.

Consider the following array:

Num

57	48	79	65	15	33	52
1	2	3	4	5	6	7

Sorting `Num` in ascending order using selection sort proceeds as follows:

1st pass

- Find the smallest number in positions 1 to 7; the smallest is 15, found in position 5.
- Interchange the numbers in positions 1 and 5. We get this:

Num

15	48	79	65	57	33	52
1	2	3	4	5	6	7

2nd pass

- Find the smallest number in positions 2 to 7; the smallest is 33, found in position 6.
- Interchange the numbers in positions 2 and 6. We get this:

Num

15	33	79	65	57	48	52
1	2	3	4	5	6	7

3rd pass

- Find the smallest number in positions 3 to 7; the smallest is 48, found in position 6.
- Interchange the numbers in positions 3 and 6. We get this:

Num

15	33	48	65	57	79	52
1	2	3	4	5	6	7

4th pass

- Find the smallest number in positions 4 to 7; the smallest is 52, found in position 7.
- Interchange the numbers in positions 4 and 7. We get this:

Num

15	33	48	52	57	79	65
1	2	3	4	5	6	7

5th pass

- Find the smallest number in positions 5 to 7; the smallest is 57, found in position 5.
- Interchange the numbers in positions 5 and 5. We get this:

Num

15	33	48	52	57	79	65
1	2	3	4	5	6	7

6th pass

- Find the smallest number in positions 6 to 7; the smallest is 65, found in position 7.
- Interchange the numbers in positions 6 and 7. We get this:

Num

15	33	48	52	57	65	79
1	2	3	4	5	6	7

The array is now sorted.

If we let h go from 1 to 6, on each pass:

- We find the smallest number from locations h to 7.
- If the smallest number is in location s, we interchange the numbers in locations h and s.
- For an array of size n, we make n-1 passes. In our example, we sorted 7 numbers in 6 passes.

The following is an outline of the algorithm:

```
for h = 1 to n - 1
    s = location of smallest number from Num[h] to Num[n]
    swap Num[h] and Num[s]
endfor
```

In Section 7.10, we wrote a function to return the position of the smallest number in an array. Here it is for easy reference (we rename the argument Num to List since the function can work with strings and characters, as well as numbers):

```
function getSmallest(List, lo, hi)
# Return the location of the smallest item in List[lo:hi]
    small = lo
    for h = lo+1 : hi
        if List[h] < List[small] small = h end
    end
    small
```

```
end # getSmallest
```

With `getSmallest`, we can code the algorithm, above, as a function `selectionSort`. To make it general, we also tell the function which *portion* of the array to sort by specifying subscripts `lo` and `hi`. Instead of the loop going from `1` to `n-1` as in the algorithm, it now goes from `lo` to `hi-1`, just a minor change for greater flexibility.

```
function selectionSort(List, lo, hi)
# Sort List[lo:hi] in ascending order
    for h = lo : hi-1
        s = getSmallest(List, h, hi)
        List[h], List[s] = List[s], List[h] # swap the values in locations h and
        s
    end
end # selectionSort
```

We test `selectionSort` with the following:

```
function main()
    A = [57, 48, 79, 65, 15, 33, 52]
    selectionSort(A, 1, 7)
    for a in A print("$a ") end; println("\n")

    B = ["nu", "ra", "bu", "xi", "pi", "os", "io"]
    selectionSort(B, 1, 7)
    for b in B print("$b ") end; println()
end

main()
```

When run, it produced this output: the numbers in A, sorted, and the strings in B, sorted.

```
15 33 48 52 57 65 79
```

```
bu io nu os pi ra xi
```

Again, note how seamlessly Julia lets us sort different types of arrays with the same code.

As a matter of interest, if we always want to sort the entire array, the header for `selectionSort` can simply be this:

```
function selectionSort(List)
```

The function can proceed assuming the subscripts range from `1` to `length(List)`.

We have sorted the list in *ascending* order. We can sort `List[1:n]` in *descending* order with the following algorithm:

```
for h = 1 to n-1
    b = position of biggest number from Num[h] to Num[n]
    swap Num[h] and Num[b]
endfor
```

8.2.1 Analysis of Selection Sort

To find the smallest of k items, we make $k-1$ comparisons. On the first pass, we make $n-1$ comparisons to find the smallest of n items. On the second pass, we make $n-2$ comparisons to find the smallest of $n-1$ items. And so on, until the last pass where we make one comparison to find the smaller of two items. On the ith pass, we make $n-i$ comparisons to find the smallest of $n-i+1$ items. We have this:

Total number of comparisons = $1 + 2 + ... + n-1 = \frac{1}{2} n(n-1) \approx \frac{1}{2} n^2$

We say selection sort is of order $O(n^2)$ ("big O n squared"). The constant ½ is not important in "big O" notation since, as n gets very big, the constant becomes insignificant.

Swapping two items requires three assignments. On each pass, we swap two items. We make n-1 passes so we make $3(n-1)$ assignments in all. Using "big O" notation, we say that the number of assignments is $O(n)$. The constants 3 and 1 are not important as n gets large.

Does selection sort perform any better if there is order in the data? No. One way to find out is to give it a sorted list and see what it does. If you work through the algorithm, you will see that the method is oblivious to order in the data. It will make the same number of comparisons every time, regardless of the data.

As an exercise, modify the programming code so that it counts the number of comparisons and assignments made in sorting a list using selection sort.

8.3 Insertion Sort

Consider the same array as before:

Num

57	48	79	65	15	33	52
1	2	3	4	5	6	7

Think of the numbers as cards on a table and picked up one at a time in the order in which they appear in the array. We first pick up 57, then 48, then 79, and so on, until we pick up 52. However, as we pick up each new number, we add it to our hand in such a way that the numbers in our hand are all sorted.

When we pick up 57, we have just one number in our hand. We consider one number to be sorted.

When we pick up 48, we add it in front of 57 so our hand contains this:

    48 57

When we pick up 79, we place it after 57 so our hand contains this:

    48 57 79

When we pick up 65, we place it after 57 so our hand contains this:

    48 57 65 79

At this stage, four numbers have been picked up and our hand contains them in sorted order.

When we pick up 15, we place it before 48 so our hand contains this:

    15 48 57 65 79

When we pick up 33, we place it after 15 so our hand contains this:

    15 33 48 57 65 79

Finally, when we pick up 52, we place it after 48 so our hand contains this:

    15 33 48 52 57 65 79

The numbers are sorted in ascending order.

The method described illustrates the idea behind *insertion* sort. The numbers in the array will be processed one at a time, from left to right. This is equivalent to picking up the numbers from the table, one at a time. Since the first number, by itself, is sorted, we will process the numbers in the array starting from the second.

When we come to process Num[h], we can assume that Num[1] to Num[h-1] are sorted. We then insert Num[h] among Num[1] to Num[h-1] so that Num[1] to Num[h] are sorted. We will then go on to process Num[h+1]. When we do so, our assumption that elements Num[1] to Num[h] are sorted will be true.

Sorting Num in ascending order using insertion sort proceeds as follows:

1ˢᵗ pass

- Process Num[2], that is, 48. This involves placing 48 so that the first two numbers are sorted; Num[1] and Num[2] now contain the following:

Num

48	57	79	65	15	33	52
1	2	3	4	5	6	7

The rest of the array remains unchanged.

2ⁿᵈ pass

- Process Num[3], that is, 79. This involves placing 79 so that the first three numbers are sorted; Num[1] to Num[3] now contain the following:

Num

48	57	79	65	15	33	52
1	2	3	4	5	6	7

The rest of the array remains unchanged.

3ʳᵈ pass

- Process Num[4], that is, 65. This involves placing 65 so that the first four numbers are sorted; Num[1] to Num[4] now contain the following:

Num

48	57	65	79	15	33	52
1	2	3	4	5	6	7

The rest of the array remains unchanged.

4ᵗʰ pass

- Process Num[5], that is, 15. This involves placing 15 so that the first five numbers are sorted. To simplify the explanation, think of 15 as being taken out and stored in a simple variable (key, say) leaving a "hole" in Num[5]. We can picture this as follows:

key

15

Num

48	57	65	79		33	52
1	2	3	4	5	6	7

The insertion of 15 in its correct position proceeds as follows:

- Compare 15 with 79; it is smaller, so move 79 to location 5, leaving location 4 free. This gives the following:

key

15

Num

48	57	65		79	33	52
1	2	3	4	5	6	7

- Compare 15 with 65; it is smaller, so move 65 to location 4, leaving location 3 free. This gives the following:

key		Num						
15		48	57		65	79	33	52
		1	2	3	4	5	6	7

- Compare 15 with 57; it is smaller, so move 57 to location 3, leaving location 2 free. This gives the following:

key		Num						
15		48		57	65	79	33	52
		1	2	3	4	5	6	7

- Compare 15 with 48; it is smaller, so move 48 to location 2, leaving location 1 free. This gives the following:

key		Num						
15			48	57	65	79	33	52
		1	2	3	4	5	6	7

- There are no more numbers to compare with 15, so it is inserted in location 1, giving this:

key		Num						
15		15	48	57	65	79	33	52
		1	2	3	4	5	6	7

- We express the logic of placing 15 (key) by comparing it with the numbers to its left, starting with the nearest one like this: As long as key is less than Num[k], for some k, move Num[k] to location Num[k+1] and go on to consider Num[k-1], providing it exists. It won't exist when k is 1. In this case, the process stops, and key is inserted in location 1.

5th pass

- Process Num[6], that is, 33. This involves placing 33 so that the first six numbers are sorted. This is done as follows:
  - Store 33 in key, leaving location 6 free.
  - Compare 33 with 79; it is smaller, so move 79 to location 6, leaving location 5 free.
  - Compare 33 with 65; it is smaller, so move 65 to location 5, leaving location 4 free.
  - Compare 33 with 57; it is smaller, so move 57 to location 4, leaving location 3 free.
  - Compare 33 with 48; it is smaller, so move 48 to location 3, leaving location 2 free.
  - Compare 33 with 15; it is bigger, so insert 33 in location 2. This gives the following:

key		Num						
33		15	33	48	57	65	79	52
		1	2	3	4	5	6	7

- We express the logic of placing 33 by comparing it with the numbers to its left, starting with the nearest one like this: As long as key is less than Num[k], for some k, we move Num[k] to position Num[k+1] and move on to consider Num[k-1], providing it exists. If key is greater than or equal to Num[k] for some k, then key is inserted in position k+1. Here, 33 is greater than Num[1] and so is inserted into Num[2].

6th pass

- Process Num[7], that is, 52. This involves placing 52 so that the first seven (all) numbers are sorted. This is done as follows:
    - Store 52 in key, leaving location 7 free.
    - Compare 52 with 79; it is smaller, so move 79 to location 7, leaving location 6 free.
    - Compare 52 with 65; it is smaller, so move 65 to location 6, leaving location 5 free.
    - Compare 52 with 57; it is smaller, so move 57 to location 5, leaving location 4 free.
    - Compare 52 with 48; it is bigger, so insert 52 in location 4. This gives the following:

key		Num						
52		15	33	48	52	57	65	79
		1	2	3	4	5	6	7

The array is now completely sorted.

The following is an outline to sort the first n elements of an array, Num, using insertion sort:

```
for h = 2 to n do
    insert Num[h] among Num[1] to Num[h-1] so that Num[1] to Num[h] are sorted
endfor
```

At the heart of the sort is the idea of adding a new element to an already sorted list so that the list remains sorted. Specifically, given a sorted list of items from Num[m] to Num[n-1], we want to add a new item (Num[n]) to the list so that Num[m] to Num[n] are sorted.

We write the function insertInPlace to perform this task. We use the more general parameter, List, since we may want to sort non-numeric data as well.

```
function insertInPlace(List, m, n)
# List[m:n-1] is sorted in ascending order
# insert List[n] so that List[m:n] are sorted
    newItem = List[n]
    for k = n-1 : -1 : m
        if newItem >= List[k]
            List[k+1] = newItem
            return
        end
        List[k+1] = List[k]
    end
    List[m] = newItem # All items have moved up; insert in first position
end # insertInPlace
```

Now that we have insertInPlace, we can write insertionSort as follows:

```
function insertionSort(List, lo, hi)
# sort List[lo:hi] in ascending order
    for h = lo+1 : hi
        insertInPlace(List, lo, h)
    end
end # insertionSort
```

We test insertionSort with the following:

```
function main()
    A = [57, 48, 79, 65, 15, 33, 52]
    insertionSort(A, 1, 7)
    for a in A print("$a ") end; println("\n")

    B = ["nu", "ra", "bu", "xi", "pi", "os", "io"]
```

```
    insertionSort(B, 1, 7)
    for b in B print("$b ") end; println()
  end

  main()
```

When run, it produced this output: the numbers in A, sorted, and the strings in B, sorted.

```
15 33 48 52 57 65 79

bu io nu os pi ra xi
```

If, for instance, we want to sort items 2 to 6 of the array B, we just call `insertionSort` like this:

```
insertionSort(B, 2, 6)
```

It will sort only that portion of B, leaving the rest unchanged.

Note, again, that `insertionSort` makes no assumption about the *type* of values `List` contains. They will sort a list of integers, floating-point numbers, characters or strings.

8.3.1 Analysis of Insertion Sort

In processing item h, we can make as few as one comparison (if `Num[h]` is bigger than `Num[h-1]`) or as many as h-1 comparisons (if `Num[h]` is smaller than all the previous items). For random data, it is expected that we would make $\frac{1}{2}(h-1)$ comparisons, on average. Hence, the average total number of comparisons to sort n items is as follows:

$$\sum_{h=2}^{n} \tfrac{1}{2}(h-1) = \tfrac{1}{2}\{1 + 2 + \cdots + n - 1\} = \tfrac{1}{4}\,n(n-1) \approx \tfrac{1}{4}n^2$$

We say insertion sort is of order $O(n^2)$ ("big O n squared"). The constant $\frac{1}{4}$ is not important as n gets large.

Each time we make a comparison, we also make an assignment. Hence, the total number of assignments is also $\frac{1}{4}\,n(n-1) \approx \frac{1}{4}\,n^2$.

We emphasize that this is an average for random data. Unlike selection sort, the actual performance of insertion sort depends heavily on the data supplied. If the given array is already sorted, insertion sort will quickly determine this by making n-1 comparisons. In this case, it runs in $O(n)$ time. One would expect that insertion sort will perform better the more order there is in the data.

If the given data is in descending order, insertion sort performs at its worst since each new number has to travel all the way to the beginning of the list. In this case, the number of comparisons is $\frac{1}{2}\,n(n-1) \approx \frac{1}{2}\,n^2$. The number of assignments is also $\frac{1}{2}\,n(n-1) \approx \frac{1}{2}\,n^2$.

Thus, the number of comparisons made by insertion sort ranges from n-1 (best) to $\frac{1}{4}\,n^2$ (average) to $\frac{1}{2}\,n^2$ (worst). The number of assignments is always the same as the number of comparisons.

As an exercise, modify the code so that it counts the number of comparisons and assignments made in sorting a list using insertion sort.

8.3.2 Sort Unlimited Data

Because of the way it sorts, insertion sort has the advantage that it doesn't need to know/store *all* its elements up front before sorting. In others words, when dealing with item k, it doesn't need to know anything about the items that come *after* k.

This enables us to write the sort, as we fetch the data, for *any* amount of data that may be supplied. As we get each new number, we expand the array to hold it. At the end, the array is exactly the size of the amount of numbers supplied, and it is sorted.

We write Program P8.1 which reads an unknown amount of numbers from `input.txt` and sorts them. Suppose `input.txt` contains this:

```
57 48 79 65 15 33 52
32 17 47 83 74
89 81 76 34 62 29
```

Program P8.1 prints this, all the numbers, sorted:

```
15 17 29 32 33 34 47 48 52 57 62 65 74 76 79 81 83 89
```

```
# Program P8.1 - Insertion Sort Unlimited
function insertInPlace(List)
# n = length(List); List[1] to List[n-1] are sorted
# List[n] is newItem; insert so that List[1:n] are sorted
    n = length(List)
    newItem = List[n]
    for k = n-1 : -1 : 1
        if newItem >= List[k]
            List[k+1] = newItem
            return
        end
        List[k+1] = List[k]
    end
    List[1] = newItem # All items have moved up; insert in first position
end # insertInPlace

function sortControl(inn, List)
    while (line = readline(inn)) != ""      # get the data, one line at a time
        lnum = [parse(Int, x) for x in split(line)] # get numbers on one line
        for num in lnum              # for each new number
            push!(List, num)         # add it to the array
            insertInPlace(List)  # place it so array is sorted
        end
    end # while
end # sortControl

function main()
    inn = open("input.txt", "r")
    numList = Array{Int64}(undef,0) # create a list with no elements
    sortControl(inn, numList)
    for num in numList
        print("$num ")
    end
    println()
end # main

main()
```

8.4 Sort Parallel Arrays

It is common to have related information in different arrays. We may have two arrays `Name` and `Id` such that `Id[h]` is an identification number associated with `Name[h]`, as shown here.

	Name	**Id**
1	Samlal, Rawle	8742
2	Williams, Mark	5418
3	Delwin, Mac	4833
4	Taylor, Victor	4230
5	Mohamed, Abu	8583
6	Singh, Krishna	2458
7	Tawari, Taradutt	5768
8	Abdool, Zaid	7746

Consider the problem of sorting the names in alphabetical order. At the end, we would want each name to have its correct ID number. So, for example, after the sorting is done, Name[1] should contain Abdool, Zaid and Id[1] should contain 7746.

To achieve this, each time a name is moved during the sorting process, the corresponding ID number must also be moved. Since the name and ID number must be moved "in parallel", we say we are doing a *parallel sort*.

We rewrite insertInPlace but now it will be given *two* arrays (Name and Id) and two other arguments m and n. The function assumes Name[m] to Name[n-1] are sorted in ascending order and Name[n] contains the name to be inserted. It will insert Name[n] so that Name[m] to Name[n] are sorted. It will ensure that a name remains with its ID; we move an ID whenever we move a name. We name the function parallelInsertInPlace.

```
function parallelInsertInPlace(Name, Id, m, n)
# Name[m] to Name[n-1] are sorted in ascending order
# Insert Name[n] so that Name[m] to Name[n] are sorted
    newName = Name[n]
    idn = Id[n]
    for k = n-1 : -1 : m
        if newName >= Name[k]
            Name[k+1] = newName
            Id[k+1] = idn
            return
        end
        Name[k+1] = Name[k]
        Id[k+1] = Id[k]
    end
    Name[m] = newName # All items have moved up; insert in first position
    Id[m] = idn
end # parallelInsertInPlace
```

We can now write parallelInsertSort which calls parallelInsertInPlace repeatedly.

```
function parallelInsertSort(Name, Id, lo, hi)
# sort Name[lo] to Name[hi] in ascending order
    for h = lo+1 : hi
        parallelInsertInPlace(Name, Id, lo, h)
    end
end # parallelInsertSort
```

We test `parallelInsertSort` with the following:

```
function testParallelSort()
    Name = ["Samlal, Rawle", "Williams, Mark","Delwin, Mac", "Taylor, Victor",
            "Mohamed, Abu","Singh, Krishna", "Tawari, Taradutt", "Abdool, Zaid"]
    Id = [8742,5418,4833,4230,8583,2458,5768,3313]

    parallelInsertSort(Name, Id, 1, length(Id))
    println("The sorted names and IDs are\n")
    for i = 1 : length(Id)
        @printf("%-18s %d\n", Name[i], Id[i])
    end
end # testParallelSort
```

When run, it produces the following output:

```
The sorted names and IDs are

Abdool, Zaid        3313
Delwin, Mac         4833
Mohamed, Abu        8583
Samlal, Rawle       8742
Singh, Krishna      2458
Tawari, Taradutt    5768
Taylor, Victor      4230
Williams, Mark      5418
```

Tip: Julia provides another way to iterate through parallel arrays: use the standard function `zip`. The following will produce the same list of names/ID as above.

```
for (nmi, idi) in zip(Name, Id)
    @printf("%-18s %d\n", nmi, idi)
end
```

(`nmi`, `idi`) are set to (`Name[1]`, `Id[1]`), then (`Name[2]`, `Id[2]`, etc. You can generalize this to an arbitrary number of lists. If the array sizes are different, iteration stops when the shortest ends.

We alert you that "parallel arrays" can be more conveniently stored and sorted using *structures*. We will discuss an example in Section 9.3.1 after we've learnt a bit about structures.

8.5 Binary Search

Binary search is a very fast method for searching a list of items for a given one, *providing the list is sorted* (either ascending or descending). To illustrate the method, consider a list of 11 numbers, sorted in ascending order.

Num

17	24	31	39	44	49	56	66	72	78	83
1	2	3	4	5	6	7	8	9	10	11

Suppose we wish to search for 56. The search proceeds as follows:

- First, we find the middle item in the list. This is 49 in position 6. Compare 56 with 49; 56 is bigger, so we know that if 56 is in the list, it *must* be *after* position 6, since all numbers *before* are less than 49. In our next step, we confine our search to locations 7 to 11.
- Next, we find the middle item from locations 7 to 11. This is the item in location 9, 72.

- We compare 56 with 72. Since 56 is smaller, we know that if 56 is in the list, it *must* be *before* location 9, since numbers *after* 9 are bigger than 72. In our next step, we confine our search to locations 7 to 8.

- Next, we find the middle item from locations 7 to 8. In this case, we can choose either item 7 or item 8. The algorithm we write will choose the smaller index, 7, the number 56.

- We compare 56 with 56. Since they are the same, our search ends successfully; it finds the required item in location 7.

Suppose we were searching for 60. The search will proceed as above until we compare 60 with 56 (in location 7).

- Since 60 is bigger, we know that if 60 is in the list, it must be *after* position 7, since the numbers are in ascending order. This is just one location, 8.

- We compare 60 with item 8, that is, 66. Since 60 is smaller, we know that if 60 is in the list, it must be before position 8. Since it can't be *after* position 7 *and before* position 8, we conclude it is not in the list.

At each stage, we confine our search to some portion of the list. Let us use the variables lo and hi as the subscripts which define this portion. In other words, our search will be confined to the numbers from Num[lo] to Num[hi], inclusive.

Initially, we want to search the entire list so that we will set lo to 1 and hi to 11, in this example.

How do we find the subscript of the middle item? We will use this calculation:

```
mid = (lo + hi) ÷ 2         # could also use mid = div(lo+hi, 2)
```

Since integer division will be performed, the fraction, if any, is discarded. For example when lo is 1 and hi is 11, mid becomes 6; when lo is 7 and hi is 11, mid becomes 9; and when lo is 7 and hi is 8, mid becomes 7.

As long as lo is less than or equal to hi, they define a non-empty portion of the list to be searched. When lo is equal to hi, they define a single item to be searched. If lo ever gets *bigger* than hi, it means we have searched the entire list and the item was not found.

Based on these ideas, we can now write a function binarySearch. To be more general, we will write it so the calling function can specify in which *portion* of the array it wants the search to look for the item.

Thus, the function must be given the item to be searched for (key), the array (list), the start position of the search (lo) and the end position of the search (hi). For example, to search for the number 56 in the array Num, above, we can issue the following call:

```
binarySearch(56, Num, 1, 11)
```

The function must tell us the result of the search. If the item is found, the function will return its location. If not found, it will return -1. The call above returns 7 since Num[7] contains 56.

The function is shown as part of Program P8.2 which tests it.

```
# Program P8.2 - Test Binary Search Function
function binarySearch(key, List, lo, hi)
    # Search for key from List[lo:hi].
    # If found, return its location; otherwise, return -1
    while lo <= hi
        mid = (lo+hi)÷2
        if key == List[mid] return mid end # found
        if key < List[mid]
            hi = mid - 1
```

```
        else
            lo = mid + 1
        end
    end
    return -1 # lo and hi have crossed; key not found
end # binarySearch

function testBinarySearch()
    word = ["bu","id","io","mu","nu","od","os","pi","ra","so","xi"]
    print("Search for? ")
    key = readline()
    ans = binarySearch(key, word, 1, length(word))
    if ans == -1
        println("$key not found")
    else
        println("$key found in location $ans")
    end
end # testBinarySearch

testBinarySearch()
```

As before, there is nothing in the way binarySearch is written that restricts it to searching an array of a particular type. It will search whatever we give it, number or string. We show this by testing with the String array

```
word = ["bu","id","io","mu","nu","od","os","pi","ra","so","xi"]
```

Here are the results we get when we run it with various words as input.

```
Search for? pi
pi found in location 8

Search for? bu
bu found in location 1

Search for? xi
xi found in location 11

Search for? os
os found in location 7

Search for? gold
gold not found
```

8.6 Word Frequency Count

Let's write a program to read an English passage and count the number of times each word appears. The output consists of an alphabetical listing of the words and their frequencies.

We can use the following outline to develop our program:

```
while there is input
    get a word
    search for word
    if word is in the table
        add 1 to its count
    else
        add word to the table
        set its count to 1
    endif
endwhile
print table
```

This is a typical "search and insert" situation. We search for the next word among the words stored so far. If the search succeeds, we need only increment its count. If the search fails, the word is put in the table, and its count set to 1.

A major design decision here is how to search the table, which, in turn, will depend on where and how a new word is inserted in the table. The following are two possibilities:

1. A new word is inserted in the next free position in the table. This implies that a sequential search must be used to look for an incoming word since the words would not be in any particular order. This method has the advantages of simplicity and easy insertion, but searching takes longer as more words are put in the table.

2. A new word is inserted in the table in such a way that the words are always in alphabetical order. This may entail moving words that have already been stored so the new word may be slotted in the right place. However, since the table is in order, a binary search can be used to search for an incoming word.

   For this method, searching is faster, but insertion is slower than in (1). Since, in general, searching is done more frequently than inserting, (2) might be preferable.

Another advantage of (2) is that, at the end, the words will already be in alphabetical order and no sorting will be required. If (1) is used, the words will need to be sorted to obtain the alphabetical order.

We write our program using the approach in (2). The complete program is shown as Program P8.3.

```
# Program P8.3 - Word Frequency Count

# Read a file with arbitrary words; count frequency of each word
# A word is a string of letters; any non-letter is a delimiter
using Printf

function getNextWord(inn::IOStream)
# A word is defined as a contiguous sequence of letters
    ch = ' '        # necessary for ch to be known to the whole function
    while !eof(inn) && !isletter(ch) # Search for next letter
        ch = read(inn, Char)
    end
    if eof(inn) return nothing end  # None found; end of file reached

    # At this point, ch contains the first letter of the word
    wrd = string(ch)   # convert a single letter to String
    ch = read(inn, Char)
    while isletter(ch) # as long as we get a letter
        wrd *= ch       # add it to the word
        ch = read(inn, Char)
    end
    return wrd
end # endGetNextWord

function binarySearch(key, List, lo, hi)
# Search for key from List[lo:hi].
# If found, return its location; otherwise, return -1
    while lo <= hi
        mid = (lo+hi)÷2
        if key == List[mid] return mid end # found
        if key < List[mid]
            hi = mid - 1
        else
            lo = mid + 1
        end #if
    end #while
```

```
        return lo # not found; should be inserted in location lo
    end # binarySearch

function main()
    inn = open("passage.txt", "r")
    out = open("output.txt", "w")

    # start with empty word list
    WordList = Array{String}(undef,0)
    Frequency = Array{Int64}(undef,0)

    while (word=getNextWord(inn)) != nothing
        word = lowercase(word) # so that If and if treated the same
        numWords = length(WordList)
        loc = binarySearch(word, WordList, 1, numWords)
        if loc <= numWords && word==WordList[loc] # word already met
            Frequency[loc] += 1
        else # this is a new word; create a new element in the list
            insert!(WordList, loc, word)
            insert!(Frequency, loc, 1)
        end
    end

    println(out, "Words        Frequency\n")
    for h = 1 : length(WordList)
        @printf(out, "%-15s %2d\n", WordList[h], Frequency[h])
    end

    close(inn)
    close(out)

end # main

main()
```

Suppose the file `passage.txt` contains the following data (from *If* by *Rudyard Kipling*):

```
If you can dream—and not make dreams your master;
 If you can think—and not make thoughts your aim;
If you can meet with Triumph and Disaster
 And treat those two impostors just the same...
If you can fill the unforgiving minute
 With sixty seconds' worth of distance run,
Yours is the Earth...
```

When Program P8.3 was run with this data, it produced the following output:

```
Words        Frequency

aim             1
and             4
can             4
disaster        1
distance        1
dream           1
dreams          1
earth           1
fill            1
if              4
impostors       1
is              1
just            1
make            2
master          1
meet            1
minute          1
```

not	2
of	1
run	1
same	1
seconds	1
sixty	1
the	3
think	1
those	1
thoughts	1
treat	1
triumph	1
two	1
unforgiving	1
with	2
worth	1
you	4
your	2
yours	1

Comments on Program P8.3

- For our purposes, we assume a word begins with a letter and consists of letters only. If you want to include other characters (such as a hyphen or apostrophe), you need change only the `getNextWord` function.

- When a new word is found, the arrays `WordList` and `Frequency` expand to accommodate the word. This is accomplished with the `insert!` function. Consider this statement

  ```
  insert!(WordList, loc, word)
  ```

  This *inserts* word at `WordList[loc]`. The indices of the following items, if any, increase by 1. In theory, an unlimited number of words can be accommodated.

- There is no limit on the length of a word.

- All words are converted to lowercase so that, for instance, `The` and `the` are counted as the same word.

- We wrote `binarySearch` so that if the word is found, its location (`loc`, say) is returned. If not found, the location in which the word *should be inserted* is returned. In `main`, the test

  ```
  word == WordList[loc]
  ```

  tells us if it was found. If `false`, the new word must be inserted at index `loc`.

- If the location returned by `binarySearch` is greater than the current number of words in `WordList`, we have a new word; this one must be inserted after all the current words.

8.7 Merge Sorted Lists

Merging is the process by which two or more ordered lists are combined into one ordered list. For example, given two lists of numbers, `A` and `B`, as follows:

```
A: 21 28 35 40 61 75
B: 16 25 47 54
```

They can be combined into one ordered list, `C`, as follows:

```
C: 16 21 25 28 35 40 47 54 61 75
```

The list `C` contains all the numbers from lists `A` and `B`. How can the merge be performed?

One way to think about it is to imagine that the numbers in the given lists are stored on cards, one per card, and the cards are placed face up on a table, with the smallest at the top. We can imagine the lists A and B as follows:

```
21      16
28      25
35      47
40      54
61
75
```

We look at the top two cards, 21 and 16. The smaller, 16, is removed and placed in C. This exposes the number 25. We have this:

```
21      25
28      47
35      54
40
61
75
```

The top two cards are now 21 and 25. The smaller, 21, is removed and added to C, which now contains 16 21. This exposes the number 28. We have this:

```
28      25
35      47
40      54
61
75
```

The top two cards are now 28 and 25. The smaller, 25, is removed and added to C, which now contains 16 21 25. This exposes the number 47. We have this:

```
28      47
35      54
40
61
75
```

The top two cards are now 28 and 47. The smaller, 28, is removed and added to C, which now contains 16 21 25 28. This exposes the number 35. We have this:

```
35      47
40      54
61
75
```

The top two cards are now 35 and 47. The smaller, 35, is removed and added to C, which now contains 16 21 25 28 35. This exposes the number 40. We have this:

```
40      47
61      54
75
```

The top two cards are now 40 and 47. The smaller, 40, is removed and added to C, which now contains 16 21 25 28 35 40. This exposes the number 61. We have this:

```
61      47
75      54
```

The top two cards are now 61 and 47. The smaller, 47, is removed and added to C, which now contains 16 21 25 28 35 40 47. This exposes the number 54. We have this:

```
61      54
75
```

The top two cards are now 61 and 54. The smaller, 54, is removed and added to C, which now contains 16 21 25 28 35 40 47 54. The list B has no more numbers.

We copy the remaining elements (61 75) of A to C, which now contains the following:

    16 21 25 28 35 40 47 54 61 75

The merge is now completed.

At each step of the merge, we compare the smallest remaining number of A with the smallest remaining number of B. The smaller of these is added to C. If the smaller comes from A, we move on to the next number in A; if the smaller comes from B, we move on to the next number in B.

This is repeated until all the numbers in either A or B have been used. If all the numbers in A have been used, we add the remaining numbers from B to C. If all the numbers in B have been used, we add the remaining numbers from A to C.

We can express the logic of the merge as follows:

```
while (at least one number remains in both A and B)
    if (smallest in A < smallest in B)
        add smallest in A to C
        move on to next number in A
    else
        add smallest in B to C
        move on to next number in B
    endif
endwhile
if (A has ended)
    add remaining numbers in B to C
else
    add remaining numbers in A to C
endif
```

Given two sorted lists A and B, the function merge in Program P8.4 merges them and returns the merged list.

 # Program P8.4 - Merge Sorted Lists

```
function merge(A, B)
# Given sorted arrays A and B, merge A and B into C; return C
    # Create an array of the same type as A
    C = Array{typeof(A[1]),1}(undef,length(A)+length(B))
    k = 0 # k will index C
    m = length(A); n = length(B)

    i = 1 # i points to the first (smallest) element in A
    j = 1 # j points to the first (smallest) element in B

    while i <= m && j <= n # as long as we have elements in A and B
        if A[i] < B[j]  # smaller element in A; copy to C
            C[k+=1] = A[i]
            i += 1
        else
            C[k+=1] = B[j]  # smaller element in B; copy to C
            j += 1
        end
    end # while

    for a = i : m # copy remaining elements of A, if any
        C[k+=1] = A[a]
    end

    for b = j : n # copy remaining elements of B, if any
        C[k+=1] = B[b]
```

```
        end
        return C
    end
    function testMerge()
        A = [21, 28, 35, 40, 61, 75]
        B = [16, 25, 47, 54]

        C = merge(A, B)

        for c in C print("$c ") end
        println()
    end # testMerge

    testMerge()
```

We wrote a simple function `testMerge` to test if the function is working correctly, using the sample data above. When run, it prints the following, the result of merging A and B:

```
16 21 25 28 35 40 47 54 61 75
```

Once again, we observe that `merge` makes no assumption about what *types* of values A and B may contain. As long as they can be compared with each other, the function will work. Note, however, it won't work if, for instance, A contains integers and B contains strings since we cannot use `<` to compare a number with a string.

To show the versatility of `merge`, suppose we replace A and B in `testMerge` with the following:

```
A = ["id", "mu", "od", "xi"]
B = ["bu", "io", "nu", "os", "pi", "ra"]
```

With no other change, when run, the program will print this:

```
bu id io mu nu od os pi ra xi
```

There's more. We can merge a *portion* of A with a *portion* of B, for example, A[1:3] with B[2:5], using this:

```
C = merge(A[1:3], B[2:5])
```

When we do, the following will be printed:

```
id io mu nu od os pi
```

While we can admire the advantages (flexibility, versatility) of specifying arguments without a fixed type, there are times when we may want Julia to check that an argument *is* of a given type. So, for instance, if we want to ensure that `merge` is called with integer arrays, we can write this:

```
function merge(A::Array{Int64}, B::Array{Int64})
```

If we call `merge` with A and B as integer arrays, things will work as before. However, if we try this:

```
A = ["id", "mu", "od", "xi"]
B = ["bu", "io", "nu", "os", "pi", "ra"]
C = merge(A, B)
```

we will get an error message:

```
MethodError: no method matching merge(::Array{String,1}, ::Array{String,1})
```

In effect, it says there is no function `merge` which takes two `String` arrays as arguments:

Julia lets us write whichever version of `merge` best suits our needs.

EXERCISES 8

1. In the voting problem of Section 7.10, print the results in alphabetical order by candidate name. Do not use any predefined sorting functions.

2. In the voting problem of Section 7.10, print the results in descending order by candidate score. Do not use any predefined sorting functions.

3. Write a function to sort a `Float64` array in *ascending* order using selection sort. Do the sort by finding the *largest* number on each pass.

4. Write a program to find out, for a class of students, the number of families with 1, 2, 3, ... up to 8 or more children. The data consists of the number of children in each pupil's family. Print the results in decreasing order by family-size popularity. That is, print the most popular family-size first and the least popular family-size last.

5. A survey of 10 pop artists is made. Each person votes for an artist by specifying the number of the artist (a value from 1 to 10). Write a program to read the names of the artists, followed by the votes, and find out which artist is the most popular.

   Print a table of the results with the most popular artist first and the least popular last.

6. The *median* of a set of *n* numbers (not necessarily distinct) is obtained by arranging the numbers in order and taking the number in the middle. If *n* is odd, there is a unique middle number. If *n* is even, then the *average* of the two middle values is the median. Write a program to read a set of positive integers and print their median.

7. The *mode* of a set of *n* numbers is the number which appears most frequently. For example, the mode of 7 3 8 5 7 3 1 3 4 8 9 is 3.

   Write a program to read a set of numbers and print their mode.

   Write an efficient program to find the mode if it is known that the numbers all lie between 1 and 999, inclusive, with no restriction on the amount of numbers supplied.

8. An array `Num` contains `k` numbers sorted in descending order. Write a function `insertInPlace` which, given `Num` and another number `x`, inserts `x` in its proper position such that `Num` is sorted in descending order.

9. A multiple-choice examination consists of twenty questions. Each question has five choices, labelled A, B, C, D and E. The first line of data contains the correct answers to the twenty questions in the first 20 consecutive character positions, for example:

   `BECDCBAADEBACBAEDDBE`

   Each subsequent line contains the answers for one candidate. Data on a line consists of a candidate number (an integer), followed by one or more spaces, followed by the twenty answers given by the candidate in the next twenty *consecutive* character positions. An X is used if a candidate did not answer a particular question. You may assume all data are valid and stored in a file `exam.dat`. A sample line is:

   `4325    BECDCBAXDEBACCAEDXBE`

   Points for a question are awarded as follows:– correct answer: 4 ; wrong answer: -1; no answer: 0.

   Write a program to process the data and print a report consisting of candidate number and the total points obtained by the candidate, *in ascending order by candidate number*. At the end, print the average points gained by the candidates and those with the highest score.

10. You are given two integer arrays A and B each of maximum size 500, containing numbers in arbitrary order. The variables m and n indicate how many numbers are stored in A and B, respectively.

   Write code to merge the elements of A and B into another array C of size m+n such that C contains the numbers in *ascending* order.

11. An array A contains integers that first increase in value and then decrease in value, for example:

   Num

17	24	31	83	78	72	66	56	49	44	39
1	2	3	4	5	6	7	8	9	10	11

   It is unknown at which point the numbers start to decrease. Write efficient code to copy the numbers from A to another array B so that B is sorted in ascending order. Your code must take advantage of the way the numbers are arranged in A. (*Hint*: perform a merge starting at both ends.)

12. An anagram is a word or phrase formed by rearranging the letters of another word or phrase. Examples of one-word anagrams are: sister/resist and senator/treason. We can get more interesting anagrams if we ignore letter case and punctuation marks. Examples are: Time-table/Bet I'm Late, Clint Eastwood/Old West Action and Woman Hitler/Mother-in-law.

   Write a function which, given two strings, returns true if the strings are anagrams of each other and false if they are not.

CHAPTER 9

Structures

In this chapter, we will explain the following:

- What is a structure (`struct`)
- How to declare a structure
- How to pass a structure to a function
- How to work with an array of structures
- How to search an array of structures
- How to sort an array of structures
- How to declare/use nested structures
- How to use structures to manipulate fractions

9.1 The Need for Structures

In Julia, a structure (denoted by the keyword `struct`) is a collection of one or more variables, possibly of different types, grouped together under a single name for convenient handling.

There are many situations in which we want to process data about a certain entity or object but the data consists of items of various types. For example, the data for a student (the *student record*) may consist of several *fields* such as a name, address and telephone number (all of type string), number of courses taken (integer), fees payable (floating-point), names of courses (string), grades obtained (character), and so on.

The data for a car may consist of manufacturer, model and registration number (string), seating capacity and fuel capacity (integer), and mileage and price (floating-point). For a book, we may want to store author and title (string), price (floating-point), number of pages (integer), type of binding—hardcover, paperback, spiral (string)—and number of copies in stock (integer).

Suppose we want to store data for 100 students in a program. One approach is to have a separate array for each field and use subscripts to link the fields together. Thus, `Name[i]`, `Address[i]`, `Fees[i]`, and so on, refer to the data for the ith student.

The problem with this approach is that if there are many fields, the handling of several parallel arrays becomes clumsy and unwieldy. For example, suppose we want to pass a student's data to a function via the argument list. This will involve the passing of several arrays. Also, if we are sorting the students by name, say, each time two names are interchanged, we have to write statements to interchange the data in the other arrays as well. In such situations, Julia structures are convenient to use.

© The Author(s), under exclusive license to Springer Nature Switzerland AG 2021
N. Kalicharan, *Julia - Bit by Bit*, Undergraduate Topics in Computer Science,
https://doi.org/10.1007/978-3-030-73936-2_9

9.2 How to Write a `struct` Declaration

Consider the problem of storing a date in a program. A date consists of three parts: the day, the month, and the year. Each of these parts can be represented by an integer. For example, the date "September 14, 2006" can be represented by the day, 14; the month, 9; and the year, 2006. We say that a date consists of three *fields*, each of which is an integer.

If we want, we can also represent a date by using the *name* of the month, rather than its number. In this case, a date consists of three fields, one of which is a string and the other two are integers.

We can declare a *date type* as a *structure* using the keyword `struct`. Consider this declaration:

```
struct Date
    day
    month
    year
end
```

It consists of the keyword `struct` followed by some name we choose to give to the structure (`Date`, in the example). (In this book, for the most part, we use the *convention* of starting a `struct` name with an uppercase letter.) This is followed by the fields, one per line, followed by `end`.

If necessary, we could declare a type for any of the fields, like this:

```
struct Date
    day::Int64
    month::String
    year:Int64
end
```

These declarations *could* be written as follows, if we so choose:

```
struct Date day; month; year end
struct Date day::Int64; month::String; year::Int64 end
```

We use a semi-colon to separate consecutive fields.

Once we've defined a `struct`, we can create variables of that type, like this:

```
dob = Date(14,"Nov",2015)
```

This declares `dob` to be a `Date` variable with the given value. We can picture `dob` as follows:

	day	month	year
dob	14	Nov	2015

We refer to the fields of `dob` with `dob.day`, `dob.month` and `dob.year`. *A field is specified by the struct name, followed by a period, followed by the field name.*

The following illustrates some of what we can do with `dob`:

```
julia> dob = Date(14,"Nov",2015)
Date(14, "Nov", 2015)

julia> dob.day
14

julia> dob.month
"Nov"

julia> dob.year
2015

julia> println("$(dob.month) $(dob.day), $(dob.year)")
Nov 14, 2015
```

What we *cannot* do is *change* the *value* of a *field*. Suppose we try this:

```
dob.day = 25
```

We will get the following message:

```
Error: immutable struct of type Date cannot be changed
```

Why? Because, like a `String`, and unless declared otherwise, a `struct` is *immutable*. Once assigned, we *cannot* change the value of an *individual* field. However, we *can* assign a new value to the entire `struct`, like here:

```
julia> dob = Date(29,"Oct",1980)
Date(29, "Oct", 1980)
```

`dob` has a new value; the old one has been replaced.

In many applications, immutable structs (like immutable strings) will suffice. For those times when we may need to modify the fields of a `struct`, Julia lets us declare it as `mutable`, like this (if we wish, we can declare a type for any or all of the fields):

```
mutable struct Date
    day
    month
    year
end
```

Now we can change the value of individual fields, which we couldn't do with an immutable `struct`.

```
julia> dob1 = Date(28,"Sep",1955)
Date(28, "Sep", 1955)

julia> dob1.day = 25
25

julia> dob1.month = "Jun"
"Jun"

julia> println(dob1)
Date(25, "Jun", 1955)
```

Immutable structs are processed more efficiently than mutable ones. Make sure you really need a `mutable struct` before deciding to use one. To "protect" you, Julia's default is *immutable*.

9.2.1 Pass `struct` as Argument to a Function

We can pass a `struct` as an argument to a function. Let's write one which prints a date in the format `Dec 25, 2001`.

```
function printDate(d::Date)
    println("$(d.month) $(d.day), $(d.year)")
end
```

It can be used as follows:

```
julia> chmas = Date(25,"Dec",2001);
julia> printDate(chmas)
Dec 25, 2001
```

Next, we write a function to read a date and return it in a `Date struct`. It assumes the date is stored on three lines, in a file designated by `inn`. For example, suppose the file contains this:

```
15
February
1949
```

The function will read the file and return the `struct Date(15,"February",1949)`. Here is getDate:

```
function getDate(inn)
    d = parse(Int64, readline(inn))
    m = readline(inn)
    y = parse(Int64, readline(inn))
    Date(d,m,y)
end
```

The statement

```
printDate(getDate(inn))
```

will print this:

```
February 15, 1949
```

One question which arises is this: can a function change the value of a `struct` argument passed to it, *with the change known in the calling function*? The question arises only in the case of a `mutable struct` since, by definition, we can't change an immutable one.

To answer, let's define the following (`mDate` indicates mutable date):

```
mutable struct mDate
    day; month; year
end
```

We write a function which adds 1 to the year of the given date:

```
function changeDate(d::mDate)
    d.year += 1
end
```

Let's test it:

```
julia> mday = mDate(14,"September",2006);

julia> changeDate(mday);

julia> print(mday)
mDate(14, "September", 2007)
```

As we see, the function has changed the value of its argument. This confirms that a `struct` argument is passed "by reference"; the called function has access to the original argument. If the argument is a `mutable struct`, the called function can change its value.

Suppose we want to store information about students. For each student, we want to store their name, age, and gender (male or female). We can declare the following `struct`:

```
struct Student
    name; age; gender
end
```

We can now create variables of type `Student`, as follows:

```
stud1 = Student("Harry",27,'M')
stud2 = Student("Sally",23,'F')
```

Each of `stud1` and `stud2` will have its own fields—`name`, `age`, and `gender`. We can refer to these as follows:

```
stud1.name stud1.age stud1.gender
stud2.name stud2.age stud2.gender
```

As declared, `stud1` and `stud2` are immutable. We can do this (assign the entire structure to another variable):

```
stud3 = stud2
stud2 = stud1
```

But we cannot change an individual field in any of them.

9.3 Array of Structures

Suppose we want to store data on 40 students. We will need an array of size 40, and each element of the array will hold the data for one student. Thus, each element will have to be a `struct`—we need an "array of structures", a `struct` array.

We can declare the array with the following:

```
Pupil=Array{Student}(undef,40)
```

This allocates storage for `Pupil[1]`, `Pupil[2]`, `Pupil[3]`, ..., up to `Pupil[40]`. Each element `Pupil[i]` consists of three fields that can be referred to as follows:

```
Pupil[i].name    Pupil[i].age    Pupil[i].gender
```

In this example, we will take a slightly different approach. We will not declare `Pupil` to be of some fixed, pre-determined size (like `40`, above). Similar to what we did before, we will declare `Pupil` to be of size `0`; when we get data for a new student, we will expand `Pupil` using the `push!` function.

Also, we will not use an end-of-data marker—the program will read data until there is no more. There is also no need to cater for any given maximum number of students—the `Pupil` array grows as we get more students.

The first thing we need to do is fetch the data and store in the array. Assume we have data in the following format (name, age, gender):

```
"Mohamed, Sherila" 33 F
"Williams, Mark" 29 M
"Charles, Sandra" 24 F
"Layne, Dennis" 49 M
```

Suppose the data are stored in a file `students.txt` and `inn` is declared as follows:

```
inn = open("students.txt", "r")
```

Using the functions—`getString`, `getInteger`, `getChar`—that we wrote previously, we can read one student's data as follows:

```
name = getString(inn)
age = getInteger(inn)
gen = getChar(inn)
```

Study the following carefully:

```
name = getString(inn)
while name != nothing
    age = getInteger(inn)
    gen = getChar(inn)
    push!(Pupil,Student(name,age,gen)) # add this student to the list
    name = getString(inn)
end
```

A key statement is this:

```
push!(Pupil,Student(name,age,gen))
```

After values are fetched for name, age and gen, Student(name,age,gen) creates a struct out of them and push! adds it as the new last item in the array Pupil.

At the end, Pupil contains exactly the number of students' data supplied, no more, no less; length(Pupil) will tell us how many.

Putting it all together, we write Program P9.1 which reads the data and prints them in a slightly different format. We assume the functions—getString, getInteger, getChar—are available in the file GetDataFunctions.jl.

```julia
# Program P9.1 - Struct Fundamentals
# Declare a struct; read data into struct array; print data
include("GetDataFunctions.jl")

struct Student
    name; age; gender
end

function main()
    inn = open("students.txt", "r")
    Pupil=Array{Student}(undef,0)

    while (name = getString(inn)) != nothing
        age = getInteger(inn)
        gen = getChar(inn)
        push!(Pupil,Student(name,age,gen)) # add this student to the list
    end
    println("\nNumber of students: $(length(Pupil))\n")

    for p in Pupil
        println("$(p.name): $(p.age) $(p.gender)")
    end
end # main

main()
```

With the data above in students.txt, the program produced the following output:

```
Number of students: 4

Mohamed, Sherila: 33 F
Williams, Mark: 29 M
Charles, Sandra: 24 F
Layne, Dennis: 49 M
```

Where to place struct: Julia requires that a struct declaration be placed *at the top level*, that is, *outside* of any function. It is conventional to place it at the head of the program. But note, for instance, in P9.1, we could have placed it before or after main() (but not *inside* main).

Let's build on this example. Assuming students' data have been stored in a struct array, we write a function to search for a given name. Here it is:

```julia
function search(List, key, lo, hi)
# Search for key in struct List[lo:hi]; 'key' is a name
    for h = lo:hi
        if key == List[h].name return h end
    end
    -1
end # search
```

The only change (and the only giveaway that we are dealing with a struct) from our previous search is the reference List[h].name. This is necessary since we must compare the search item, key, with the name field of the struct.

The function might be called as follows:

```
ans = search(Pupil, "Charles,Sandra", 1, 4)
```

`"Charles,Sandra"` will be found in location 3, so `ans` is 3.

The call `search(Pupil,"Layne, Sandy",1,4)` returns `-1` since `"Layne, Sandy"` is not in the list.

9.3.1 Sort `struct` Array

Suppose we want the list of students in alphabetical order by name. It will be required to sort the array `Pupil`. The following uses an insertion sort to do the job. The process is identical to sorting an ordinary array except that the `name` field is used to govern the sorting.

```
function insertionSort(List, lo, hi)
# sort List[lo:hi] in ascending order
    for h = lo+1 : hi
        insertInPlace(List, lo, h)
    end
end # insertionSort

function insertInPlace(List, m, n)
# List[m:n-1] is sorted in ascending order
# insert List[n] so that List[m:n] are sorted
    newItem = List[n]
    for k = n-1 : -1 : m
        if newItem.name >= List[k].name  # compare name fields
            List[k+1] = newItem
            return
        end
        List[k+1] = List[k]
    end
    List[m] = newItem
end # insertInPlace
```

To sort the array `Pupil`, and print it, we can use the following:

```
insertionSort(Pupil, 1, length(Pupil))
for p in Pupil
    println("$(p.name): $(p.age) $(p.gender)")
end
```

When executed, the following is printed:

```
Charles, Sandra: 24 F
Layne, Dennis: 49 M
Mohamed, Sherila: 33 F
Williams, Mark: 29 M
```

Observe this statement in the function `insertInPlace`:

```
List[k+1] = List[k]
```

This assigns *all* the fields of `List[k]` to `List[k+1]`.

If we want to sort the students in order by age, all we need to change is the `if` condition. To sort in ascending order by age, we write this:

```
if newItem.age >= List[k].age
```

To sort in descending order by age, we write this:

```
if newItem.age <= List[k].age
```

We could even separate the list into male and female students by sorting on the gender field. Since *F* comes before *M* in alphabetical order, we can put the females first by writing this:

```
if newItem.gender >= List[k].gender
```

And we can put the males first by writing this:

```
if newItem.gender <= List[k].gender
```

We've used this example to illustrate how structures can be accessed and manipulated. The end result of sorting was not as important as the process of working with structures. Indeed, if all we want to do is sort, Julia provides many options. For example, to sort the `Pupil` array by `name`, in *ascending* order, we can write this:

```
sort!(Pupil, by = v -> v.name)
```

To sort in *descending* order by name, we write this (using the option `rev=true`):

```
sort!(Pupil, by = v -> v.name, rev=true)
```

When we use `sort!`, the sort is done "in place", meaning the contents of the array is changed to the sorted order. To do a non-destructive sort, we drop the exclamation mark:

```
Psorted = sort(Pupil, by = v -> v.name)
```

The sorted list is stored in `Psorted`; `Pupil` is unchanged.

Next, suppose we want to sort a list of persons alphabetically. If two or more persons have the same last name, their first names determine their order. We illustrate with the following:

```
struct Person
    first; last; age
end

person = Array{Person}(undef,5) # declares person[1:5] of type Person

person[1]=Person("Ernie","Smith",52)
person[2]=Person("Mary","Jones",21)
person[3]=Person("John","Jones",26)
person[4]=Person("Carl","Smith",26)
person[5]=Person("Liam","Jones",26)
```

Consider this statement:

```
sList = sort(person, by = v -> v.last)
```

It sorts `person` by last name and stores the sorted list in `sList`. This is `sList`:

```
Person("Mary", "Jones", 21)
Person("John", "Jones", 26)
Person("Liam", "Jones", 26)
Person("Ernie", "Smith", 52)
Person("Carl", "Smith", 26)
```

Suppose we print the items in `sList` as follows:

```
for p in sList
    println("$(p.last), $(p.first) $(p.age)")
end
```

We get this:

```
Jones, Mary 21
Jones, John 26
Jones, Liam 26
Smith, Ernie 52
Smith, Carl 26
```

The names are sorted by last name. However, ties are listed in the same order as they appear in the data. This is a result of *stable* sorting. If we need ties to be broken by first name, we must do a bit more, like this:

```
sList = sort(person, by=v -> (v.last, v.first))
```

This sorts by last name, then by first name, producing true alphabetical order:

```
Jones, John 26
Jones, Liam 26
Jones, Mary 21
Smith, Carl 26
Smith, Ernie 52
```

9.4 Nested Structures

Julia lets us use a structure as part of the definition of another structure—a structure within a structure, called a *nested* structure. Consider the Person structure declared in the last section. Suppose that, instead of age, we want to store the student's date of birth. This might be better since a student's date of birth is fixed, whereas his/her age changes, and the field would have to be updated every year.

Consider the following:

```
struct Name
    first; middle; last
end

struct Date
    day; month; year
end

struct Person
    name::Name
    dob::Date
    gender::Char
end

db=Date(10,"December",1960)
nm=Name("Mary",'R',"Ramroop")
mrr=Person(nm,db,'F')
```

The following shows how we can access the various fields and subfields of mrr.

```
julia> db=Date(10,"December",1960)
Date(10, "December", 1960)

julia> nm=Name("Mary",'R',"Ramroop")
Name("Mary", 'R', "Ramroop")

julia> mrr=Person(nm,db,'F')          # Consists of structs Name, Date and a Char
Person(Name("Mary", 'R', "Ramroop"), Date(10, "December", 1960), 'F')

julia> println("$(mrr.name)")         # This is a struct
Name("Mary", 'R', "Ramroop")

julia> println("$(mrr.name.first)")
Mary
julia> println("$(mrr.name.middle)")
R
julia> println("$(mrr.name.last)")
Ramroop

julia> println("$(mrr.dob)")          # This is a struct
Date(10, "December", 1960)
```

```
julia> println("$(mrr.dob.day)")
10

julia> println("$(mrr.dob.month)")
December

julia> println("$(mrr.dob.year)")
1960

julia> println("$(mrr.gender)")
F
```

A structure may be nested as deeply as you want. The dot (.) operator associates from left to right. If a, b and c are structures, the construct

```
a.b.c.d
```

is interpreted as

```
((a.b).c).d
```

9.5 Fractions

In this section, we discuss an example which involves working with structures. It deals with fractions.

A fraction is the ratio of two integers, so we can represent one by two integer values: one for the numerator and the other for the denominator. For example, 5/9 is represented by the two numbers 5 and 9.

We use the following structure to represent a fraction:

```
struct Fraction
    num::Int64; den::Int64
end
```

If f is variable of type Fraction, we can store 5/9 in f with this:

```
f.num = 5
f.den = 9
```

We can picture f like this:

```
          num     den
      ┌───────┬───────┐
f     │   5   │   9   │
      └───────┴───────┘
```

We can also read a line with two integers representing a fraction and store them in f like this:

```
julia> n, d = [parse(Int, x) for x in split(readline())]
3 5
julia> f = Fraction(n, d)
Fraction(3, 5)
```

We write a program to illustrate the basics of working with fractions. It requests two integers, reads them, and prints the corresponding fraction. It is shown as P9.2.

 # Program P9.2 - Read/Print Fraction

```
struct Fraction
    num::Int64; den::Int64
end

function printFraction(f::Fraction)
    println("$(f.num)/$(f.den)")
```

```
end # printFraction

function main()
    print("Enter numerator and denominator: ")
    n, d = [parse(Int, x) for x in split(readline())]   # read two numbers
    f = Fraction(n, d)   # create a fraction from them
    printFraction(f)
end # main

main()
```

Here is a run:

```
Enter numerator and denominator: 8 13
8/13
```

9.5.1 Manipulate Fractions

We can write functions to perform various operations on fractions. For instance, since

$$\frac{a}{b} + \frac{c}{d} = \frac{ad+bc}{bd}$$

we can write a function to return the sum of two fractions as follows:

```
function addFrac(a::Fraction, b::Fraction)
    Fraction(a.num*b.den + a.den*b.num, a.den*b.den)
end # addFrac
```

Similarly, we can write functions to subtract, multiply and divide fractions.

```
function subFrac(a::Fraction, b::Fraction)
    Fraction(a.num*b.den - a.den*b.num, a.den*b.den)
end # subFrac
```

```
function mulFrac(a::Fraction, b::Fraction)
    Fraction(a.num*b.num, a.den*b.den)
end # mulFrac
```

```
function divFrac(a::Fraction, b::Fraction)
    Fraction(a.num*b.den, a.den*b.num)
end # divFrac
```

To show how they can be used, we write Program P9.3

```
# Program P9.3 - Manipulate Fractions
struct Fraction
    num::Int64; den::Int64
end

function strFrac(f::Fraction) # convert f to a string
    "$(f.num)/$(f.den)"
end # strFrac

function redFrac(f::Fraction) # reduce fraction to its lowest terms
    d = gcd(f.num, f.den)      # divide num and den by their gcd
    Fraction(f.num÷d, f.den÷d)
end

function addFrac(a::Fraction, b::Fraction)
    Fraction(a.num*b.den + a.den*b.num, a.den*b.den)
```

```
end # addFrac

function subFrac(a::Fraction, b::Fraction)
    Fraction(a.num*b.den - a.den*b.num, a.den*b.den)
end # subFrac

function mulFrac(a::Fraction, b::Fraction)
    Fraction(a.num*b.num, a.den*b.den)
end # mulFrac

function divFrac(a::Fraction, b::Fraction)
    Fraction(a.num*b.den, a.den*b.num)
end # divFrac

function main()
    print("Enter numerator and denominator: ")
    n1, d1 = [parse(Int, x) for x in split(readline())]
    f1 = Fraction(n1, d1)
    print("Enter numerator and denominator: ")
    n2, d2 = [parse(Int, x) for x in split(readline())]
    f2 = Fraction(n2, d2)

    f3 = addFrac(f1, f2)
    println(strFrac(f1)*" + "*strFrac(f2)*" = "*strFrac(f3))

    f3 = subFrac(f1, f2)
    println(strFrac(f1)*" - "*strFrac(f2)*" = "*strFrac(f3))

    f3 = mulFrac(f1, f2)
    println(strFrac(f1)*" × "*strFrac(f2)*" = "*strFrac(f3))

    f3 = divFrac(f1, f2)
    println(strFrac(f1)*" ÷ "*strFrac(f2)*" = "*strFrac(f3))

    f3 = Fraction(12,42)
    println(strFrac(f3)*" = "*strFrac(redFrac(f3)))
end # main

main()
```

The following is a sample run:

```
Enter numerator and denominator: 1 5
Enter numerator and denominator: 1 7
1/5 + 1/7 = 12/35
1/5 - 1/7 = 2/35
1/5 × 1/7 = 1/35
1/5 ÷ 1/7 = 7/5
12/42 = 2/7
```

9.5.2 Rational Numbers

We have used fractions mainly to illustrate some of the ways structures can be manipulated in Julia. And that is how you would have to work with fractions in most other languages. However, to work with fractions in Julia, you can use the standard type Rational.

A Rational variable is used to represent the exact ratios of integers. It is constructed using the // operator. For example, we can create a Rational variable f34 with this:

```
julia> f34 = 3//4;
julia> typeof(f34)
Rational{Int64}
```

If the numerator and denominator of a rational have common factors, they are reduced to lowest terms such that the denominator is non-negative; we say the rational is `normalized`. Note these:

```
julia> 8//12
2//3
julia> -8//12
-2//3
julia> 8//-12
-2//3
julia> -8//-12
2//3
```

This normalized form for a ratio of integers is unique so, for instance, `2//3`, `8//12` and `14//21` all represent the *same* `Rational` number. We can test for equality of rational values by checking for equality of the numerator and denominator. The normalized numerator and denominator of a rational value can be extracted using the `numerator` and `denominator` functions. We have this:

```
julia> numerator(2//3)
2
julia> denominator(2//3)
3
```

But how about these?

```
julia> numerator(8//12)
2
julia> denominator(8//12)
3
```

Really? Yes, because the `Rational` is reduced to its lowest terms (`2//3`) *before* `numerator` and `denominator` are applied. Note the following:

```
julia> 8//12 == 16//24    # both reduced to 2//3 before being compared
true
julia> numerator(8//12) == numerator(16//24) # both first reduced to 2//3
true
```

We can compare two rationals directly so we hardly ever need to compare the numerator and denominator individually.

```
julia> 8//12 < 15//20     # 2/3 < 3/4? Yes
true
julia> 8//12 > 15//20     # 2/3 > 3/4? No
false
```

We can apply the usual arithmetic operators:

```
julia> 1//4 + 1//3
7//12
julia> 1//3 - 1//4
1//12
julia> 1//3 * 1//4
1//12
julia> 1//3 / 1//4
4//3
```

Answers are always reduced to lowest terms:

```
julia> 4//8 + 3//12    # 1//2 + 1//4
3//4
```

```
julia> 4//8 + 9//12    # 1//2 + 3//4
5//4
```

We can convert a rational to floating-point using float:

```
julia> b = float(9//12)
0.75
```

```
julia> typeof(b)
Float64
```

We can use rational numbers with other numeric types in a seamless way:

```
julia> 3//4 - 1/4    # 3//4 is promoted to 3/4
0.5
```

```
julia> 3//4 + 2    # 2 is promoted to 2//1
11//4
```

```
julia> 3//4 + 2/1    # 3//4 is promoted to float; / means float division
2.75
```

We now rewrite Program P9.3 as P9.4 to illustrate a simple use of Rational numbers.

 # Program P9.4 - Manipulate Rationals (Fractions)

```
function main()
    print("Enter numerator and denominator: ")
    n1, d1 = [parse(Int, x) for x in split(readline())]
    f1 = n1//d1        # make a rational number from n1, d1

    print("Enter numerator and denominator: ")
    n2, d2 = [parse(Int, x) for x in split(readline())]
    f2 = n2//d2        # make a rational number from n2, d2

    println("$f1 + $f2 = $(f1 + f2)")
    println("$f1 - $f2 = $(f1 - f2)")
    println("$f1 x $f2 = $(f1 * f2)")
    println("$f1 / $f2 = $(f1 / f2)")
    println("12/42 = $(12//42)")
end # main

main()
```

The following is a sample run:

```
Enter numerator and denominator: 1 5
Enter numerator and denominator: 1 7
1//5 + 1//7 = 12//35
1//5 - 1//7 = 2//35
1//5 x 1//7 = 1//35
1//5 / 1//7 = 7//5
12/42 = 2//7
```

We get the same output as that obtained from P9.3, with much less effort.

9.6 Voting Problem Revisited

This example will be used to illustrate several points concerning the passing of arguments to functions. It further highlights the differences between array arguments and simple-variable arguments. To do so, we will write a program to solve the voting problem we met in Section 7.11. Here it is again:

In an election, there are seven candidates. Each voter is allowed one vote for the candidate of his/her choice. The vote is recorded as a number from 1 to 7. The number of voters is unknown beforehand. Any vote which is not a number from 1 to 7 is an invalid (spoilt) vote.

A file, `votes.txt`, contains the names of the candidates. The first name is considered as candidate 1, the second as candidate 2, and so on. The names are followed by a blank line (the program will stop reading names when it hits the blank line), followed by the votes in free format. Write a program to read the data and evaluate the results of the election. Print all output to the file, `results.txt`.

Your output should specify the total number of votes, the number of valid votes and the number of spoilt votes. This is followed by the votes obtained by each candidate and the winner(s) of the election.

Suppose the file `votes.txt` contains the following data:

```
Victor Ali
Denise Duncan
Keith Khan
Michael Ali
Anisa Sawh
Carol Khan
Gary Oliver

3 1 2 5 4 3 5 3 5 3 2 8 1 6 7 7 3 5
6 9 3 4 7 1 2 4 5 5 1 4
```

Your program should send the following output to `results.txt`:

```
Invalid vote: 8
Invalid vote: 9

Number of voters: 30
Number of valid votes: 28
Number of spoilt votes: 2

Candidate        Score

Ali, Victor        4
Duncan, Denise     3
Khan, Keith        6
Ali, Michael       4
Sawh, Anisa        6
Khan, Carol        2
Oliver, Gary       3

The winner(s)
Khan, Keith
Sawh, Anisa
```

We now explain how we can solve this problem using Julia structures. Consider this declaration:

```
mutable struct Person
    first::String
    last::String
    votes::Int64
end
```

It's declared `mutable` since the `votes` field will change as votes are accumulated. We could also use the following and let Julia work out the types based on how we use them:

```
mutable struct Person
    first; last; votes
end
```

Next, we declare a `struct` array of type `Person` to hold the data for each candidate:

```
Candidate = Array{Person}(undef,0)
```

We start with an empty array (size `0`). When we read the name of the next candidate, we will allocate a new entry in `Candidate` to hold his/her data.

In the function `getNames`, we read a name, use `split` to break it up into `first` and `last` and then execute this statement (in the function `Candidate` is known as `Cand`):

```
push!(Cand, Person(first,last,0))
```

This creates a new entry in `Candidate` with the new name and the `votes` field set to `0`.

After all the names are read, `getNames` returns the number of candidates in the election.

We call `getNames` from `main` like this:

```
numCand = getNames(inn, Candidate) # returns number of candidates
```

Here is `getNames`:

```
function getNames(inn, Cand::Array{Person})
    # get the names of the candidates; count them
    if (aName = readline(inn)) == ""
        println("No names supplied")
        exit(1)
    end
    while aName != ""
        first, last = split(aName)
        push!(Cand, Person(first,last,0))  # add name to the list
        aName = readline(inn)
    end
    return length(Cand)    # number of candidates
end # getNames
```

Next, we must read and process the votes. This is handled by the function `processVotes`. This is its header:

```
function processVotes(inn, out, Cand::Array{Person})
```

We read votes line by line. The following reads one line of votes and stores them in the array `Num`:

```
line = readline(inn)
Num = [parse(Int, x) for x in split(line)]
```

We then process each vote in `Num`. Processing vote `v` involves checking that it is valid. If it is, we add 1 to the score for candidate `v` (`Cand[v].votes += 1`). We process one line of votes with this:

```
for v in Num
    if v < 1 || v > numCand
        println(out, "Invalid vote: $v")
        spoiltVotes += 1
    else
        Cand[v].votes +=1
        validVotes += 1
    end
end
```

Using the sample data, the array `Candidate` will contain the values shown below after all the votes have been tallied.

	first	last	votes
1	Victor	Ali	4
2	Denise	Duncan	3
3	Keith	Khan	6
4	Michael	Ali	4
5	Anisa	Sawh	6
6	Carol	Khan	2
7	Gary	Oliver	3

It remains only to print the results. This is done with the function `printResults`.

A name is given as separate words, like `"Victor"` and `"Ali"`, but we want to print it like this:

```
Ali, Victor
```

We do the conversion like this for `Cand[c]`:

```
aName = Cand[c].last * ", " * Cand[c].first
```

To find the winner, we first find the largest value (`winVote`) in the `votes` field. We then go through the array, printing those candidates with `winVote` votes.

In our example, `winVote` will be set to 6. We then "step through" the array, looking for those candidates with 6 votes. This way, we will find all the candidates, if there is more than one, with the highest vote and declare them as winners.

Putting all the pieces together, we get Program P9.5, a program to solve the voting problem using a `struct`.

```
# Program P9.5 - Vote Counting using struct
using Printf
mutable struct Person
    first; last; votes
end
function getNames(inn, Cand)
# get the names of the candidates; count them
    if (aName = readline(inn)) == ""
        println("No names supplied")
        exit(1)
    end
    while aName != ""
        first, last = split(aName)
        push!(Cand, Person(first,last,0))  # add name to the list
        aName = readline(inn)
    end
    return length(Cand) # number of candidates
end # getNames
function printResults(out, Cand::Array{Person}, valid, spoilt)
    println(out, "\nNumber of voters: $(valid + spoilt)")
    println(out, "Number of valid votes: $valid")
    println(out, "Number of spoilt votes: $spoilt")
    println(out, "\nCandidate      Score\n")

    for c in Cand
        @printf(out, "%-15s %3d\n", c.last*", "*c.first, c.votes)
    end
```

```
    winVote = Cand[1].votes
    for c in Cand[2:end]
        if (c.votes > winVote) winVote = c.votes end
    end

    println(out, "\nThe winner(s)")
    for c in Cand
        if c.votes == winVote
            println(out, "$(c.last), $(c.first)")
        end
    end
end # printResults

function processVotes(inn, out, Cand::Array{Person})
    validVotes = spoiltVotes = 0
    numCand = length(Cand)
    while (line = readline(inn)) != "" # get the data, one line at a time
        Num = [parse(Int, x) for x in split(line)] # all the numbers on one line
        for v in Num
            if v < 1 || v > numCand
                println(out, "Invalid vote: $v")
                spoiltVotes += 1
            else
                Cand[v].votes +=1
                validVotes += 1
            end
        end
    end # while
    validVotes, spoiltVotes # return values
end # processVotes

function main()
    inn = open("votes.txt", "r")
    out = open("results.txt", "w")

    Candidate = Array{Person}(undef,0)
    numCand = getNames(inn, Candidate)

    valid, spoilt = processVotes(inn, out, Candidate)
    printResults(out, Candidate, valid, spoilt)

    close(inn)
    close(out)
end # main

main()
```

We showed a sample run at the beginning of this section.

9.6.1 On using isless in sort

Program P9.5 prints the results in the order in which the names were supplied in the data. But that may not be the most useful way to present the results. One possibility is to print the results in alphabetical order by last name. We can do so with the function resultsByName:

```
function resultsByName(out, Cand::Array{Person,1})
    println(out, "\nResults sorted by name")
    sc = sortperm(Cand, by=v->(v.last, v.first))
    for c in sc
        aName = Cand[c].last*", "*Cand[c].first
        @printf(out, "%-15s %3d\n", aName, Cand[c].votes)
    end
end # resultsByName
```

If this function is called from `main` after the votes have been tallied, it will print this, the results sorted in alphabetical order by name:

```
Results sorted by name
Ali, Michael      4
Ali, Victor       4
Duncan, Denise    3
Khan, Carol       2
Khan, Keith       6
Oliver, Gary      3
Sawh, Anisa       6
```

Observe that persons with the same last name are arranged in order by their first name.

Yet another possibility is to sort the results in *descending order by votes received*, that is, with the winner(s) at the top of the list. Consider this function, `resultsByVote`:

```
function resultsByVote(out, Cand::Array{Person})
    sort!(Cand, by=v->v.votes, rev=true)
    println(out, "\nResults in descending order by score")
    for c in Cand
        aName = c.last*", "*c.first
        @printf(out, "%-15s %3d\n", aName, c.votes)
    end
end # resultsByVote
```

In `sort!` the option `rev=true` is used to sort in reverse order, in this case, descending.

If called from `main` after the votes have been tallied, it will print this, the results sorted in descending order by votes received:

```
Results in descending order by score
Khan, Keith       6
Sawh, Anisa       6
Ali, Victor       4
Ali, Michael      4
Duncan, Denise    3
Oliver, Gary      3
Khan, Carol       2
```

Looks correct, doesn't it? And the numbers are. But wait. The `Ali` boys with the same score of 4 are not listed in alphabetical order. Not a big deal but it would be nice if persons who tie are listed in alphabetical order.

Be alert to what we would like to do. We want to sort the list in *descending* order by votes and, within ties, in *ascending* order by name.

Unfortunately, this is not so easy to do using standard options in `sort`. Not easy, but not too difficult. It just requires a little more work, using the `lt=isless` option in `sort`. To use it, you must precede `resultsByVote` with this directive:

```
import Base.isless
```

We can then write `resultsByVote` as follows, identical to the version above, except for a change in the arguments to `sort!`.

```
function resultsByVote(out, Cand::Array{Person})
    sort!(Cand, lt=isless)
    println(out, "\nResults in descending order by score")
    for c in Cand
        aName = c.last*", "*c.first
        @printf(out, "%-15s %3d\n", aName, c.votes)
    end
end # resultsByVote
```

To complete the job, we must define what `isless` means for `Person` structures. It's a powerful mechanism which gives us great flexibility in how we sort.

For instance, consider this:

```
function isless(a::Person, b::Person)
    a.votes < b.votes
end
```

This says that, in sorting, `Person a` is considered less than `Person b` if the `votes` field of a is less than the votes field of b, and, in that case, a will appear earlier in the sorted order than b. With these changes, calling `resultsByVote` will print this, the results sorted in ascending order by `votes`:

```
Khan, Carol       2
Duncan, Denise    3
Oliver, Gary      3
Ali, Victor       4
Ali, Michael      4
Khan, Keith       6
Sawh, Anisa       6
```

Observe that ties appear in the order the names appeared in the original list.

If, for whatever reason, we wanted to sort in alphabetical order by *first name*, all we have to do is change `isless` to this:

```
function isless(a::Person, b::Person)
    a.first < b.first
end
```

And we would get this:

```
Sawh, Anisa       6
Khan, Carol       2
Duncan, Denise    3
Oliver, Gary      3
Khan, Keith       6
Ali, Michael      4
Ali, Victor       4
```

We hope you're starting to see the power and versatility of `isless`.

Now to the task at hand: sort in *descending* order by votes and, within ties, in *ascending* order by name. Here is `isless`:

```
function isless(a::Person, b::Person)
    if a.votes > b.votes          # higher votes come earlier in sorted order
        true
    elseif a.votes < b.votes      # lower votes come later in sorted order
        false
    elseif a.last == b.last       # votes are the same: if last names are the same
        a.first < b.first         # use first name to determine order
    else
        a.last < b.last           # otherwise, order by last name
    end
end
```

With these changes, we finally get the results sorted in descending order by `votes` and, within ties, in alphabetical order by name.

```
Khan, Keith        6
Sawh, Anisa        6
Ali, Michael       4
Ali, Victor        4
Duncan, Denise     3
Oliver, Gary       3
Khan, Carol        2
```

EXERCISES 9

1. Write a program to read names and phone numbers into a `struct` array. Request a name and print the person's phone number. Use binary search to look up the name.

2. Write a function that, given two Date structures, `d1` and `d2`, returns `-1` if `d1` comes before `d2`, `0` if `d1` is the same as `d2`, and `1` if `d1` comes after `d2`.

3. Write a function that, given two Date structures, `d1` and `d2`, returns the number of days that `d2` is ahead of `d1`. If `d2` comes before `d1`, return a negative value.

4. A time in 24-hour clock format is represented by two numbers; for example, `16 45` means the time 16:45, that is, 4:45 p.m.

   (a) Using a structure to represent a time, write a function that, given two time structures, `t1` and `t2`, returns the number of minutes from `t1` to `t2`. For example, if the two given times are `16 45` and `23 25`, your function should return `400`.

   (b) Modify the function so that it works as follows: if `t2` is less than `t1`, take it to mean a time for the next day. For example, given the times `20:30` and `6:15`, take this to mean 8.30 p.m. to 6.15 a.m. of the next day. Your function should return `585`.

5. A length, specified in meters and centimeters, is represented by two integers. For example, the length 3m 75cm is represented by `3 75`. Using a structure to represent a length, write functions to compare, add, and subtract two lengths.

6. A file contains the names and distances jumped by athletes in a long-jump competition. Using a structure to hold a name and distance (which is itself a structure as in Exercise 5), write a program to read the data and print a list of names and distance jumped in order of merit (best jumper first).

7. A data file contains registration information for six courses—CS20A, CS21A, CS29A, CS30A, CS35A, and CS36A. Each line of data consists of a seven-digit student registration number followed by six (ordered) values, each of which is `0` or `1`. A value of `1` indicates that the student is registered for the corresponding course; `0` means the student is not. Thus, `1 0 1 0 1 1` means that the student is registered for CS20A, CS29A, CS35A, and CS36A, but not for CS21A and CS30A.

   You may assume that there are no more than 100 students and a registration number `0` ends the data.

   Write a program to read the data and produce a class list for each course. Each list consists of the registration numbers of those students taking the course.

8. At a school's bazaar, activities were divided into stalls. At the close of the bazaar, the manager of each stall submitted information to the principal consisting of the name of the stall, the income earned, and its expenses. Here are some sample data:

```
"Bran Tub" 2300.00 1000.00
"Putt The Ball" 900.00 1000.00
```

(a) Create a structure to hold a stall's data.

(b) Write a program to read the data and print a report consisting of the stall name and net income (income - expenses), in order of decreasing net income (that is, with the most profitable stall first and the least profitable stall last). In addition, print the number of stalls, the total profit or loss of the bazaar, and the stall(s) that made the most profit.

9. An anagram is a word or phrase formed by rearranging the letters of another word or phrase. Examples of one-word anagrams are: sister/resist and senator/treason. We can get more interesting anagrams if we ignore letter case and punctuation marks. Examples are: Time-table/Bet I'm Late, Clint Eastwood/Old West Action and Woman Hitler/Mother-in-law.

An input file contains one word or phrase per line. Write a program to read the file and output all words/phrases (from the file) that arc anagrams of each other. Print a blank line between each group of anagrams.

Hint: Use an array of struct. Each struct has two fields—phrase and code, say: code consists of all the letters of phrase, converted to one case and arranged in ascending order. Some examples:

```
Bet I'm Late abeeilmtt
Time-table abeeilmtt
```

If you sort the array by the code field, all anagrams will occupy consecutive entries.

Sample input
```
Time-table
Woman Hitler
Clint Eastwood
Bet I'm Late
Mother-in-law
Old West Action
```

Sample output
```
Bet I'm Late
Time-table

Clint Eastwood
Old West Action

Mother-in-law
Woman Hitler
```

CHAPTER 10

Dictionaries and Sets

In this chapter, we will explain the following:

- What is a dictionary (`Dict`)
- How to create and use dictionaries
- How to implement a letter-frequency program using a `Dict`
- What is a `Set`
- Operations on sets: `union`, `union!`, `intersect`, etc.
- How to use a `Set` to find all unique words in an input file
- How to build a thesaurus from lines of synonyms
- How to generate all combinations and permutations of a set
- How to write a program to evaluate a hand in *Scrabble*

10.1 Dictionaries

In a dictionary, we look-up a word to find its meaning. In computing terminology, the word we search for is called the `key` and the meaning is its `value`. A *dictionary* is a data structure which lets us associate keys with values. Julia provides the type `Dict` for working with dictionaries.

In the game of *Scrabble*, each letter has a point-value. The first four are A-1, B-3, C-3, D-2. We could create a dictionary of these letters (we call it `Scrb`) like this:

```
julia> Scrb = Dict('A' => 1, 'B' => 3, 'C' => 3, 'D' => 2)
Dict{Char,Int64} with 4 entries:
  'C' => 3
  'D' => 2
  'A' => 1
  'B' => 3
```

Some observations:

- The keys *are in no particular order*, indicating that *a dictionary is an unordered collection of (key, value) pairs*.
- The keys are *unique*. We cannot have two entries with the same key. In an English dictionary, we can have several entries for the same word (`run`, say). In a `Dict`, they would have to be distinguished in some way, like `run1`, `run2`, etc.
- Values can be duplicated. We can have the same value associated with more than one key. Here, `'B'` and `'C'` both have the value 3.
- Above, we let Julia determine the type of the keys as `Char` and the type of the values as `Int64`. We also have the option of specifying the types ourselves:
  ```
  Scrb = Dict{Char,Int64}('A' => 1, 'B' => 3, 'C' => 3, 'D' => 2)
  ```

© The Author(s), under exclusive license to Springer Nature Switzerland AG 2021
N. Kalicharan, *Julia - Bit by Bit*, Undergraduate Topics in Computer Science,
https://doi.org/10.1007/978-3-030-73936-2_10

The types, separated by a comma, are written in curly brackets right after the word Dict.

We can access the elements of Scrb using the *keys as subscripts* (enclosed by square brackets):

```julia
julia> Scrb['B']
3

julia> Scrb['D']
2
```

We can extract the *keys* from the dictionary using the function keys:

```julia
julia> ScrbKeys = keys(Scrb);

julia> print(ScrbKeys)
['C', 'D', 'A', 'B']
```

Caution: Even though this may *look* like an array, it is not. For instance, note this:

```julia
julia> ScrbKeys[1]
ERROR: MethodError: no method matching
getindex(::Base.KeySet{Char,Dict{Char,Int64}}, ::Int64)
```

Essentially, this says ScrbKeys is of type Base.KeySet and array indexing does not apply to it.

Nevertheless, using collect, we can *create* an "array of keys" with this:

```julia
julia> ScrbKeysArr = collect(ScrbKeys)
4-element Array{Char,1}:
 'C'
 'D'
 'A'
 'B'
```

Now, we can access ScrbKeysArr with array indexing:

```julia
julia> ScrbKeysArr[3]
'A'
```

If we need the keys in sorted order, we can use this:

```julia
julia> ScrbKeysSorted = sort(ScrbKeysArr)
4-element Array{Char,1}:
 'A'
 'B'
 'C'
 'D'
```

We could have combined all of the above in one statement:

```julia
julia> ScrbKeysSorted = sort(collect(keys(Scrb)))
4-element Array{Char,1}:

 'A'
 'B'
 'C'
 'D'
```

If we wish to print the dictionary in order by keys, we could do so with this:

```julia
julia> for key in sort(collect(keys(Scrb)))
           println("$key => $(Scrb[key])")
       end
A => 1
B => 3
C => 3
D => 2
```

If we need to work with the values only, we could extract them with the function `values`:

```
julia> ScrbVals = values(Scrb)
Base.ValueIterator for a Dict{String,Int64} with 4 entries. Values:
  3
  2
  1
  3
```

The order of the values correspond with the order we would get with `keys(Scrb)`.

Note, again, that `ScrbVals` is *not* an array and attempting to access `ScrbVals[1]`, say, will give an error. However, we can *iterate* through the values like this:

```
julia> for v in ScrbVals print("$v ") end
3 2 1 3
```

Tip: The `Pair()` function is a synonym for `=>`. `Pair('B',3)` is the same as `'B' => 3`.

We *could* have created the original `Dict` `Scrb` with this:

```
julia> Scrb = Dict(Pair('A',1), Pair('B',3), Pair('C',3), Pair('D',2))
Dict{Char,Int64} with 4 entries:
  'C' => 3
  'D' => 2
  'A' => 1
  'B' => 3
```

Assuming `'X'` and `'M'` are not yet among the keys of `Scrb`, here's how we can add them:

```
julia> Scrb['X'] = 10 # this adds a new entry with 'X' as key
10
```

(If `'X'` was already a key, this would change its value to `10`.)

We can use the function `push!` to add a new entry to a dictionary.

```
julia> push!(Scrb, Pair('M', 3))
Dict{Char,Int64} with 6 entries:
  'C' => 3
  'M' => 3
  'D' => 2
  'A' => 1
  'X' => 10
  'B' => 3
```

Again, note the entries are in no particular order.

After we discuss `Sets` in Section 10.2, we will show (in 10.4) how to find all the words which can be formed from a given set of tiles in the game of *Scrabble*.

For now, we illustrate how to use a `Dict` by writing a program to solve the *Letter Frequency* problem we met in Section 7.6.

10.1.1 Letter Frequency

Given some text as input, we want to determine the frequency with which each letter of the alphabet is used.

To solve it, we'll use a `Dict`; we call it `LetterFreq`.

Each entry in `LetterFreq` will be indexed by a `Char`; e.g. `LetterFreq['a']` will hold the number of times a occurs in the input. We declare `LetterFreq` like this, initially with no entries:

```
LetterFreq = Dict{Char, Int64}()
```

When we read a letter c, the following is executed:

```
LetterFreq[c] = get(LetterFreq, c, 0) + 1
```

Here, we introduce the function get. Its general form is

```
get(D, k, dflt)
```

where D is a Dict, k is a key and dflt is a 'default' value. If k is present in D, get returns D[k]; if it's not present, dflt is returned.

If the letter c is already in the dictionary LetterFreq, its frequency is retrieved with get, 1 is added to it, and this becomes the new value of LetterFreq[c].

If c is not in the dictionary, get returns the default value 0, 1 is added to it, and 1 is stored in a newly-created entry LetterFreq[c].

After all the input has been read and processed, we print the dictionary. But recall a dictionary is in no particular order. We use this statement to put the keys in alphabetical order:

```
sort(collect(keys(LetterFreq)))
```

The details are shown in Program P10.1.

```
# Program P10.1 - Letter Frequency
using Printf

function tolowercase(ch::Char)
# If ch is a letter, return its lowercase equivalent; else return '0'
    if isletter(ch) return lowercase(ch) end
    return '0'
end # tolowercase

function LetterFrequency(LetterFreq::Dict, inn)
    while !eof(inn)
        ch = read(inn, Char)
        if (c = tolowercase(ch)) != '0'
            LetterFreq[c] = get(LetterFreq, c, 0) + 1
        end
    end
end # LetterFrequency

function main()
    inn = open("input.txt", "r")
    out = open("output.txt", "w")

    LetterFreq = Dict{Char, Int64}()
    LetterFrequency(LetterFreq, inn)

    println(out, "Letter Frequency\n")
    for ch in sort(collect(keys(LetterFreq)))
        @printf(out, "%4c %8d\n", ch, LetterFreq[ch])
    end
    close(inn)
    close(out)
end # main

main()
```

Suppose we are given the following in the file input.txt:

```
To be or not to be?
That is the question
```

The program sends this to the file output.txt:

```
Letter Frequency
    a      1
    b      2
    e      4
    h      2
    i      2
    n      2
    o      5
    q      1
    r      1
    s      2
    t      7
    u      1
```

Note that only those letters which appeared in the input are stored in the dictionary; hence only those appear in the output.

10.1.2 Dict Functions - haskey, in, delete!

We'll use this dictionary in the examples which follow:

```
julia> D = Dict(["A" => ">= 80", "B" => "65-79", "C" => "50-64"])
Dict{String,String} with 3 entries:
  "B" => "65-79"
  "A" => ">= 80"
  "C" => "50-64"
```

The function haskey(D, k) returns true if the key k is in the dictionary D and false if it's not.

```
julia> haskey(D, "B")
true

julia> haskey(D, "D")
false
```

We can ask if a (key => value) item belongs to D, in two ways, using in:

```
julia> ("B" => "65-79") in D     # brackets required
true

julia> in(("B" => "65-79"), D)  # brackets required
true
```

We can delete a key k (and its associated entry) from a dictionary D with delete!(D, k):

```
julia> delete!(D, "B")
Dict{String,String} with 2 entries:
  "A" => ">= 80"
  "C" => "50-64"
```

As a reminder, we can *add* an entry to a dictionary with a simple assignment:

```
julia> D["B"] = "65-79"
"65-79"

julia> D["F"] = "< 50"
"< 50"

julia> D
Dict{String,String} with 4 entries:
  "B" => "65-79"
  "A" => ">= 80"
  "C" => "50-64"
  "F" => "< 50"
```

10.2 Sets

In mathematics, a *set* is an *unordered* collection of *unique* elements. This means a set cannot have more than one of the same item unlike an array. Also, items in an array A have an order imposed by their indices: A[1] comes before A[2] which comes before A[3], etc. There is no such notion of ordering in a set. Put another way, there is no first, second or last item in a set.

An easy way to create a set is to assign elements to it, like this:

```
julia> S = Set([11, 13, 17, 19])
Set{Int64} with 4 elements:
  13
  19
  17
  11
```

The round brackets () enclose the argument to Set, [11,13,17,19].

This creates a set called S with the values shown. Since all the elements are integers, Julia tags the set as Int64. Also, the response emphasizes that the elements are in no particular order. It would make no sense to ask for the first (or any specific) element of S.

Compare with this (without the word Set, we get an array):

```
julia> A = [11, 13, 17, 19]
4-element Array{Int64,1}:
  11
  13
  17
  19
```

This is an Int64 array whose elements are A[1]=11, A[2]=13, A[3]=17 and A[4]=19. We can access the elements using a subscript, and the elements are in the order we supplied them.

So how do we access the elements of a set? Like this, using in:

```
julia> for p in S print("$p ") end
13 19 17 11
```

As you see, we can process each item in a set but can make no assumptions about the *order* in which they will be processed.

We can also ask if a specific item is present in a set, also with in:

```
julia> if 15 in S print("It's there!") else print("It's not there!") end
It's not there!
julia> if 17 in S print("It's there!") else print("It's not there!") end
It's there!
```

Here are some other examples of set creation:

```
julia> Fruit = Set(["mango","plum","fig"])
Set{String} with 3 elements:
  "fig"
  "mango"
  "plum"
```

Julia recognizes that all the arguments are String and creates a String set called Fruit. But how about this?

```
julia> Fruit = Set(["mango",10,"plum",15])
Set{Any} with 4 elements:
  10
  "mango"
```

```
"plum"
15
```

Now that the set contains strings and numbers, it is a set of `Any`.

It's worthwhile to point out the difference between `Set(["abc"])` and `Set("abc")`.

```
A = Set(["abc"])
Set{String} with 1 element:
 "abc"
```

There is one string within the square brackets so Julia creates a set with that one element. But, without the square brackets, we have this:

```
julia> A = Set("abc")
Set{Char} with 3 elements:
 'a'
 'c'
 'b'
```

Without the square brackets, Julia treats the string `"abc"` as a set of three characters (`Char`), and creates the set accordingly.

Caution: Here is something else to be aware of:
```
julia> A = Set{String}["ab","53"]
ERROR: MethodError: Cannot `convert` an object of type String to an object of type
Set{String}
```

This occurs because we omitted the parentheses `()` that enclose the argument to a `Set()`.

When we include the parentheses, we get this:
```
julia> A = Set{String}(["ab","53"])
Set{String} with 2 elements:
 "53"
 "ab"
```

10.2.1 Set Operations

Julia provides many functions for working with sets. We discuss the more common of these.

union

The *union* of two sets A and B contains all the elements which belong to either A or B, *without duplication*. (It is usually written as A ∪ B.) In Julia, *union* is performed using the functions `union` and `union!`.

For example,

```
julia> F1 = Set(["mango", "chenet", "plum"])
Set{String} with 3 elements:
 "mango"
 "chenet"
 "plum"

julia> F2 = Set(["guava", "chenet", "mango"])
Set{String} with 3 elements:
 "guava"
 "mango"
 "chenet"

julia> F3 = union(F1, F2)
Set{String} with 4 elements:
```

```
    "guava"
    "mango"
    "chenet"
    "plum"
```

"mango" and "chenet" appear in both sets but appear once in the union. To emphasize, elements in a set are *unique*.

Above, we saw that if a string constant is used where a set is expected, it is treated as a set with the individual characters in the string as elements of the set. Note the following:

```
julia> s = "1010cc";

julia> S1 = Set(["a", "b"]);

julia> union(s, S1)
5-element Array{Any,1}:
 '1': ASCII/Unicode U+0031 (category Nd: Number, decimal digit)
 '0': ASCII/Unicode U+0030 (category Nd: Number, decimal digit)
 'c': ASCII/Unicode U+0063 (category Ll: Letter, lowercase)
 "b"
 "a"
```

The unique characters of s are 1, 0 and c. These are "unioned" with the two strings in S1.

Attention: union resulted in an Array, not a Set.

But look what happens if we merely reverse the order of the arguments:

```
julia> union(S1, s)
Set{Any} with 5 elements:
  '0'
  '1'
  'c'
  "b"
  "a"
```

We end up with a Set, not an Array. If the first argument is a Set *variable*, the result is a Set.

Even if we put square brackets around [s], this is an *expression*, not a variable. If it's the first argument, the result is an Array:

```
julia> union([s], S1)
3-element Array{String,1}:
 "1010cc"
 "b"
 "a"
```

And, again, compare with this (the first argument, S1, is a Set variable; the result is a Set):

```
julia> union(S1, [s])
Set{String} with 3 elements:
  "1010cc"
  "b"
  "a"
```

If we union two strings, the individual characters of both strings are treated as set elements; the result is an Array:

```
julia> union("ab3c","b13a")
5-element Array{Char,1}:
 'a': ASCII/Unicode U+0061 (category Ll: Letter, lowercase)
 'b': ASCII/Unicode U+0062 (category Ll: Letter, lowercase)
 '3': ASCII/Unicode U+0033 (category Nd: Number, decimal digit)
 'c': ASCII/Unicode U+0063 (category Ll: Letter, lowercase)
 '1': ASCII/Unicode U+0031 (category Nd: Number, decimal digit)
```

A useful rule to remember is that set operations are meant to apply to sets. If we apply union to a set and a string (or even two strings), Julia will try to make the best sense of it. It will interpret a string as a "set of characters", ignoring their order (or duplicates) in the string.

Tip: In union(A, B), if A is a Set variable, the result is a Set; if not, the result is an Array.

---

union!

Closely related to union is union!. As might be expected, union! changes one of its arguments, the first one:

```
julia> S1 = Set(["a", "b"]);

julia> S2 = Set(["b", "c"]);

julia> union!(S1,S2)
Set{String} with 3 elements:
  "c"
  "b"
  "a"

julia> println(S1)
Set(["c", "b", "a"])

julia> println(S2)
Set(["c", "b"])
```

The statement union!(S1,S2) sets S1 to the union of S1 and S2; S2 is unchanged.

In the following, note a subtle difference between union and union!.

```
julia> typeof(S2)
Set{String}

julia> union(S2, "mp")
Set{Any} with 4 elements:
  "c"
  "b"
  'p'
  'm'
```

But,

```
julia> union!(S2, "mp")
ERROR: MethodError: Cannot `convert` an object of type Char to an object of type String
```

There is no problem with union as "mp" is converted to a Set of Char; we union a set of String with a set of Char to get a set of Any.

With union!, since S2 is a set of String and also the result of the union, the second argument *must* be a set of String. We can get around this by converting the String "mp" to a set:

```
julia> union!(S2, ["mp"])
Set{String} with 3 elements:
  "c"
  "mp"
  "b"
```

To pursue the example:

```
julia> println(S2)
Set(["c", "mp", "b"])

julia> S3 = union(S2, "hff")
```

```
Set{Any} with 5 elements:
  'f'
  "c"
  "mp"
  'h'
  "b"
```

Since S3 is a set of Any, we can now do this union (which would give an error if S3 was a set of String):

```
julia> union!(S3, "ef")  # set of Any and set of Char
Set{Any} with 6 elements:
  'f'
  "c"
  "mp"
  'h'
  "b"
  'e'
```

intersect and intersect!

The *intersection* of two sets A and B contains those elements which belong to both sets. (It is usually written as A ∩ B.) In Julia, *intersection* is performed using the functions intersect and intersect!.

For example,

```
julia> S1 = Set(["a", "b", "c", 1, 2, 3]);

julia> println(S1)
Set(Any["c", 2, 3, "b", "a", 1])

julia> S2 = Set(["c", "d", "e", 3, 5, 7]);

julia> println(S2)
Set(Any[7, "c", "e", 3, 5, "d"])

julia> S3 = intersect(S1, S2);

julia> println(S3)
Set(Any["c", 3])
```

Here, the intersection is assigned to S3; S1 and S2 are unchanged.

We use intersect! when we want to *replace* the contents of one of the sets by the intersection, like this:

```
julia> intersect!(S1, S2);  # replace S1 by S1 ∩ S2; S2 is unchanged

julia> println(S1)
Set(Any["c", 3])

julia> println(S2)
Set(Any[7, "c", "e", 3, 5, "d"])
```

delete!

We use delete! to remove individual elements from a set:

```
julia> S = Set(["a", "b", "c"]);

julia> delete!(S, "b")
Set{String} with 2 elements:
  "c"
  "a"
```

The general format is `delete!(S, d)` where `S` is a set and `d` is the item to be deleted.

Relational operators applied to Sets

We can apply any of the six relational operators to sets.

==	equal to (set equality)
!=	not equal to
>	greater than (proper superset)
>=	greater than or equal to (superset)
<	less than (proper subset)
<=	less than or equal to (subset)

We illustrate with the following examples:

```julia
julia> A = Set(["a", "b", "c", "d"]);

julia> B = Set(["b", "c"]);

julia> C = Set(["b", "c"]);

julia> A > B  # A is a superset of B
true

julia> B < A  # B is a subset of A
true

julia> B >= A  # B is not a superset of A
false

julia> A != B
true

julia> B == C
true

julia> B != C
false

julia> B < C   # not a proper subset
false

julia> B <= C  # but a subset
true

julia> B > C  # not a proper superset
false

julia> B >= C  # but a superset
true
```

`setdiff` and `setdiff!`

The *difference* of two sets A and B (usually written A - B) contains those elements which belong to A but not to B. In Julia, *set difference* is performed using the functions `setdiff` and `setdiff!`.

```julia
julia> S1 = Set(["a","b","c",1,2,3]);

julia> S2 = Set(["c","d","e",1,3,5]);

julia> SD12 = setdiff(S1, S2);
```

```
julia> println(SD12)
Set(Any[2, "b", "a"])

julia> SD21 = setdiff(S2, S1);

julia> println(SD21)
Set(Any["e", 5, "d"])
```

In the usual meaning of !, setdiff! *replaces* the first argument by the difference of the two sets:

```
julia> setdiff!(S1, S2);

julia> println(S1)
Set(Any[2, "b", "a"])
```

Suppose we reset S1 to Set(["a","b","c",1,2,3]) and do setdiff(S2, S1). We get this:

```
julia> setdiff!(S2, S1);

julia> println(S2)
Set(Any["e", 5, "d"])
```

10.2.2 Find All Unique Words

We now write a program (P10.2) to fetch words from a file with arbitrary punctuation. It keeps track of all the different words found, ignoring the case of the letters: to and To are treated as the same word.

A Set is appropriate to use here since it does not allow duplicates. It frees us from having to check if we've seen a word before. If we try to add a word that's already in the set, it is ignored.

After all the words have been fetched, the program prints the *number* of unique words found, the Set of words and an alphabetical listing of the words

The function length (which we've used before to get the length of a string), when applied to a Set, returns the *number of elements* in the set.

```
# Program P10.2 - Find All Unique Words
# A word is a string of letters; any non-letter is a delimiter

function getNextWord(inn::IOStream)
# A word is defined as a contiguous sequence of letters
    ch = ' '         # necessary for ch to be known to the whole function
    while !eof(inn) && !isletter(ch) # Search for next letter
        ch = read(inn, Char)
    end
    if eof(inn) return nothing end   # None found; end of file reached

    # At this point, ch contains the first letter of the word
    wrd = string(ch)   # convert a single letter to String
    ch = read(inn, Char)
    while isletter(ch) # as long as we get a letter
        wrd *= ch        # add it to the word
        ch = read(inn, Char)
    end
    return wrd
end # getNextWord

function main()
    inn = open("input.txt", "r")
    WordList = Set{String}()

    while (word = getNextWord(inn)) != nothing
        union!(WordList, [lowercase(word)]) # add to list; ignore duplicates
    end
```

```
    close(inn)

    print("Number of unique words: $(length(WordList))\n\n")

    print("Words in set\n$WordList \n")

    print("\nWords in order\n")
    for w in sort(collect(WordList)) print("$w ") end
    println()
end # main

main()
```

Suppose `input.txt` contains this:

```
To be or not to be?
That is the question. No?
```

When run, the program prints this:

```
Number of unique words: 9

Words in set
Set(["question", "or", "that", "not", "is", "the", "to", "no", "be"])

Words in order
be is no not or question that the to
```

10.3 Thesaurus

We use this example to illustrate some of the power and convenience of Julia functions/operations.

Problem

Write a program to read and store a thesaurus based on the following.

Data for the program consists of lines of input. Each line contains a (variable) number of distinct words, all of which are synonyms of each other. For example:

```
flower blossom
live reside dwell
```

You may assume words consist of letters only and are separated by one or more spaces.

A word can appear on more than one line. If a word appears on more than one line then all words on those lines are to be considered synonyms. For example:

```
live reside dwell
inhabit live lodge
```

All five (distinct) words are considered synonyms of each other.

After all the input has been read and processed, print a listing of the groups of synonyms. Within each group, print the members in alphabetical order. And print the entire thesaurus sorted by the first word in each group.

Suppose you are given the following data:

```
live reside dwell
flower blossom
perplex confuse bewilder confound
inhabit live lodge
bloom flower bud
```

Your program should print this:

```
bewilder confound confuse perplex
bloom blossom bud flower
dwell inhabit live lodge reside
```

Before looking at the solution, it would be instructive to spend some time and think about how you might solve this problem.

We use a `Dict` called `Thes`, with keys `1`, `2`, etc. `Thes[1]` holds the first set of synonyms, `Thes[2]` the second set, and so on. We read the data line by line. For each line, we break it up into individual words using `split`, and store them in a `Set` called `words`.

Here's an outline of the processing required:

```
get the words on a line; store in a Set called words
for each w in words
    if w is in any existing word set (Thes[k], say)
        union!(Thes[k], words)
        # nothing more to do for this line of words
    end
end
if none of the words is in any Thes[k]
    add these words as a new set to Thes
end
```

After all the data is read, and the thesaurus built, we call `printResults` to produce the required output.

Keep in mind that `Thes` is a dictionary (`Dict`) of `Set`s. And neither a `Set` nor a `Dict` is stored in any particular order. Suppose we decide to print `Thes` with this:

```
for (k, v) in Thes
    for wrd in v
        print(out, "$wrd ")
    end
    println(out)
end
```

We will get this output:

```
bloom bud blossom flower
perplex bewilder confound confuse
reside live dwell inhabit lodge
```

The information is correct; synonyms are grouped together but they are listed in no particular order. (Compare with the required output above.)

We must do some sorting but we cannot apply `sort` directly to a `Dict` or a `Set`. We must first store the data in an `Array`. Consider this:

```
tList = Array{Array{String}}(undef, length(Thes))
```

For the sample data, `length(Thes)` is 3, so `tList` is an array of size 3. But what kind of array?

Each element of `tList` is an "array of `String`s". Now consider this:

```
for n in keys(Thes)
    tList[n] = sort(collect(Thes[n]))
end
```

- n takes on the values 1, 2, 3 (not necessarily in that order).
- `collect(Thes[n])` converts the `Set` `Thes[n]` to an `Array`.

- **sort** sorts the array in ascending order.

Because of the order in which the data was supplied,

- **Thes[1]** is the *live* set
- **Thes[2]** is the *flower* set
- **Thes[3]** is the *perplex* set

When the **for n in keys(Thes)** loop above is executed, we end up with this:

```
tList[1] = ["dwell", "inhabit", "live", "lodge", "reside"]
tList[2] = ["bloom", "blossom", "bud", "flower"]
tList[3] = ["bewilder", "confound", "confuse", "perplex"]
```

Within each group, the words are sorted.

The last step is to sort by the first word in each group. Fortunately, that's easy (when you know how;). All we need is this:

```
sort!(tList)
```

This rearranges the elements of **tList** in ascending order by the first word in each group:

```
tList[1] = ["bewilder", "confound", "confuse", "perplex"]
tList[2] = ["bloom", "blossom", "bud", "flower"]
tList[3] = ["dwell", "inhabit", "live", "lodge", "reside"]
```

When we print this, we get the final required output:

```
bewilder confound confuse perplex
bloom blossom bud flower
dwell inhabit live lodge reside
```

All the details are captured in the Program P10.3. It's a feather in Julia's cap that such a non-trivial problem can be solved so neatly and concisely using standard features.

```
# Program P10.3 - Thesaurus
function processWord(w, wordSet::Set, Thes::Dict)
# check if w is in any set of synonyms
    for k in keys(Thes)
        if w in Thes[k]
            union!(Thes[k], wordSet)
            return true
        end
    end # for k
    false
end # processWord

function printResults(out, Thes::Dict)
    tList = Array{Array{String}}(undef, length(Thes))

    for n in keys(Thes)
        tList[n] = sort(collect(Thes[n]))
    end
    sort!(tList)

    for synonyms in tList
        for wrd in synonyms
            print(out, "$wrd ")
        end
        println(out)
    end
end # printResults

function main()
    inn = open("thesaurus.txt", "r")
```

```
        out = open("output.txt", "w")
        Thes = Dict()

        setNo = 0
        while (line = readline(inn)) != ""
            words = Set([w for w in split(line)])
            seen = false
            for w in words
                if (seen = processWord(w, words, Thes)) break end
                # seen is true if w is found in an existing set
            end
            if !seen
                setNo += 1
                Thes[setNo] = words
            end
        end # while

        printResults(out, Thes)

        close(inn)
        close(out)
    end

    main()
```

10.4 Scrabble

In the game of *Scrabble*, each letter of the alphabet is worth a certain number of points based on how often they appear in English words. In the standard game, points are allocated as follows:

```
1 point   - A E I O U L N S T R
2 points  - D G
3 points  - B C M P
4 points  - F H V W Y
5 points  - K
8 points  - J X
10 points - Q Z
```

There is also a varying *number of tiles* for each letter: A-9, B-2, C-2, D-4, E-12, F-2, G-3, H-2, I-9, J-1, K-1, L-4, M-2, N-6, O-8, P-2, Q-1, R-6, S-4, T-6, U-4, V-2, W-2, X-1, Y-2, Z-1.

At the start of the game, a player chooses 7 tiles at random. We will try to solve this problem:

Given 7 tiles, find all the valid words which can be made from them and the number of points each word is worth.

What's a valid word? Any word found in our 'dictionary', the file scrabble.txt. We will elaborate on this later.

To keep the discussion manageable, we will start with three tiles: A, S, T. For the moment, we will assume the tiles are all different. Later, we will discuss how to handle cases where we have more than one of the same letter, as can happen in the real game.

First, we look at all the possible combinations of these three letters: we look at 1-letter 'words', 2-letter 'words' and 3-letter 'words'. We observe that not every letter combination, say, (e.g. ST) is a valid word. Here are the possibilities:

- 1-letter: A, S, T
- 2-letter: AS, AT, ST
- 3-letter: AST

That's a total of 7 possibilities of letter-combinations. With *n* tiles, the total number of possibilities will be 2^n-1. But that's not all we have to worry about.

For the combination AST, there are 6 ways we can arrange the letters, each a possible word: AST, ATS, SAT, STA, TAS, TSA. Of these, only SAT is a legitimate English word (we're not counting common abbreviations like AST, TSA). Three letters can be arranged in 3! = 6 ways. We say there are 6 *permutations* of the letters AST. A set of *n* distinct letters can be arranged in *n*! ways.

Our first task is to enumerate all the combinations and, for each combination, find all its permutations. Further, for each permutation, determine whether the 'word' is in the dictionary.

We've seen that the 3-letter combination AST can be arranged in 3! = 6 ways. Each of the three 2-letter combinations can be arranged in 2! = 2 ways. And, of course, each 1-letter combination can be 'arranged' in 1! = 1 way. This gives a total of 6+6+3 =15 possibilities we need to check.

As a matter of interest, for 4 tiles, the number is 1!4 + 2!6 + 3!4 + 4!1 = 64. And, for 7 tiles, the number is 1!7+2!21+3!35+4!35+5!21+6!7+7!1 = 13699.

```julia
julia> f(x)= factorial(x);
julia> 7f(1)+ 21f(2)+ 35f(3)+35f(4)+21f(5)+7f(6)+f(7)
13699
```

Let's tackle the problem of generating all *combinations* of *n* letters. We'll illustrate with *n*=3.

We will use a *bit-string* of length 3. Using 3 bits, we can count from 0 to 7 like this:

```
000 - 0
001 - 1
010 - 2
011 - 3
100 - 4
101 - 5
110 - 6
111 - 7
```

We show how to use this to generate all subsets of the 3-letter set [A, S, T]. The first bit *from the right* is assigned to A, the second to S and the third to T.

A 1 indicates the corresponding letter is present in the set and 0 indicates its absence.

So, for instance, 001 represents {A} and 101 represents {A, T}. We have this:

```
000 - 0 represents []
001 - 1 represents [A]
010 - 2 represents [S]
011 - 3 represents [A,S]
100 - 4 represents [T]
101 - 5 represents [A,T]
110 - 6 represents [S,T]
111 - 7 represents [A,S,T]
```

We will use Julia's versatile string function to help us solve this problem. We demonstrate by writing Program P10.3 to generate all subsets of a given set.

 # Program P10.3 - Generate all subsets of a given set

```
function moreCombinations(BC::String) # binary counter of length(BC) bits
# there are more combinations if BC contains at least one 0
    '0' in BC
end # moreCombinations

function incrCount(BC::String)
# String BC[1:n] holds a binary counter; add 1 to it.
```

```
        ct = parse(Int, BC, base=2)
        string(ct+1, base=2, pad=length(BC))
    end # incrCount

function getCombination(BC::String, Item::Array{Char})
# Return array of those items which correspond to 1s in BC[1:n]
# Last bit in BC matches first in Set. Counting in BC proceeds from right to
left.
# The least significant bit is BC[n]; most significant BC[1]
        combi = Array{Char}(undef, 0)
        n = length(BC)
        for k = 1:n
            if BC[n+1-k] == '1'
                push!(combi, Item[k])
            end
        end
        combi
end # getCombination

function main()
        Tiles = ['A', 'S', 'T']
        Size = length(Tiles)

        BC = string(0, base=2, pad=Size)
        while moreCombinations(BC)
            BC = incrCount(BC)
            thisCombi = getCombination(BC, Tiles) #Items identified by this
            combination
            println("$(BC[1:Size]) = $thisCombi")
        end
end # main

main()
```

When run, the program produced the following output:

```
001 = ['A']
010 = ['S']
011 = ['A', 'S']
100 = ['T']
101 = ['A', 'T']
110 = ['S', 'T']
111 = ['A', 'S', 'T']
```

BC holds the binary counter. It is initialized to three zero bits, 000, in this example. Each time the function incrCount is called, it adds 1 to the counter. When the counter reaches all 1s (111), there are no more combinations; moreCombinations returns false.

For each value of BC, the corresponding elements in Tiles are printed. Note that the values in BC are to be interpreted from right to left. So, for instance, 011 means take the first and second elements of the set but not the third: ['A', 'S'].

To cater for a different set of tiles, all you need to do is change the assignment to Tiles.

The next (sub)problem to solve is this: Given a combination of letters, generate all its permutations. (And, later, for each permutation, check if it's in the dictionary.) How can we generate the permutations? Program P10.4 shows how.

 # Program P10.4 - Generate all permutations of a given string

```
function swap(T::String, k, i)
# swap T[i] and T[k] in string T; recall T is immutable
# We must convert to an array, swap in the array; then re-create string
```

```
    C = collect(T)
    C[k], C[i] = C[i], C[k]
    T = join(C)
end #swap
function permute(T::String, k, n, perms)
    if k == n
        push!(perms, T) #Permutation found; add it to perms
    else
        for i = k : n
            T = swap(T, k, i)
            permute(T, k+1, n, perms)
        end
    end
end # permute
function pmain()
    Tiles = ['A', 'S', 'T']
    Size = length(Tiles)
    AllPerms = Set()
    tStr = join(Tiles)
    permute(tStr, 1, Size, AllPerms)
    sortedPerms = sort(collect(AllPerms))
    for s in sortedPerms
        println("$s")
    end
end # pmain

pmain()
```

When run with the tiles chosen (A, S, T), it produced the following output, the 6 sorted permutations of AST:

```
AST
ATS
SAT
STA
TAS
TSA
```

Generating all permutations of a set is a non-trivial task that is best solved using *recursion*. It would help to review Section 5.4 or you will have to take it on faith that the function permute will store all permutations of the string S[1:n] in AllPerms when called as follows:

```
permute(S, 1, n, AllPerms)
```

We cannot call sort directly on a Set. We first use collect(AllPerms) to create an "array of strings" on which we can then call sort.

Next, we combine programs P10.3 and P10.4. Given a set sTiles, it prints all permutations of all subsets of sTiles. For the sample tiles (A, S, T), it produces the following output:

```
001 = ['A']
A
010 = ['S']
S
011 = ['A', 'S']
AS SA
100 = ['T']
T
101 = ['A', 'T']
AT TA
110 = ['S', 'T']
```

```
ST TS
111 = ['A', 'S', 'T']
AST ATS SAT STA TAS TSA
```

The combined program is shown as P10.5.

```
# Program P10.5 - Generate all permutations of all subsets of a given string
function moreCombinations(BC::String) # binary counter of n bits
# there are more combinations if BC contains at least one 0
    '0' in BC
end # moreCombinations

function incrCount(BC::String)
# String BC[1:n] holds a binary counter; add 1 to it.
    ct = parse(Int, BC, base=2)
    string(ct+1, base=2, pad=length(BC))
end # incrCount
function getCombination(BC::String, Item::Array{Char})
# Return array of those items which correspond to 1s in BC[1:n]
# Last bit in BC matches first in Set
    combi = Array{Char,1}(undef, 0)
    n = length(BC)
    for k = 1:n
        if BC[n+1-k] == '1'
            push!(combi, Item[k])
        end
    end
    combi
end # getCombination

function swap(T::String, k, i)
# swap S[i] and S[k] in string S; recall S is immutable
# We must convert to an array, swap in the array; then re-create string
    C = collect(T)
    C[k], C[i] = C[i], C[k]
    T = join(C)
end #swap

function permute(T::String, k, n, perms)
    if k == n
        push!(perms, T) #Permutation found; add it to perms
    else
        for i = k : n
            T = swap(T, k, i)
            permute(T, k+1, n, perms)
        end
    end
end # permute

function printPermsOfCombi(aCombination::Array{Char})
    S = join(aCombination) # convert to a string
    AllPerms = Set()
    permute(S, 1, length(S), AllPerms)
    for s in sort(collect(AllPerms)) print("$s ") end
    println()
end # printPermsOfCombi

function main()
    sTiles = ['A', 'S', 'T']
    Size = length(sTiles)

    BC = string(0, base=2, pad=Size)
    while moreCombinations(BC)
        BC = incrCount(BC)
```

```
            thisCombi = getCombination(BC, sTiles) # items identified by this
            combination
            println("$(BC[1:Size]) = $thisCombi")
            printPermsOfCombi(thisCombi)
        end
    end # main

    main()
```

Now that we've written the various helper functions, we return to the original problem:

Given 7 tiles, find all the valid words which can be made from them and the number of points each word is worth.

We will use a `Dict` called `Tiles` to store each letter tile and its associated value. We illustrate with the first nine letters:

```
Tiles = Dict('A'=>1,'B'=>3,'C'=>3,'D'=>2,'E'=>1,'F'=>4,'G'=>2,'H'=>4,'I'=>1)
```

Recall, the items in a `Dict` are stored by Julia in no particular order. To ensure that the keys (the letters) are in alphabetical order, we use this:

```
KeysSorted = sort(collect(keys(Tiles))) # ensure keys in alpha order
```

`KeysSorted` is an array of `Char` containing the letters of `Tiles`, in order.

We'll use Hand (an array of Char) to store the tiles we're playing with, those in our hand:

```
Hand = ['A', 'S', 'T']
```

This is the *only* statement we'll need to change to work with a different hand.

Given a value of the binary counter (one bit for each letter in `Hand`), we want to return a list of the items in `Hand` which correspond to 1s in the counter (we call it `subHand`). We delegate this task to the function `getSubHand`.

```
function getSubHand(BC::String, Hand:Array{Char})
# Return array of those items which correspond to 1s in BC
# Last bit in BC matches first in Hand
    subHand = Array{Char}(undef, 0)
    n = length(BC)
    for k = 1:n
        if BC[n+1-k] == '1' push!(subHand, Hand[k]) end
    end
    subHand
end # getSubHand
```

In Program P10.5 we saw how to generate all the permutations of a given string. Now we delegate that task to the function `getPermsOfHand`:

```
function getPermsOfHand(aCombination::Array{Char})
    S = join(aCombination) # convert to a string
    AllPerms = Set()
    permute(S, 1, length(S), AllPerms)
    return AllPerms # a set of permutations
end # getPermsOfCombi
```

Consider this statement:

```
perms = getPermsOfHand(['A', 'B', 'C'])
```

perms will be a `Set`—the set of all permutations of A, B, C—each permutation returned as a string, like this

```
Set{Any} with 6 elements:
"BCA"
"CBA"
"CAB"
"BAC"
"ACB"
"ABC"
```

Each permutation is a potential word which will be checked against those in the dictionary (stored in WordList).

The function, evaluateHand, is given a Hand (set of tiles) and WordList). It calls getPermsOfHand (described above) to generate a set of all the permutations of Hand. It then creates and returns a set of all the permutations (words), if any, found in WordList.

```
function evaluateHand(Hand::Array{Char}, WordList::Set{String})
# Go through all the permutations of Hand. For each, check if in list of words
# If yes, add to the set of words found; return that set
    AllPerms = getPermsOfHand(Hand) # a set
    pSorted=sort(collect(AllPerms)) # convert to array of strings and sort
    ansSet= Set{String}()
    for p in pSorted
        if p in WordList
            union!(ansSet, [p])
        end
    end
    ansSet
end # evaluateHand
```

We promised to print the number of points each word is worth. To do so, we write the function tilesInHandValue as follows:

```
function tilesInHandValue(Hand::Array{Char}, WordList::Set{String})
# return total value of tiles in Hand
    tval = 0
    for h in Hand
        tval += Tiles[h]
    end
    tval
end # tilesValue
```

This function highlights the convenience of using a Dict here. For each letter h in Hand, we use it as a subscript to Tiles to retrieve the value of that tile.

The overall logic of the program is handled by main. It does the following:

- Read the words in the dictionary from the file scrabble.txt and store them in WordList, an array of strings.
- Set Hand to the tiles we will use for this game. We could also have read the tiles if supplied as data.
- Initialize the binary counter, BC, to all zeros; the length of BC is the same as the number of tiles being used.
- BC is used to generate all the possible combinations of the letters being used.
- getSubHand returns the subset of letters identified by a given combination.
- Call evaluateHand to do the work described above.
- Call printWordList to print, in alphabetical order, all the words which can be made from the chosen set of tiles. For each word, print the word and its point value.

Putting it all together, we write program P10.6 which generates all the words which can be made from a chosen set of tiles.

```
# Program P10.6 - Scrabble - Analyze words for a given set of tiles
using Printf
function moreCombinations(BC::String) # binary counter of n bits
# there are more combinations if BC contains at least one 0
    '0' in BC
end # moreCombinations

function incrCount(BC::String)
# String BC[1:n] holds a binary counter; add 1 to it.
    ct = parse(Int, BC, base=2)
    string(ct+1, base=2, pad=length(BC))
end # incrCount

function swap(T::String, k, i)
# swap T[i] and T[k] in string T; recall T is immutable
# We must convert to an array, swap in the array; re-create string
    C = collect(T)
    C[k], C[i] = C[i], C[k]
    T = join(C)
end #swap

function permute(T::String, k, n, perms)
    if k == n
        push!(perms, T)
    else
        for i = k : n
            T = swap(T, k, i)
            permute(T, k+1, n, perms)
        end
    end
end # permute

function tilesInHandValue(Hand, Tiles::Dict{Char, Int64})
# return total value of tiles in Hand; works if Hand is String or Char array
    tval = 0
    for h in Hand
        tval += Tiles[h]
    end
    tval
end # tilesValue

function getWordList(WordList::Set{String})
# The words can be supplied in free format, any number per line, separated by whitespace
    inn = open("scrabble.txt", "r")

    while (line = readline(inn)) != ""
        words = split(line)
        for w in words
            push!(WordList, uppercase(w))
        end
    end
    close(inn)
end # getWordList

function getSubHand(BC::String, Hand::Array{Char})
# Return array of those items which correspond to 1s in BC
    subHand = Array{Char}(undef, 0)
    n = length(BC)
    for k = 1:n
        if BC[n+1-k] == '1'
            push!(subHand, Hand[k])
```

```
                end
            end
            subHand
    end # getSubHand

    function getPermsOfHand(aCombination::Array{Char})
        S = join(aCombination) # convert to a string
        AllPerms = Set()
        permute(S, 1, length(S), AllPerms)
        AllPerms # a set of permutations
    end # getPermsOfCombi

    function evaluateHand(Hand::Array{Char}, WordList::Set{String})
    # Go through all the permutations of Hand. For each, check if in list of words
    # If yes, add to the set of words found; return that set
        AllPerms = getPermsOfHand(Hand) # a set
        pSorted=sort(collect(AllPerms)) # convert to array of strings and sort
        ansSet= Set{String}()
        for p in pSorted
            if p in WordList
                union!(ansSet, [p])
            end
        end
        ansSet
    end # evaluateHand

    function printWordList(WordList::Set{String}, Tiles::Dict{Char, Int64})
    # WordList is a Set so words are in random order; we sort them before printing
        sortedWords = sort(collect(WordList))
        println("\nWords    Value\n")
        for w in sortedWords
            @printf("%-7s %4d\n", w, tilesInHandValue(w, Tiles))
        end
    end # printWordList

    function main()
        WordList = Set{String}()
        getWordList(WordList)  # Words in the dictionary

        Tiles = Dict('A'=>1,'B'=>3,'C'=>3,'D'=>2,'E'=>1,'F'=>4,'G'=>2,'H'=>4,'I'=>1)
        Hand = ['A', 'B', 'D', 'E', 'F', 'G', 'H'] # array of Char
        hSize = length(Hand)
        println("Letters in Hand: $Hand")

        AllWords = Set{String}()
        BC = string(0, base=2, pad=hSize) # Binary counter same size as Hand
        while moreCombinations(BC)
            BC = incrCount(BC)
            subHand = getSubHand(BC, Hand) # items identified by this combination
            tv = tilesInHandValue(subHand, Tiles)
            words = evaluateHand(subHand, WordList) # words from permutations of
            subHand
            if !isempty(words)
                #println("$words - Value: $tv")
                union!(AllWords, words)
            end
        end
        printWordList(AllWords, Tiles)
    end # main

main()
```

Suppose the following words are stored in scrabble.txt:

aged bed ace bad bag bed beg cab cad bead egg gaffe fad had haggle he
hag hid hide die fender bend fib bade cage face be head deaf fed fond

When run, Program P10.6 prints this:

```
Letters in Hand: ['A', 'B', 'D', 'E', 'F', 'G', 'H']

Words   Value

AGED    6
BAD     6
BADE    7
BAG     6
BE      4
BEAD    7
BED     6
BEG     6
DEAF    8
FAD     7
FED     7
HAD     7
HAG     7
HE      5
HEAD    8
```

Duplicate Tiles

Nothing in our discussion so far made any assumption about whether the tiles in a hand are unique or not. As in the real game, we can pick more than one of the same tile. For instance, suppose we have this:

```
Hand = ['A', 'B', 'B', 'A']
```

If we were to print a word each time one is found, we may get something like this (we assume these words are all in `WordList`):

```
Set(["A"]) - Value: 1
Set(["AB"]) - Value: 4
Set(["AB"]) - Value: 4
Set(["A"]) - Value: 1
Set(["AB"]) - Value: 4
Set(["BAA"]) - Value: 5
Set(["AB"]) - Value: 4
Set(["BAA"]) - Value: 5
Set(["BABA"]) - Value: 8
```

We have several repetitions. This reflects the fact that BAA, for instance, can be formed from two different combinations of letters: 1, 2, 4 and 1, 3, 4. Of course, they are the same word so we would want to print it once.

Therein lies the reason why we used a Set to store the words found. A set does not permit duplicates. If we tried to add a word that was already there, the attempt is ignored. For this example, the program would print this:

```
Letters in Hand: ['A', 'B', 'B', 'A']

Words   Value

A       1
AB      4
BAA     5
BABA    8
```

EXERCISES 10

1. Write a program to create a directory of names and phone numbers using a `Dict`. Request a name and print the person's phone number. If the name isn't found, ask if the name should be added to the directory. If yes, ask for the phone number and add the new entry.

2. Consider the voting problem of Section 7.9. Solve it using two dictionaries—both with integer keys. One stores the names of the candidates and the other keeps track of their scores.

3. A length, specified in meters and centimeters, is represented by two integers. For example, the length 3m 75cm is represented by [3, 75]. A file contains the names and distances jumped by athletes in a long-jump competition. Here are some sample data:

```
Adam 3 75
Kyle 4 25
Fred 3 90
```

Use a `Dict` to hold a name (the key) and distance (an array value). For the above data, your program should create this:

```
LongJump = Dict("Adam"=>[3,75], "Kyle"=>[4,25], "Fred"=>[3,90])
```

Write a program to read the data and print a list consisting of name and distance jumped in order of merit (best jumper first).

For the sample data, your program should print the following under a suitable heading:

```
Kyle 4m 25cm
Fred 3m 90cm
Adam 3m 75cm
```

4. A data file contains registration information for five courses—CS20A, CS25A, CS30A, CS35A, and CS40A. Each line of data consists of a seven-digit student registration number followed by five (ordered) values, each of which is 0 or 1. A value of 1 indicates that the student is registered for the corresponding course; 0 means the student is not. Thus, 1 1 0 0 1 means that the student is registered for CS20A, CS25A and CS40A, but not for CS30A and CS35A.

Write a program to read the data and produce a class list for each course. Each list consists of the registration numbers of those students taking the course. *Hint*: you can use the following to iterate through all the (key, value) entries in a dictionary D:

```
for (k, v) in D
```

Sample input:
```
1234567 1 1 0 0 1
2345678 1 0 1 0 1
3456789 1 1 1 1 1
```

Sample output:
```
CS20A: 2345678 3456789 1234567
CS25A: 3456789 1234567
CS30A: 2345678 3456789
CS35A: 3456789
CS40A: 2345678 3456789 1234567
```

Modify the program to print each class list in order by student number, like this:

```
CS20A: 1234567 2345678 3456789
CS25A: 1234567 3456789
CS30A: 2345678 3456789
CS35A: 3456789
CS40A: 1234567 2345678 3456789
```

5. At a school's bazaar, activities were divided into stalls. At the close of the bazaar, the manager of each stall submitted information to the principal consisting of the name of the stall, the income earned, and its expenses. Here are some sample data:

```
"Bran Tub" 2300.00 1000.00
"Putt The Ball" 900.00 1000.00
```

Write a program to read the data and print a report consisting of the stall name and net income (income - expenses), in order of decreasing net income (that is, with the most profitable stall first and the least profitable stall last). In addition, print the number of stalls, the total profit or loss of the bazaar, and the stall(s) that made the most profit.

Use a `Dict` to store the data with the name of the stall as the key and a two-element `Float` array as the value.

6. On a telephone keypad, letters are assigned to numbers as follows:

2 - ABC, 3 - DEF, 4 - GHI, 5 - JKL, 6 - MNO, 7 - PQRS, 8 - TUV, 9 - WXYZ

Suppose you press 8 2 6 (TUV)(ABC)(MNO). If we take one letter from each group, there are 27 ($3 \times 3 \times 3$) possible 3-letter combinations: TAM, TAN, TAO, TBM, etc. Of these 27, only some are English words: tam, tan, tao, van.

If you press 7 2 5 3, there are $4 \times 3 \times 3 \times 3 = 108$ possible combinations. Only a few of these are actual words, like pale, rake, sake and sale.

You are given a set of words stored in the file dict.txt. This is the dictionary. Words on a line are separated by spaces. A blank line indicates the end of the dictionary.

Following the dictionary is a set of 'digit strings', one per line. For each string, print, in alphabetical order, all possible 'dictionary' words which can be formed from that string.

Write all output to the file output.txt.

Sample input

```
good home gone boy any hood hoof help
yard ward ware box bow cow

4663
269
2345
4357
9273
```

Sample output

```
4663: gone good home hood hoof
269: any bow box boy cow
2345:
4357: help
9273: ward ware yard
```

Appendix A - Install Julia/Atom/Juno

Install and run Julia

Go to `https://julialang.org/downloads/` and download the appropriate version for your operating system. We'll illustrate using the Windows 64-bit installer. As of this writing, we have this: Current stable release: v1.5.3 (Nov 9, 2020).

We will install the compiler in this folder: `C:\Julia-1.5.3`. (You can give it any name you want.)

Download the installer (`julia-1.5.3-win64.exe`) and run it. When asked for the place to install the compiler (Select Installation Directory), type `C:\Julia-1.5.3`.

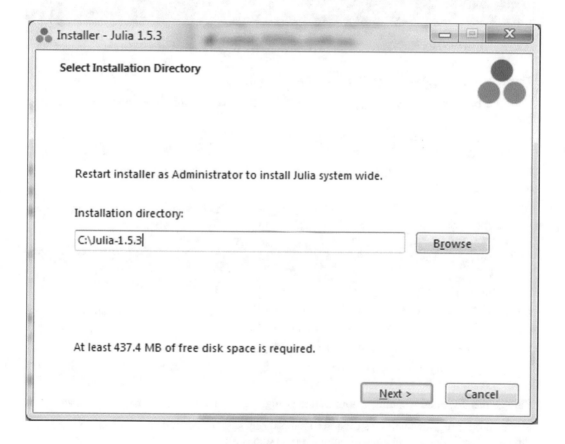

When the installation process is completed, the folder `C:\Julia-1.5.3` would have been created, if it wasn't created before. In it would be a folder called `bin` and, in `bin`, would be the compiler `julia.exe`. The *path* to the compiler is this: `C:\Julia-1.5.3\bin\julia.exe`. We can start the compiler by double-clicking on this file. When we do, we'll get this (but in colour):

© The Author(s), under exclusive license to Springer Nature Switzerland AG 2021
N. Kalicharan, *Julia - Bit by Bit*, Undergraduate Topics in Computer Science,
https://doi.org/10.1007/978-3-030-73936-2

This is called the `Julia REPL` (Read-Eval-Print-Loop).

This is a place where we can type commands at the `julia>` prompt, and have them executed immediately.

```
julia> println("Welcome to Julia")
Welcome to Julia
```

In the next step, you would store your program in a file and have Julia execute the program directly from the file.

Assume we have created a folder `C:\JuliaPrograms` in which we will store all our programs. And suppose we have stored the following program in the file `Welcome.jl`:

```
function welcome()
    println("Welcome to Julia")
end

welcome()
```

Caution: The file must be created with a text editor (like Notepad). You can use a word processor but be sure to save it as a text file. Also, make sure the name ends with `.jl`, not `.txt`.

We could execute the program using the `include` command, as follows:

```
julia> include("C:\\JuliaPrograms\\Welcome.jl")
Welcome to Julia
```

Since \ has a special meaning within a Julia string, we must use \\ in a string to represent \.

Since all our programs will be stored in `C:\JuliaPrograms`, we can tell Julia this is our "working directory" by issuing a "change directory" command (`cd`):

```
julia> cd("C:\\JuliaPrograms")
```

If we ever want to know what is the "current working directory", we can use the `pwd` command:

```
julia> pwd()
"C:\\JuliaPrograms"
```

We can now run a program by specifying just the name of the file:

```
julia> include("Welcome.jl")
Welcome to Julia
```

For another example, suppose the file `Greeting.jl` contains the following program:

```
function greet()
    print("Hi, what's your name? ")
    name = readline()
    println("Delighted to meet you, $name")
end

greet()
```

The following is a sample run (`Julia` is underlined to indicate it's typed by the user):

```
julia> include("Greeting.jl")
Hi, what's your name? Julia
Delighted to meet you, Julia
```

Install Atom and Juno

We can do a lot working with Julia this way but it has its limitations, especially when we are developing a big program and we need to make changes and quickly test the effects of those changes. To work more flexibly with our programs, we need to install `Atom` and `Juno`. These have been called "the perfect duo for Julia development". According to its creators, `Atom` is "a hackable text editor for the 21st Century". There is a plugin for almost anything. `Juno` is a great IDE (Integrated Development Environment) meant for Julia development.

First `Atom`.

You can download `Atom` here:

```
http://docs.junolab.org/stable/man/installation/#.-Install-Atom-1
```

After downloading, install and launch it. When asked "Register as Atom://URI handler?", click `Yes`. *Alert*: installation may take several minutes.

The next step is to install `Juno`.

In `Atom`, go to `File > Settings` (or just type `Ctrl-,`)

Choose `Install` from the left panel. In the search box that appears, type `uber-juno`. The following will come up:

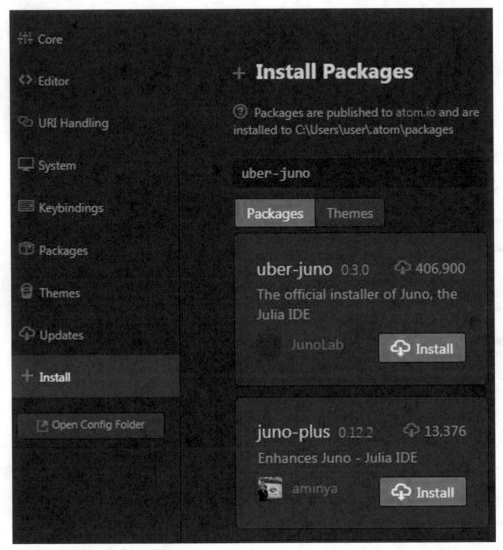

Click `Install` in the `uber-juno` box. (You may see a different version number from the one shown here.) Wait a few moments until you get confirmation that `Juno` was installed. (The `Install` button will change to `Uninstall` and a `Juno` menu will appear at the top of the screen, next to `File Edit View`...) If this question pops up: Julia-Client: Open Juno-specific panes on startup?, click `No`.

The next step is critical since this is when you tell `Juno` where the `Julia` compiler is installed. If you accepted the default location the installer chose, it should be here:

    C:\Users\user\AppData\Local\Programs\Julia 1.5.3\bin\julia.exe

In our case, because we chose `C:\Julia-1.5.3` as the installation directory, it would be here:

    C:\Julia-1.5.3\bin\julia.exe

Wherever it is, we need to tell Juno.

Bring up the `Settings` window (type `Ctrl-,`) if it's not already open.

Click on `Packages` in the left panel, then click the down arrow on `Community Packages` from the right panel. If necessary, scroll until you see `julia-client` (bottom of picture below).

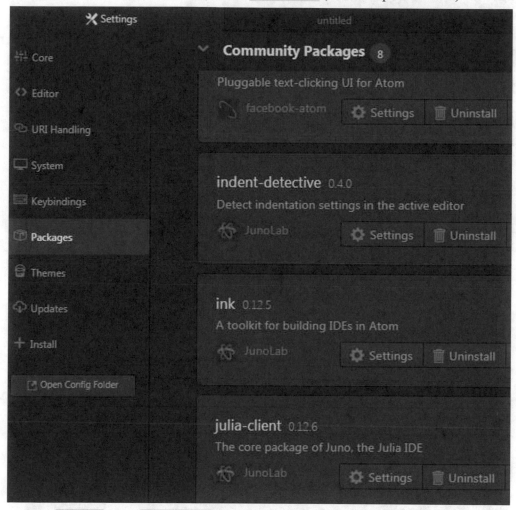

Click on `Settings` in the `julia-client` box. The first option should be `Julia Path`. Click in the box and type or paste the path to the `julia.exe` file.

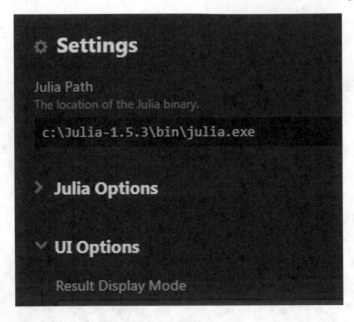

You're all set. You can close the `Settings` tab at the top of the screen.

Running Programs

Above, we wrote two programs—`Welcome.jl` and `Greeting.jl`—and stored them in the folder `C:\JuliaPrograms`.

Launch `Atom` and choose `File > Open Folder` (`Ctrl-Shift-O`). Navigate to `C:\JuliaPrograms` and select it. You should see this:

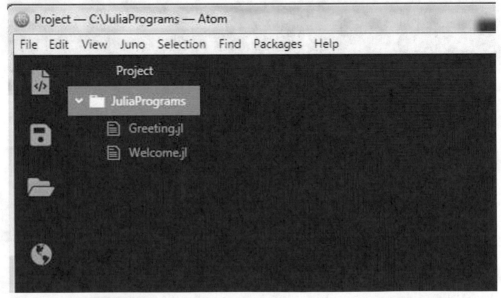

If you click on `Greeting.jl`, the program will appear on the right-hand-side.

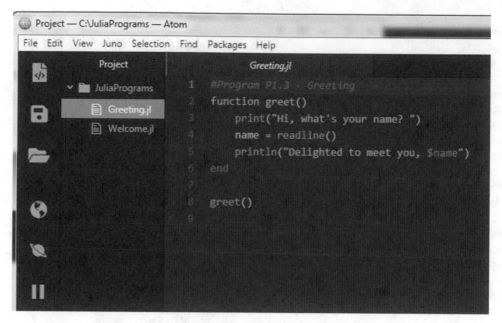

To work with the Julia REPL, choose the following icon from the left side panel:

or choose Open REPL from the Juno menu.

You can now run any of your programs at the Julia> prompt using include(…), like this:

```
julia> include("Greeting.jl")
Hi, what's your name? Julia
Delighted to meet you, Julia
```

You can also write a program in Atom. Choose File -> New File (Ctrl+N). Type your program and save it (as Test.jl, say) in the folder C:\JuliaPrograms. You can now run Test.jl from the julia> prompt with include("Test.jl").

Index

! 55
&& 55
@printf 30, 38
|| 55
abundant numbers 124
algorithm 4
algorithm, develop 5
algorithm, program for 5
alphabetic 10
alphanumeric 10
anagram 229, 251
and, && 55
argmax, string function 150
argmin, string function 150
argument to a function 113
array of characters 174
array of structures 234
array
    argument to function 194
    declaration 182
    expand as needed 202
    largest 195
    smallest 196
    store values 186
    variable 182
    zero-length 202
Arrays 181
ASCII character set 10, 140
assignment float32 float64 42
assignment operator 45
average
    (prompt) 98
    find 26
    from file 85
    values in array 190

big integers 118
binary search 219
Bool 56
Boolean expressions 53
break in for 82
break in while 104

ceil 47
Celsius 78
Char
    functions 143
    type 142

print 146
read 146
character
    array 174
    compare 149
    control 10
    digit 10
    letter 10
    lowercase 10
    newline 14
    set 140
    special 10
    uppercase 10
Characters 140
children's game, count-out 205
classify triangle 68
close 96
cmp, compare strings 156
collect function 174
combinations 121
comments 17
compare characters 149
compare strings 156
compilers 1
concatenate strings 161
condition 54
constant, symbolic 21, 65
continue in for 82
continue in while 104
count (prompt) 98
counting 85

data 4
data types 9
decimal to binary 129
declare an array 182
deficient numbers 124
delete! 256, 261
deleteat! 175
Dictionaries 252
digit string to integer 151
document program 8
dynamic binding 111

eachindex, string function 178
Easter Sunday 71
escape sequence 15
expand an array 202
expressions, mixed 44

factorial 118
Fahrenheit 78
Fibonacci numbers 128
field width 38
file not found 193
file pointer 93
file reading 83, 92
file writing 100
fill function 185
findfirst, string function 170
findlast, string function 171
findnext, string function 171
findprev, string function 173
firstindex, string function 177
float32, print 41
float64, print 41
floating-point expressions 43
floating-point numbers 40
floor 47
for statement 72
for, nested 90
fractions 239
functions
    delete! 256, 261
    fill 185
    gcd 99, 116
    getString 166
    haskey 256
    how argument is passed 113
    in 256
    intersect 261
    intersect! 261
    isless 247
    keys 253
    max 197
    maximum 197
    mean 191
    min 197
    minimum 197
    Pair 254
    setdiff 262
    setdiff! 262
    square 6, 27, 110
    std 191
    SubString 158
    swap 114
    union 258
    union! 260
    values 254

var 191
    zeros 185
Functions 109

gcd 99, 116
    to find lcm 118
    recursive 128
Geography quiz program 167
getString function 166
greatest common divisor 99, 116

haskey 256
hcf 116
highest common factor 116

identifiers 20
if 56
if...else 61
if...elseif...else 66
in 256
index a string 157
insert! 175
insertion sort 212
insertion sort, analysis 216
install Julia/Atom/Juno 279
Int 34
integer expressions 36
integers, big 118
intersect 261
isless in sort 247

join 175
Julia Programming 11
    alphabet 18
    basics 18
    tokens 18

keep count 85
keys function 253

languages 1
largest 86, 88
largest in array 195
lastindex, string function 159, 177
lcm 118
letter frequency 191, 254
letter position in alphabet 125
longest word 89
lowercase to/from uppercase 144

`max` function 197
`maximum` function 197
`maximum`, string function 150\
maze 133
`mean` function 191
median 228
merge sorted lists 224
Merging 207
`min` function 197
`minimum` function 197
`minimum`, string function 150
mixed expressions 44
mode 228
multiplication tables 75

nested `for` 90
nested structures 238
`nextind`, string function 177
not, `!` 55
Numbers, 23
numbers, floating-point 40
numbers, rational 241
numeric 10

`occursin`, string function 174
operator, assignment 45
operator, updating 45
operators, precedence 37
or, `||` 55
overloading 112

`Pair` function 254
palindrome 164
pass argument to function 113
path through maze 133
perfect numbers 124
permutations of a string 269
pointer to file 93
polymorphism 112
`power` function 132
precedence of operators 37
`prevind`, string function 177
prime numbers, generate 206
print integer, field width 38
print working directory 94
`print/println` 13
`printf` 30, 38
program debugging 7
program testing 7,64
programs 1
`pwd` 94

range indexing of a string 158
rational numbers 241
read floating-point 25
read from file 83,92
read integer 23
read several numbers from one line 33
recursion 126
recursive `gcd` 128
relational expressions 53
relational operators 53
relational operators, Sets 262
reserved words 20
`round` 48
`RoundDown` 49
`RoundNearestTiesAway` 48
`RoundNearestTiesUp` 48
`RoundToZero` 49
`RoundUp` 49

scope rule 74
Scrabble 267
search, binary 219
search, sequential 207
Searching 207
selection sort 209
    analysis 211
sequential search 207
`setdiff` 262
`setdiff!` 262
Sets 257
simple variable 182
smallest 89
    in array 196
sort
    insertion 212
    parallel arrays 217
    selection 209
    `struct` array 234
    unlimited data 216
Sorting 207
`square` function 110
`square`, area of 6, 27
standard deviation, `std` 191
static binding 111
`std`, standard deviation 191
store values in array 186
string concatenation 161
string function
    `argmax` 150
    `argmin` 150
    `eachindex` 178

findfirst 170
findlast 171
findnext 171
findprev 173
firstindex 177
lastindex 177
maximum 150
minimum 150
nextind 177
occursin 174
prevind 177
thisind 179
string indexing 157
string, compare 156
string, print 155
Strings 140
struct
    array 234
    array, sort 236
    declaration 234
    declaration, where to place 235
    argument to a function, 232
Structures 230
structures, nested 238
SubString function 158
sum numbers (prompt) 97
sum of divisors 123
sum of two lengths 59
swap two variables 114
symbolic constant 21, 65

temperature conversion 78
thesaurus 264
thisind, string function 179
Towers of Hanoi 130
triangle 68
trunc 47

union 258
union! 260
unlimited data sort 216
updating operator 45
uppercase to/from lowercase 144

values function 254
var, variance function 191
variable, print 16
variables 4
variance 191
voting problem 198, 243

while statement 95
word frequency 221
working directory 94
write to file 100

zero-length array 202
zeros function 185

Printed in the United States
by Baker & Taylor Publisher Services